# VOCABULARY POWER 2

## PRACTICING ESSENTIAL WORDS

## Kate Dingle • Jennifer Recio Lebedev

PEARSON
Longman

**Vocabulary Power 2: Practicing Essential Words**

Pearson Education, 10 Bank Street, White Plains, NY 10606

**Staff credits**: The people who made up the *Vocabulary Power 2* team, representing editorial, production, design, and manufacturing, are Rhea Banker, Christine Edmonds, Stacey Hunter, Laura Le Dréan, Francoise Leffler, Christopher Leonowicz, Amy McCormick, Edith Pullman, and Barbara Sabella.

**Cover and text design**: Barbara Sabella

**Cover photos**: (wave) © P. Wilson/zefa/Corbis; (car) © Schlegelmilch/Corbis; (windmills) © Firefly Productions/Corbis; (bulb) © Chris Rogers/Corbis; (train) © Tim Bird/Corbis; (volcano) © Jim Sugar/Corbis; (type) © Don Bishop/Getty Images; (shuttle) © Stock Trek/Getty Images

**Text composition**: Laserwords, Inc.

**Text font**: 11/12.5 New Aster Medium

**Library of Congress Cataloging-in-Publication Data**
Dingle, Kate.
    Vocabulary power 2 / Kate Dingle, Jennifer Lebedev.
        p. cm.
    Includes index.
    ISBN 978-0-13-222150-4 (student bk. : alk. paper)—ISBN 978-0-13-222151-1
(answer key : alk. paper)
    1. Vocabulary. 2. Vocabulary—Problems, exercises, etc.
I. Lebedev, Jennifer. II. Title. III. Title: Vocabulary power two.
PE1449.D556 2007
428.1—dc22                                          2007003249

**LONGMAN** ON THE **WEB**

**Longman.com** offers online resources for teachers and students. Access our Companion Websites, our online catalog, and our local offices around the world.

Visit us at **longman.com**.

Printed in the United States of America
1 2 3 4 5 6 7 8 9 10 —VHG —11 10 09 08 07

# CONTENTS

Giving your students an excellent vocabulary doesn't have to be difficult. *Vocabulary Power* simplifies the process to make vocabulary acquisition effective and interesting.

## THE LATEST RESEARCH

### The Most Important Words

Research shows that it is possible but not probable for the human mind to learn 1,000 new words a year (Nation 2001). In light of this, it is no surprise that English language learners are often frustrated by their limited vocabulary. Even if they manage to learn 1,000 words a year, the words they acquire may not be those that they need for academic and professional success. *Vocabulary Power* solves this problem by teaching the words that are most worthy of their time and attention.

Of the 100,000+ words in the English language, only the 2,000 most frequent words (compiled in the General Service List) are necessary for students to understand at least 80% of daily conversation and writing (Nation 2002). If students know the 2,000 most frequent words in English, in conjunction with 570 high frequency academic words found on the Academic Word List (AWL), they may understand close to 90% of academic text (Nation 2001, Coxhead 2000). The combined knowledge of the General Service List (GSL) and the Academic Word List (AWL) will strengthen your students' ability to understand a textbook, follow an academic lecture, or read a newspaper with ease.

- **Vocabulary Power 1** teaches Low Intermediate students words from the GSL.
- **Vocabulary Power 2** teaches Intermediate students more challenging words from the GSL and words from the AWL.
- **Vocabulary Power 3** teaches Advanced students more challenging words from the AWL.

### Effective Methodology

*Vocabulary Power* is different from most vocabulary books because it is based on research on memory. Memorizing a word often requires that it be encountered seven or more times. It is important that words are not simply seen on each occasion, but encountered in new contexts, retrieved, and used (Nation 2001).

*Vocabulary Power* exposes students to each word in at least eight different contexts. This not only fixes new words in the memory, it offers learners a rich understanding of words. The eight different exposures follow a process approach, guiding the learner through the cognitive stages of noticing, retrieval, and generation. This approach teaches learners not only to recognize and understand a word, but also produce it.

## HIGH INTEREST CONTENT

*Vocabulary Power* is unique because it makes vocabulary learning enjoyable. Examples are modern and realistic. The readings are adapted from articles in current newspapers, magazines, or online news sources on a variety of up-to-date topics. Students are encouraged to apply new words to their own lives, making vocabulary more relevant and useful.

## CLASSROOM FRIENDLY FORMAT

Each chapter is organized as follows:

- **Words in Context:** understanding new words from context
- **Words and Definitions:** matching the words with their definition (or adapted definition) from the *Longman Dictionary of American English*
- **Comprehension Check:** checking comprehension of the words
- **Word Families:** expanding knowledge of the words with word families
- **Same Word, Different Meaning:** expanding knowledge of the words with multiple meanings
- **Words in Sentences:** using the words to complete sentences
- **Words in Collocations and Expressions:** understanding collocations and expressions featuring the words to improve memory and activate production
- **Words in a Reading:** using the words to complete a reading adapted from a current news article
- **Words in Discussion:** applying the words to real life with lively discussion questions
- **Words in Writing:** using the words in writing about a relevant topic

In addition:

- Ten Quizzes throughout the book make it easy for teachers and students to check the students' progress.
- The Word Builder exercises and charts in the Appendix also provide an opportunity to focus on the meaning and use of word parts.
- A complete Answer Key (for all exercises and quizzes) is provided in a separate booklet.

*Vocabulary Power* can be used as a supplement to reading, writing, grammar, or speaking classes. It can be used in class or assigned as homework. It can also be used as a self-study text. This flexibility makes the book an easy way to strengthen the academic curriculum of a class.

## REFERENCES

Coxhead, A. 2000. *A new academic word list. TESOL Quarterly, 34(2000), 213-239.*

Nation, P. 2001. *Learning Vocabulary in Another Language. Cambridge University Press: Cambridge.*

Nation, P. 2002. *Managing Vocabulary Learning. SEAMEO Regional Language Centre: Singapore.*

# ACKNOWLEDGMENTS

We are grateful to the wonderful editorial team at Longman for their contributions to this series. In particular, we would like to thank Amy McCormick, Paula Van Ells, Francoise Leffler, Stacey Hunter, and Diana Nam. We also thank Longman for allowing us to use definitions, the pronunciation table, and transcriptions from the *Longman Dictionary of American English*. This book could not have been developed without the insights of students, so we would like to thank the students at Northeastern University who piloted these materials and gave us great feedback.

# TO THE STUDENT

Do you want to improve your vocabulary, but don't know which words are most important to learn? Is studying vocabulary sometimes boring for you? Do you want to remember words easily, and know how to use them when speaking and writing? Do you need a better vocabulary to be ready for studies at the university level? If you can answer "yes" to any of these questions, this is the book for you.

### Which words are important to learn?

The English language has over 100,000 words, but you only need to know the 2,000 most common words (the General Service List) to understand 80% of daily conversation and reading. After this, learning a group of 570 special academic words (the Academic Word List) will increase your comprehension to almost 90% of academic speaking and reading. This book only teaches words from the General Service List and the Academic Word List. Whether you are preparing for academic work or simply wish to better your vocabulary, studying these words is an excellent use of your time.

### How can I remember new words easily?

To remember a word, you need to see it used several times, in different ways. Every new word in this book is taught through eight different exercises. By the end of a chapter, every word will be a part of your memory.

### How can I enjoy learning vocabulary?

Learning vocabulary should be interesting! This book can help you enjoy learning new words in four ways:

1. The examples of the words are modern and realistic. (You don't have to worry that you will sound old-fashioned or strange when you use a new word.)

2. The readings in the book come from newspapers, magazines, and online sources (such as *The New York Times* and *National Geographic*) and cover up-to-date topics like technology, music, and sports.

3. Special exercises show you common collocations (word combinations) and expressions to help you use the words in conversation and academic writing.

4. Engaging discussion questions about your opinions and your life give you the opportunity to use the words in interesting conversation.

Now that you understand how you can get a better vocabulary, you are ready to start *Vocabulary Power*.

## ABOUT THE AUTHORS

**Kate Dingle** has taught English in Poland, Italy, and the United States. Her interest in vocabulary acquisition developed at the Institute of Education, University of London, where she completed her Masters in TESOL. She now lives in Boston and is an instructor in the English Language Center at Northeastern University.

**Jennifer Recio Lebedev** received degrees in Russian Studies from Bryn Mawr and Middlebury Colleges. She began teaching English in 1996 in Moscow, Russia, where she also wrote several publications for EFL learners. Since returning to the United States in 2001, she has conducted teacher training courses and professional devolopment seminars in addition to classroom teaching at a private language school in Boston.

Key Words

| analyze | construct | distribute | master | rival |
|---------|-----------|------------|--------|-------|
| assist | debt | intend | reflect | witness |

## WORDS IN CONTEXT

*Use the sentences to guess what each key word means. Choose the meaning that is closest to that of the key word in **bold**.*

**1. analyze**
/ˈænlˌɑɪz/
-verb

- If we want to build better cars, we need to **analyze** the information we get from drivers.
- When Greg makes a serious decision, he usually **analyzes** it, thinking carefully and logically rather than using his emotions.

*Analyze* means . . .   (a.) to think about something carefully   b. to look at   c. to react to

**2. assist**
/əˈsɪst/
-verb

- If you need help finding a book in a library, a librarian can **assist** you.
- Have you ever **assisted** an elderly person across the street?

*Assist* means . . .   a. to help   b. to walk   c. to read

**3. construct**
/kənˈstrʌkt/
-verb

- It took four and a half years to **construct** the Golden Gate Bridge.
- The Pyramids of Egypt were **constructed** thousands of years ago.

*Construct* means . . .   a. to find   b. to imagine   c. to build something large

**4. debt**
/dɛt/
-noun

- AJ buys lots of expensive clothes with his credit cards, but he never pays his credit card bills. As a result, he owes the bank a lot of money; he is in **debt**.
- A company that has a lot of **debt** may have problems borrowing more money from the bank.

*Debt* means . . .   a. money you gave someone   b. money you owe someone   c. money you saved

**5. distribute**
/dɪˈstrɪbyət/
-verb

- Our organization **distributes** food and clothing to people in need.
- After the terrible storm hit the coast of Florida, water and food were **distributed** to the people who lost their houses.

*Distribute* means . . .   a. to give out   b. to talk about   c. to sell

**6. intend**
/ɪnˈtɛnd/
-verb

- Michael **intends** to become a doctor, so he is taking a lot of science classes.
- If you **intend** to buy a sports car, how much money do you need to save?

*Intend* means . . .   a. to have no interest in   b. to plan   c. to forget

7. **master**
/ˈmæstɚ/
-noun

- Jose is a **master** at cooking; he works in one of the best restaurants in San Francisco.
- Ellen is a **master** of language; she speaks Chinese, German, Russian, Spanish, and English.

*Master* means . . .

a. someone who isn't very good at something

b. someone who has average skills at something

c. someone who is very skillful at something

8. **reflect**
/rɪˈflɛkt/
-verb

- The lake is like a mirror! Look at the way it **reflects** the mountains.
- The little girl thought it was very funny to see her own face **reflected** in the window.

*Reflect* means . . .

a. to play

b. to look at

c. to show an image

9. **rival**
/ˈraɪvəl/
-noun

- In the Olympics, figure skaters became **rivals** fighting for the gold medal.
- The last time you wanted to win a game, who was your **rival**? Did this person stop you from winning?

*Rival* means . . .

a. a friend

b. a person you compete with

c. an athlete

10. **witness**
/ˈwɪtˀnɪs/
-noun

- Mrs. O'Leary was a **witness** to the bank robbery, so she told the police what the robber looked like.
- A **witness** at the scene of the accident called for help.

*Witness* means . . .

a. someone who saw something

b. an unimportant person

c. a police officer

## WORDS AND DEFINITIONS

*Match each key word with its definition.*

1. ___construct___ to build something large

2. _____ to have something in your mind as a plan or purpose

3. _____ someone who saw something, especially an accident or a crime

4. _____ to help someone do something

5. _____ money that you owe to someone

6. _____ someone who is very skillful at something

7. _____ a person, group, or organization that you compete with

8. _____ to give something to each person in a large group

9. _____ to think about something carefully in order to understand it

10. _____ to show an image as in a mirror

# COMPREHENSION CHECK

*Choose the best answer.*

1. Which of the following items CANNOT **reflect**?

    a. a mirror

    b. a tree

    c. a window

    d. a shiny piece of metal

2. If you're playing soccer, your **rival**

    a. wants you to lose.

    b. does not want to stop you.

    c. wants to help you win.

    d. is your friend.

3. Peter could go into **debt** if he

    a. is very careful with money.

    b. wears inexpensive clothing.

    c. buys a summer house in Hawaii with his credit card.

    d. eats a simple dinner every night.

4. Which of the following things did the French **construct**?

    a. the first space shuttle

    b. a mountain

    c. the Taj Mahal

    d. the Eiffel Tower

5. In her marine biology class, when Gina **analyzes** information about whales, she

    a. chats with her friends about what was on TV last night.

    b. looks carefully at the information and seriously thinks about it.

    c. draws funny pictures of fish in her notebook.

    d. sends a text message with her cell phone.

6. If you want to become a **master** at tennis, what should you do?

    a. Take lessons from an excellent coach and practice every day.

    b. Use an old tennis racket that doesn't work well.

    c. Eat fast food.

    d. Wear uncomfortable sneakers.

7. What would Bo say if he **intended** to learn French?

    a. "I need to buy a book about learning Japanese."

    b. "Tonight I'm going to listen to Czech music."

    c. "I want to study French verbs this afternoon."

    d. "I'm too lazy to learn another language."

8. Who **assists** a pilot in flying a plane?

    a. the passengers

    b. the flight attendants

    c. his wife

    d. the co-pilot

9. What might a **witness** to a violent street fight do?

    a. read about the fight in the newspaper

    b. start the fight

    c. go to the hospital

    d. call for help

10. Which of the following items would a teacher never **distribute** during a test?

    a. the answers to the test

    b. the test papers

    c. pencils

    d. pens

# WORD FAMILIES

Now that you have studied the ten key words and their basic definitions, you are ready to learn words that belong to the same family as some of the key words. A word family includes words that look alike but have different functions (noun, verb, adjective, or adverb). Their meanings are related but different.

**A.** *Look at each model phrase and decide whether the word in **bold** is used as a noun, verb, adjective, or adverb.*

| | NOUN | VERB | ADJECTIVE | ADVERB |
|---|---|---|---|---|
| **1. analyze** | | | | |
| • to think **analytically** | | | | ✓ |
| • an **analytical** mind | | | ✓ | |
| • an excellent **analysis** | ✓ | | | |
| **2. assist** | | | | |
| • to **assist** people | | | | |
| • in need of **assistance** | | | | |
| **3. intend** | | | | |
| • to **intend** to leave | | | | |
| • with the **intention** of leaving | | | | |
| **4. master** | | | | |
| • a **master** at mathematics | | | | |
| • can **master** this game | | | | |
| **5. rival** | | | | |
| • a dangerous **rival** | | | | |
| • could **rival** it | | | | |
| **6. witness** | | | | |
| • a **witness** to the accident | | | | |
| • **witness** a tornado | | | | |

**B.** *Match each of the following sentences with the definition of the word in **bold**.*

__e__ 1. Please let us know if you need any **assistance**.

____ 2. Alberto thinks **analytically**, so he can figure out math problems easily.

____ 3. No one can **rival** Diana's beauty.

____ 4. If you want to **master** the English language, you need to study every day.

____ 5. Sara's father wanted to know what Dan's **intentions** were; he asked, "Do you plan to marry my daughter or only to date her?"

____ 6. Taylor **witnessed** the bank robbery, so he described the robber to the police.

____ 7. Let's read the professor's **analysis** of the situation.

a. using methods that help you examine things carefully

b. to learn something so well that you know it completely

c. to be as good or important as someone or something else

d. to see something happen, especially an accident or a crime

e. help or support

f. a careful examination of something in order to understand it better

g. something that you plan to do

## SAME WORD, DIFFERENT MEANING

*Most words have more than one meaning. Study the additional meanings of **master, construct,** and **witness.**
Then read each sentence and decide which meaning is used.*

| | | |
|---|---|---|
| a. **master** *n.* | someone who is very skilled at something |
| b. **master** *n.* | a document from which other copies are made |
| c. **construct** *v.* | to build something large |
| d. **construct** *v.* | to form something by joining words or ideas together |
| e. **witness** *n.* | someone who sees something, especially an accident or crime |
| f. **witness** *n.* | someone who watches another person sign an official document and then signs it also |

___b___ 1. After I had made my copies, I returned the **master** to the receptionist.

_____ 2. When my grandmother signed her will, she asked me to be a **witness**.

_____ 3. The Great Wall of China was **constructed** thousands of years ago.

_____ 4. Fiona is a **master** at sailing.

_____ 5. Good writers use clear paragraphs to **construct** their essays.

_____ 6. The police took notes as the **witnesses** described the thief.

## WORDS IN SENTENCES

*Complete each sentence with one of the words from the box.*

| | | | | |
|---|---|---|---|---|
| analysis | construct | distributed | master | rivals |
| assistance | ~~debt~~ | intends | reflected | witness |

1. When Allison borrowed a lot of money to pay for her trip to India, she went into ____debt____.

2. The police officers told the family, "If you _____ anything unusual in your neighborhood, please call us."

3. If you _____ algebra, you could become a math teacher.

4. Graduate students often give professors _____ by grading papers or teaching some classes.

5. Coca Cola's success _____ Pepsi's.

6. In the Boston Marathon, water is _____ to runners throughout the race.

7. Which group will _____ the most interesting business plan?

8. Jackie _____ to become a movie star, so he is moving to Hollywood.

9. The scientists' _____ of a McDonald's hamburger shows how much fat, salt, and sugar it has.

10. The mirror _____ Karen's smile.

# WORDS IN COLLOCATIONS AND EXPRESSIONS

*Following are common collocations (word partners) and expressions with some of the key words. Read the definitions and then complete the conversations with the correct form of the collocations and expressions.*

1. **assist**
   - **assist sb in (doing sth)**     to help someone do something
2. **debt**
   - **be in debt**     to owe money
   - **fall into debt**     to start owing money
3. **master**
   - **be a master at (sth)**     to be very skillful at something
4. **rival**
   - **sibling rivalry**     competition between brothers and sisters
5. **reflect**
   - **reflect on (sth)**     to think about something

1.    JULIE:    Wow, look at Yumiko! She's won another championship.

   MARK:    That's no surprise. She has a black belt. Yumiko _____*is a master at*_____ karate. She's certainly stronger than I am!

2.    KAYLEE:    Did you see the new car that our neighbors have, Grandma? It must have cost a fortune! They must be rich.

   GRANDMA:    Don't believe it, honey. I heard they lost their jobs a year ago. They pay for everything with their credit cards, so they owe a lot of money. They _____ in _____.

   KAYLEE:    I wish I could buy a car like that.

   GRANDMA:    Don't even think about it. I don't want to see you _____ into _____, too.

3.    REPORTER:    Could you _____ your future for a moment?

   POLITICIAN:    Sure.

   REPORTER:    If you become president, what will you do to improve our country?

   POLITICIAN:    Well . . . I intend to construct more hospitals, distribute breakfast to poor students, and give unemployed people job assistance.

4.    MOTHER:    My children fight all the time! My son and my daughter both want to be the best at everything in our house.

   TEACHER:    Don't worry. It's normal for brothers and sisters to compete. That's just _____.

   MOTHER:    Do my kids fight at school, too?

   TEACHER:    No. In fact, your son always takes care of his little sister!

5.    OFFICER 1:    Why is the dog here?

   OFFICER 2:    This dog is a master at detecting smells and can _____ us _____ finding the jewel thief.

# WORDS IN A READING

*Read this article about personal finance. Complete it with words and expressions from the boxes.*

| distributes | fall into debt | ~~intend~~ | master | rivaling |
|---|---|---|---|---|

## PERSONAL FINANCE FOR TEENAGERS

When parents and teenagers talk about money, it's frequently about how much Mom and Dad are willing to give them. Many parents _____*intend*_____ to teach their children the skills necessary to
1

_____ personal finance, but they rarely explain how to write checks, handle credit cards,
2

or save for the future. As a result, many young people spend more money than they should and

_____. In fact, personal finance is rarely talked about at home, _____ only
3                                                                                                                              4

sex and drugs as the least discussed subject between teens and their parents, according to the InCharge

Institute of America, a national nonprofit organization that _____ information about
5

personal finance education.

| analyze | assist | construct | reflect | witness |
|---|---|---|---|---|

Parents can _____ their children by talking about personal finance before their
6

children go to university. The first step in learning to manage money is communication between people

who exchange thoughts and _____ a financial plan. That's why they call it personal
7

finance.

Examples from real life can help young people prepare for their financial future. A teenager who

wants a car needs to _____ how much care and money a car requires. In addition to the
8

cost of the vehicle, there's insurance, maintenance and fuel—the total of which may shock young drivers.

As parents, it's important to set a good example. If kids _____ Mom and Dad
9

running up credit card debt, it's likely that they will _____ their parents' behavior and
10

also overuse credit cards as adults. Remember, however, that it's never too late for even grown-ups to

learn how to manage their finances—and teach their kids how they did it.

*(Adapted from "Money: A Subject Teenagers Should Learn at Home." Courier—Post online, August 28, 2005.)*

## WORDS IN DISCUSSION

*Apply the key words to your own life. Read and discuss each question in small groups. Try to use the key words.*

**EXAMPLE**

The amount of **debt** which I think is okay to have: $ _0_

**A:** *Why don't you think it's okay to have **debt**?*

**B:** *Because I don't want to owe money to anyone.*

**A:** *I disagree. Sometimes you need to have **debt**, like when you borrow money to pay for college.*

1. Something I want to be **constructed** in my home town: _____

2. A subject I want to **master**: _____

3. A person whom I have **assisted**: _____

4. A place that I **intend** to visit in my lifetime: _____

5. If I become very successful, the person who will be my **rival**: _____

6. The amount of **debt** I *don't* want to have in the future: $ _____

7. Where I go when I want to **reflect** on an important decision: _____

8. Something that is often **distributed** to people in the mail: _____

9. A person whose personality I would like to **analyze**: _____

10. The most powerful storm that I have **witnessed**: _____

## WORDS IN WRITING

*Choose two topics and write a short paragraph on each. Try to use the key words.*

1. What kind of person do you **intend** to be in ten years? How long has this been your **intention**? Explain.

**EXAMPLE**

*In ten years, I **intend** to be a businesswoman who has a great job and a wonderful family. I used to think I was going to be a doctor and travel around the world, but my **intentions** changed about a year ago.*

2. Do you think that it is better to be good at many things or **a master at** one thing? Explain.

3. If you **witnessed** a poor person asking for money on the street, would you **assist** him? Do you think it would be better to give him financial **assistance** (money) or help in another way? Explain.

4. Do you believe that parents need to pay for their children's college education, or do you think that young people should borrow money and go into **debt** to pay for it? Explain.

5. Do you have an **analytical** mind, or do you follow your emotions when you make an important decision? Give an example from your past to explain your answer.

**Key Words**

| | | | | |
|---|---|---|---|---|
| available | consultant | edit | obvious | term |
| concentrate | data | issue | stiff | trial |

## WORDS IN CONTEXT

*Use the sentences to guess what each key word means. Choose the meaning that is closest to that of the key word in **bold**.*

**1. available**
/əˈveɪləbəl/
*-adjective*

- We wanted to rent bikes, but only one was **available**; we walked instead.
- I'm sorry, sir. No rooms are **available**. Why don't I give you the number of another hotel?

*Available* means . . .   a. not broken   b. for sale   ⓒ able to be used

**2. concentrate**
/ˈkɑnsənˌtreɪt/
*-verb*

- Ginny wanted to read on the way to school, but the loud conversation on the bus made it difficult for her to **concentrate**.
- Please **concentrate**. I have time to explain the instructions only once.

*Concentrate* means . . .   a. to look   b. to think carefully   c. to listen

**3. consultant**
/kənˈsʌltənt/
*-noun*

- There's a lot to know about organizing a wedding, so Shira and Tony hired a wedding **consultant** to help them prepare for theirs.
- My friend has worked as a Los Angeles police officer for fourteen years. He was recently asked to be a **consultant** for a new detective show on TV.

*Consultant* means . . .   a. someone who gives parties   b. an actor   c. someone who gives advice

**4. data**
/ˈdeɪtə or dætə/
*-plural-noun*

- The researchers will share their findings once all the **data** have been studied.
- Computers are amazing. They can store so much **data**.

*Data* means . . .   a. science   b. information   c. messages

**5. edit**
/ˈɛdɪt/
*-verb*

- The teacher agreed to **edit** my story before it was printed in the school newspaper.
- My friend videotaped my volleyball game. Later he **edited** it and added some music. Now it's like a professional film, and I'm the star!

*Edit* means . . .   a. to prepare for presentation   b. to continue   c. to look at

**6. issue**
/ˈɪʃu/
*-noun*

- My favorite class at my English school is conversation. We discuss many different **issues** from politics to education.
- Mr. Flohr asked me to rewrite my essay. He said that I needed to consider the **issue** from two different viewpoints.

*Issue* means . . .   a. a conversation   b. a subject   c. a politician

**7. obvious**
/ˈɑbviəs/
-adjective

- It's **obvious** that Sonya is in love with Mario. Just look at her big smile and happy eyes every time she talks about him!
- Quitting your job is the **obvious** solution to your problem. Stop complaining and just leave the company.

*Obvious* means . . .      a. important          b. easy to see          c. very bad

**8. stiff**
/stɪf/
-adjective

- After sitting on the plane for eight hours, my legs were very **stiff**.
- Wayne's nervousness made him rather **stiff** on the dance floor.

*Stiff* means . . .      a. cold          b. strong          c. difficult to move

**9. term**
/tɚm/
-noun

- Franklin D. Roosevelt became president of the United States in 1933. His presidency continued for three more **terms**, making it the longest in U.S. political history.
- The professor explained that we'd have to write a ten-page paper by the end of the **term**.

*Term* means . . .      a. a period of time          b. a position          c. a vacation

**10. trial**
/ˈtraɪəl/
-noun

- When a famous person goes on **trial**, journalists make it a big story, even if the crime was small.
- My aunt's favorite channel is Court TV. She loves to watch the **trials** and guess what punishment the criminals will get.

*Trial* means . . .      a. a legal process          b. prison life          c. a fight

## WORDS AND DEFINITIONS

*Match each key word with its definition.*

1. _____obvious_____ easy to notice or understand

2. _____ information or facts

3. _____ difficult to bend or move

4. _____ (something) able to be used or bought

5. _____ someone with a lot of experience in a certain area whose job is to give advice about it

6. _____ a fixed period of time

7. _____ a subject or problem that people discuss

8. _____ to prepare a piece of writing, a book, or movie for people to read or see by correcting mistakes and making changes for the better

9. _____ a legal process in which a court of law examines a case to decide if someone is guilty of a crime

10. _____ to think very carefully about something you are doing

# COMPREHENSION CHECK

*Choose the best answer.*

1. Which of the following people does NOT work for a **term**?
   a. the president of a country
   b. the mayor of a city
   c. the owner of a company
   d. the governor of a U.S. state

2. My uncle works as a **consultant**;
   a. he buys and sells shares in companies.
   b. he advises people about investing their money.
   c. he designs plans for new houses.
   d. he trains people to become chefs.

3. Who do you NOT expect to see at a **trial**?
   a. a lawyer
   b. a witness to a crime
   c. a news reporter
   d. a tourist

4. Which of the following items does NOT contain **data**?
   a. a painting
   b. a computer
   c. a cell phone
   d. a science report

5. Can you help me **edit** my report? You can
   a. type faster than me.
   b. finish the last paragraph for me.
   c. probably suggest some changes to make it better.
   d. read it and tell me if you agree with my views.

6. All of the following are **issues** parents normally discuss with children EXCEPT
   a. safety inside and outside the home.
   b. the need to study and do homework.
   c. responsibility and the need to respect rules.
   d. bills and family finances.

7. No computer was **available** in the Internet café;
   a. I had to go back home for my wallet.
   b. I asked them when the computers would be working again.
   c. I went home without checking my e-mail.
   d. I asked them how to turn the sound back on.

8. It's **obvious** that Shane is the best person for the job;
   a. no one believes he can handle the work.
   b. everyone knows he can handle the work.
   c. the company wants to consider other people in the field.
   d. he needs some additional training.

9. My body is a little **stiff** because
   a. I haven't exercised in a while.
   b. I'm on a diet.
   c. I stayed out too long in the hot sun.
   d. I just took a warm bath.

10. In which of the following situations do you NOT need to **concentrate**?
    a. taking an exam
    b. doing a difficult math problem
    c. taking a nap
    d. driving on a busy road

# WORD FAMILIES

Now that you have studied the ten key words and their basic definitions, you are ready to learn words that belong to the same family as some of the key words. A word family includes words that look alike but have different functions (noun, verb, adjective, or adverb). Their meanings are related but different.

**A.** *Look at each model phrase and decide whether the word in **bold** is used as a noun, verb, adjective, or adverb.*

|  | NOUN | VERB | ADJECTIVE | ADVERB |
|---|---|---|---|---|
| **1. available** |  |  |  |  |
| • an **available** room |  |  | ✓ |  |
| • **unavailable** information |  |  | ✓ |  |
| **2. concentrate** |  |  |  |  |
| • difficult to **concentrate** |  |  |  |  |
| • the power of **concentration** |  |  |  |  |
| **3. consultant** |  |  |  |  |
| • a wedding **consultant** |  |  |  |  |
| • a **consultation** with a lawyer |  |  |  |  |
| • to **consult** with my co-workers |  |  |  |  |
| **4. edit** |  |  |  |  |
| • to **edit** his story |  |  |  |  |
| • the **editor's** correction |  |  |  |  |
| **5. obvious** |  |  |  |  |
| • an **obvious** solution |  |  |  |  |
| • **obviously** in love |  |  |  |  |

**B.** *Read the first half of each sentence and match it with the appropriate ending.*

__b__ 1. The chess players required a lot of

_____ 2. She couldn't even look at me;

_____ 3. Any changes in our office require

_____ 4. The journalist wasn't happy with

_____ 5. Gregory called his doctor;

_____ 6. The book I wanted was

a. **unavailable** at the library.

b. **concentration**. The room fell silent.

c. the **editor's** changes to her story.

d. she was **obviously** lying.

e. **consultation**; the company president likes to be informed about everything.

f. he wanted to **consult** with someone.

## SAME WORD, DIFFERENT MEANING

Most words have more than one meaning. Study the additional meanings of **available**, **stiff**, and **term**. Then read each sentence and decide which meaning is used.

| | | | |
|---|---|---|---|
| a. | **available** *adj.* | (something) able to be used or bought | |
| b. | **available** *adj.* | (someone) not busy, free to see or talk to you | |
| c. | **stiff** *adj.* | difficult to bend or move | |
| d. | **stiff** *adj.* | more difficult, strict, or severe than usual | |
| e. | **term** *n.* | a fixed period of time | |
| f. | **term** *n.* | a word or expression that has a particular meaning | |

___f___ 1. I tried to help Hon-Ning translate the article, but there were too many technical **terms** I didn't know.

_____ 2. My neck felt **stiff** after taking a nap on the couch.

_____ 3. Littering, the crime of throwing trash on the street, can result in **stiff** fines. I read that in one Texas town a person guilty of littering could pay up to $2,000.

_____ 4. I'd like to speak with the school director. Is he **available** right now?

_____ 5. How long is the **term** of the British Prime Minister?

_____ 6. I left my cell phone at home, and there were no pay phones **available**.

## WORDS IN SENTENCES

Complete each sentence with one of the words from the box.

| | | | | |
|---|---|---|---|---|
| available | consult | ~~issue~~ | stiff | trial |
| concentration | edit | obviously | terms | unavailable |

1. Monina's decision to delay college for a year has become a(n) _____issue_____ with her parents. They hope that further discussion will change her mind.

2. I found the kind of sunglasses I was looking for, but they were _____ in the color I wanted.

3. The doctor's use of medical _____ confused the patient's family. They asked him to explain in simpler words.

4. Always take the time to _____ your writing before handing it in.

5. I lost my _____ when the students sitting behind me began to whisper.

6. The leather of my boots was kind of _____ at first, but after wearing the boots for a week, it became easier to move around in them.

7. Luc _____ didn't know the answer to the question; he looked back at the teacher with a blank face.

8. I got a speeding ticket, but I decided to fight it. On the day of my _____ the police officer didn't appear in court, so in the end I didn't have to pay a fine.

9. I'm sorry. Ms. Gerber isn't _____ right now. Would you like to leave a message?

10. Why don't you _____ with Kostya? He has a lot of knowledge about banking and money matters.

## WORDS IN COLLOCATIONS AND EXPRESSIONS

*Following are common collocations (word partners) and expressions with some of the key words. Read the definitions and then complete the conversations with the correct form of the collocations and expressions.*

| | |
|---|---|
| 1. **concentrate** | |
| • **concentrate on (sth)** | to give most of your attention to one thing |
| 2. **consult** | |
| • **consult with (sb)** | to ask for someone's permission or advice before making a decision |
| 3. **issue** | |
| • **make an issue out of (sth)** | to argue about something |
| 4. **stiff** | |
| • **stiff punishment** (*or* **fine**) | very severe punishment (*or* fine) |
| 5. **term** | |
| • **serve a term** | to hold an official position for a fixed period of time (especially in politics or education) |
| • **serve a prison term** | to remain in prison for a fixed period of time |

1. COACH: Joe, you're going to sit on the bench for the next three games.

   JOE: Coach, I know I was late for practice, but that's a _____*stiff punishment*_____. The team needs me on the field.

   COACH: Joe, I warned you. Today was the third time you came late.

2. WIFE: You're never home on Friday nights. We work all week, so when do I get to see you?

   HUSBAND: Honey, please don't _____ this. You know that Friday night is card night. My friends and I have been getting together like this for years. I need time with them, too. You and I have Saturday and Sunday together.

3. BEN: There are so many other students here! I don't think I have a chance of getting in the school play.

   LYLE: Don't worry about anyone else. Just _____ doing your best. They'd be blind not to see how good an actor you are.

   BEN: Thanks for the support. I hope you're right.

4. CRIMINAL: So what's the worst punishment I might get?

   LAWYER: I'm afraid your criminal history doesn't help. Bank robbery is a serious crime. You may have to _____ of fifteen years or more.

5. CRAIG: Do you have anything stronger than aspirin? My headache is getting worse.

   LISA: Aren't you already taking some medication? I think you should _____ your doctor before you start taking anything new.

6. JOURNALIST: Sir, do you plan to run again for office?

   MAYOR: No, I plan to _____ my last _____ as mayor of this town and then retire to a quiet life.

## WORDS IN A READING

*Read this article about computer crimes. Complete it with words and expressions from the boxes.*

| available | ~~data~~ | stiff punishments | serves (a) prison term | trial |
|---|---|---|---|---|

### PUTTING A STOP TO TEENAGE HACKING* CRIMES

Not many people connect hacking to phones. Unfortunate people like Paris Hilton, however, have learned that _____data_____ can be stolen from cell phones just as easily as from desktop
                        1
computers. Ms. Hilton's cell phone address book was taken by a seventeen-year-old hacker in Massachusetts. He then made the information _____ on the Internet, and in doing so he
                                                                            2
took away privacy from other celebrities, like tennis star Anna Kournikova and rapper Eminem.

The case went to _____, and luckily for the teenager, he was treated as a minor, not
                        3
as an adult. He will have eleven months of detention and, after release, two years of supervision. While
he _____ his _____, the boy will not be allowed to use the Internet. U.S.
                        4
Attorney Michael Sullivan, who faced the young criminal in court, stated, "Computer hacking is not
fun and games," and he warned that those who break the law, whether young or old, will receive
"_____" in the future.
      5

| concentrate on | consultant | data | edit | issue | obvious |
|---|---|---|---|---|---|

In a different case of hacking, three high school students in Panama City, Florida, entered their
school's computer system and changed grades for a friend. (They had no need to _____
                                                                                        6
their own records since they were at the top of their class in computer science and other subjects.) The
sixteen-year-olds were taken by police, and administrators now want the students removed from

*Hacking is using a computer to secretly and illegally enter someone else's computer system. The person who does so is a hacker.*

school. Principal Larry Bollinger stated that in response to the crime, Bay High School will

_____ improving computer security.
          7

The _____ of teenage hacking is handled differently from state to state, but one
          8

thing is becoming more _____ to all: stronger action is being taken against the crime.
          9

Authorities recognize the need to fight hackers of mobile phones, PDAs**, and computer systems.

Shane Coursen, senior technical _____ for Kaspersky Lab, an IT security company in
                                          10

Moscow, adds that users themselves can take steps to protect their _____. Mobile
                                                                              11

electronic equipment, as Coursen points out, includes basic security features such as passwords and

auto locks. The problem is that the average user doesn't think about security. Moreover, mobile phone

security is still in its early stages of development. The answer to the problem of hacking, though, will

come as a result of action taken by both the law and the users themselves.

*(Based on information in Gene J. Koprowski, "We'll Always Have Paris." TechNewsWorld online, October 28, 2005.)*

## WORDS IN DISCUSSION

*Apply the key words to your own life. Read and discuss each question in small groups. Try to use the key words.*

1. Name a difficult **issue** for parents to address with their children (or for children to address with their parents).

   **EXAMPLE**

   *Discussing the **issue** of freedom and responsibility is difficult for both parents and children. Children want more freedom. Parents think their children aren't responsible enough . . .*

2. What would be **obvious** to anyone about your life just by looking through your wallet?

3. Did you ever receive a **stiff punishment** for something you did? Do you think it was fair?

4. Why would someone choose *not* to store **data** electronically?

5. What are some common mistakes you must correct when you **edit** your own work?

6. Does a cell phone make you **available** all the time? When are you **unavailable** to talk to others?

7. Does music help you **concentrate** or does it make you lose your **concentration**?

8. Do you think the **trials** in movies and on TV show what happens in a real court?

9. In what kinds of situations do people hire a **consultant**? Has anyone ever held a **consultation** with you?

10. In your opinion, does **serving a** long **prison term** help a criminal in any way?

---

**PDA = Personal data assistant, a handheld computer for personal use

## ▊ WORDS IN WRITING

*Choose two topics and write a short paragraph on each. Try to use the key words.*

1. Do you **consult with** other people before making an important decision?

   **EXAMPLE**

   *When I have to make an important decision, I always **consult with** others first, just to hear other opinions. My dad has a lot of life experience, so I sometimes have a little **consultation** with him. I also **consult with** friends who work in different fields . . .*

2. Have you ever chosen to try something **obviously** difficult or dangerous? Why? Were you successful?

3. What skills does a person require to be a good newspaper or magazine **editor**? Would the job of **editing** a well-known newspaper or magazine interest you?

4. Have you ever faced **stiff** competition? Were you able to keep your **concentration**? Explain.

5. Your best friend forgot your birthday. Would you **make an issue** out of it? Why? Explain.

# CHAPTER 3

## WORDS IN CONTEXT

*Use the sentences to guess what each key word means. Choose the meaning that is closest to that of the key word in **bold**.*

1. **accurate**
   /ˈækyərɪt/
   -adjective

   • The scientist was very careful with his experiment because he wanted **accurate** results.
   • "The Earth is round" is an **accurate** statement.

   *Accurate* means . . .　　(a.) correct　　　　b. strange　　　　c. incorrect

2. **classic**
   /ˈklæsɪk/
   -adjective

   • Spaghetti is a **classic** Italian food.
   • Wooden shoes are a **classic** fashion in Holland.

   *Classic* means . . .　　a. new　　　　b. expensive　　　　c. typical or traditional

3. **critic**
   /ˈkrɪtɪk/
   -noun

   • The movie **critic** wrote that *Lord of the Rings* was a great film but too long.
   • Food **critics** decide how many stars a restaurant should have.

   *Critic* means . . .　　a. a food or movie lover　　b. someone who reports whether something is good or bad　　c. a person who reads something

4. **encourage**
   /ɪnˈkɚɪdʒ/
   -verb

   • My parents **encouraged** me to read when I was a small child, taking me to the library often and praising me when I finished books.
   • If your best friend wanted to become a doctor, would you **encourage** her to follow this dream?

   *Encourage* means . . .　　a. to give confidence and support　　b. to work hard　　c. to tell someone they can't do something

5. **exhibit**
   /ɪgˈzɪbɪt/
   -verb

   • The Tate Museum in London is **exhibiting** many of Turner's paintings.
   • The MIT museum **exhibits** a robot named Kismet.

   *Exhibit* means . . .　　a. to move　　　　b. to find　　　　c. to show

6. **firm**
   /fɚm/
   -adjective

   • The architects couldn't build the house on the beach; the foundation needed to be built on **firm** ground.
   • If you ask someone to marry you, you don't want this person to say, "Maybe"; rather, you want to hear a **firm** answer.

   *Firm* means . . .　　a. solid or definite　　b. weak or soft　　c. attractive and interesting

**7. label**
/ˈleɪbəl/
-noun

- If you want to know what ingredients are in this soup, read the **label** on the can.
- To find out how to wash your shirt, look at the **label** inside it.

*Label* means . . .
 a. a container
 b. a piece of metal
 c. a piece of paper on something that tells about it

**8. prejudice**
/ˈprɛdʒədɪs/
-noun

- "Henry, that man doesn't know you. If he hates you, it's because of the color of your skin or the place you come from. This is **prejudice**."
- If a white person won't sit next to a black person on the bus, do you think this is **prejudice**?

*Prejudice* means . . .
 a. an unfair feeling of dislike for someone
 b. having an open mind
 c. friendliness

**9. process**
/ˈprɑsɛs/
-noun

- The **process** of getting your driver's license in the United States is long. First, you should get your learner's permit; next, you should take a driving class; finally, you need to take a written test and a driving test.
- Learning a new language is a long and challenging **process**. You must practice grammar, speaking, listening, reading, and vocabulary to master the language.

*Process* means . . .
 a. discussion
 b. a series of actions that lead to a result
 c. improvement

**10. tempt**
/tɛmpt/
-verb

- I'm on a diet, so please don't **tempt** me with that chocolate cake.
- My sister **tempted** me to skip school on a beautiful spring afternoon.

*Tempt* means . . .
 a. to not be interested in
 b. to make someone want to do something
 c. to smell

## ▌WORDS AND DEFINITIONS

*Match each key word with its definition.*

1. _____*tempt*_____ to make someone want to have or do something even though they know they really should not

2. _____ to put something in a public place so that people can see it

3. _____ someone whose job is to give his/her judgment, that is, to decide whether something is good or bad

4. _____ a piece of paper that is attached to something and has information about that thing printed on it

5. _____ correct in every detail

6. _____ solid or definite, unlikely to move or change

7. _____ to help someone be confident or brave enough to do something

8. _____ typical or traditional

9. _____ a series of actions that someone does to achieve a particular result

10. _____ an unfair feeling of dislike against someone who is of a different race, sex, religion, etc.

## COMPREHENSION CHECK

*Choose the best answer.*

1. Which of the following is **accurate**?
   a. 2 + 2 = 5
   b. Ice cream is hot.
   c. The sun rises in the east and sets in the west.
   d. Very few people live in China.

2. Which of the following CANNOT be **firm**?
   a. an answer
   b. air
   c. the ground
   d. a mattress

3. Which of the people speaking is probably a **critic**?
   a. "The beginning of the concert was great, but the end was very boring."
   b. "I played music for three hours tonight."
   c. "I am so quiet; I never tell my opinion."
   d. "I wish I didn't have to clean the stadium when everyone leaves the concert tonight."

4. Which quote was said by a person who feels **prejudice**?
   a. "All people are equal."
   b. "All women are bad at business."
   c. "You can't tell what a person is like just by looking at the color of his skin."
   d. "I am happy to have neighbors from different countries."

5. If Tao **exhibits** photographs in his gallery, he
   a. doesn't take them out of his briefcase.
   b. talks about the photographs.
   c. sells the photographs.
   d. puts them on the walls of his gallery.

6. If your friend **tempts** you to skip work, he says,
   a. "Forget about work. I have tickets to the baseball game!"
   b. "You need to go to your job today."
   c. "If you skip work, you'll get in trouble."
   d. "I'll drop you off at your office."

7. Which action is NOT part of the **process** of learning a new language?
   a. memorizing new vocabulary
   b. speaking the new language
   c. studying the grammar
   d. watching TV in your native language

8. On which **label** would you probably find the words "dry clean or hand wash, cool iron"?
   a. the label on a shampoo bottle
   b. the label on a milk carton
   c. the label in a blouse
   d. the label on a box of matches

9. If Lilia likes **classic** Indian food, for her birthday meal we should
   a. create a new dish using our imaginations.
   b. make her a typical Indian dish.
   c. order food from an exciting but strange restaurant.
   d. serve breakfast food at night.

10. Which statement will **encourage** Alexandra?
   a. "You are not smart enough to become a doctor."
   b. "Why apply to medical school?"
   c. "Being a doctor is too much work for you."
   d. "You would be a great doctor! You should apply to medical school."

## ▌WORD FAMILIES

Now that you have studied the ten key words and their basic definitions, you are ready to learn words that belong to the same family as some of the key words. A word family includes words that look alike but have different functions (noun, verb, adjective, or adverb). Their meanings are related but different.

**A.** *Look at each model phrase and decide whether the word in **bold** is used as a noun, verb, adjective, or adverb.*

| | NOUN | VERB | ADJECTIVE | ADVERB |
|---|---|---|---|---|
| **1. critic** | | | | |
| • to think about the film **critically** | | | | ✓ |
| • **criticize** everybody | | ✓ | | |
| • a **critical** person | | | ✓ | |
| **2. encourage** | | | | |
| • to **encourage** people | | | | |
| • give **encouragement** | | | | |
| **3. exhibit** | | | | |
| • to **exhibit** rare books | | | | |
| • an art **exhibit/exhibition** | | | | |
| **4. prejudice** | | | | |
| • racial **prejudice** | | | | |
| • a **prejudiced** person | | | | |
| **5. process** | | | | |
| • a long **process** | | | | |
| • to **process** an application | | | | |
| **6. tempt** | | | | |
| • to **tempt** us | | | | |
| • a **tempting** offer | | | | |
| • give in to **temptation** | | | | |

**B.** *Read the first half of each sentence and match it with the appropriate ending.*

___d___ 1. Kaled does not like
_____ 2. Because of her mother's
_____ 3. Please don't
_____ 4. Joe won't be friends with a

a. **exhibition** to see interesting building designs.
b. **prejudiced** person.
c. **temptation** of going to the beach.
d. **critical** people.

_____ 5. I couldn't resist the

e. **encouragement**, Jana was confident.

_____ 6. It may take the office a long time to

f. **tempting** idea.

_____ 7. We went to an architecture

g. **process** your application.

_____ 8. Eating more dessert is a

h. **criticize** me; I am trying as hard as I can!

## ▌SAME WORD, DIFFERENT MEANING

*Most words have more than one meaning. Study the additional meanings of **critic**, **firm**, and **exhibit**. Then read each sentence and decide which meaning is used.*

| | |
|---|---|
| a. **critic** *n.* | someone whose job is to give his/her judgment about whether something is good or bad |
| b. **critic** *n.* | someone who says that someone or something is bad or wrong |
| c. **firm** *adj.* | solid or definite, not likely to move or change |
| d. **firm** *n.* | a business or small company |
| e. **exhibit** *v.* | to put something in a public place so that people can see it |
| f. **exhibit** *v.* | to show a quality, sign, emotion, etc. in a way that people easily notice |

_*b*_ 1. The queen's friends thought that she looked lovely at the party, but her **critics** said that her dress was ugly.

_____ 2. If your pet bird **exhibits** signs that it is sick, you should take it to the vet.

_____ 3. Henri works for a law **firm** in Hong Kong.

_____ 4. We plan to **exhibit** the best student photographs in the school's lobby.

_____ 5. Call us when you can give us a **firm** answer.

_____ 6. Because the movie **critic** in *The New York Times* liked the documentary, I decided to see it.

## ▌WORDS IN SENTENCES

*Complete each sentence with one of the words from the box.*

| | | | | |
|---|---|---|---|---|
| accurate | criticize | exhibit | ~~label~~ | process |
| classic | encouragement | firm | prejudice | temptation |

1. The company address was written on the package's _____*label*_____.

2. 5 + 5 = 10 is a(n) _____ statement.

3. Dad took me for many bike rides in the park when I was a child; his _____ made me love biking and helped me become a champion cyclist.

4. Look! The dog is staring at the steak on the barbecue! I bet he wants to eat our dinner. Will he resist the _____?

5. I hope to work for a large telecommunications _____.

6. A perfect society has no _____ .

7. Our boss is in a bad mood, so he probably will _____ you when you arrive late.

8. A(n) _____ design will never go out of style.

9. There is an interesting _____ of travel photographs in the library this month.

10. The _____ of becoming an American citizen is quite complicated.

## ▌WORDS IN COLLOCATIONS AND EXPRESSIONS

*Following are common collocations (word partners) and expressions with some of the key words. Read the definitions and then complete the conversations with the correct form of the collocations and expressions.*

1. **accurate**
   - **accurate information**      correct information

2. **classic**
   - **a classic example**      a typical or very good example

3. **firm**
   - **a firm handshake**      a good, strong handshake

4. **process**
   - **a natural process**      a series of actions, developments, or changes that happen naturally

5. **tempt**
   - **don't tempt me**      Don't make me want to do that!
   - **be tempted to do (sth)**      to consider doing something that may not be a good idea

1.  BUSINESSMAN 1:   It's nice to meet you. (*The two men shake hands.*)

    BUSINESSMAN 2:   It's nice to meet you, too. You have _____*a firm handshake*_____ . I like that.

2.  CHILD:   I'm not smart enough!

    TEACHER:   Some people believe that it's better to work hard than to be very intelligent. _____ is the story of the tortoise and the hare. In this story, the slow turtle beats the fast rabbit because the rabbit is lazy.

3.  JOSHUA:   I am tired of being on a diet! I know that I shouldn't, but I am _____ to eat something sweet and creamy.

    ROSEANNE:   Well, I just made your favorite cookies. Don't they smell wonderful?

    JOSHUA:   Roseanne, please, _____!

4.  STUDENT 1:   Jeff ruined our report! It's filled with mistakes. His facts are completely inaccurate.

    STUDENT 2:   Maybe the teacher won't notice.

STUDENT 1:     Impossible. Look, he wrote that the capital of Turkey is Madrid. Come on. Let's correct all the mistakes. This report has to present _____.

5.     ELENA:     I'm so homesick. I miss Russia and feel so lonely in the United States!

       DANIEL:     Don't worry. Being homesick is part of _____ of getting used to life in a new country. Everyone goes through it. You'll feel better in a few months.

## ▌WORDS IN A READING

*Read this article about music. Complete it with words and expressions from the boxes.*

| are tempted | ~~classic~~ | encouragement | exhibiting | labels |

### SALSA MUSIC ENERGIZES JAPAN

When most people imagine Salsa dancing, they think of hot, Latin countries. After all, *salsa* is the name for a variety of music and dance with Latin and Afro-Caribbean roots. The popularity of salsa is reaching new parts of the world, however, and serious salsa dancers now can be found even in the most unlikely of places: Japan.

Salsa music is completely different from formal, ____classic____ Japanese music—and that's exactly
                                                          1
why dancers here _____ to try salsa. By choosing salsa, dancers can rebel against their
                         2
orderly society. Salsa gives young Japanese the _____ they need to express their emotions.
                                                              3
Japan is _____ unmistakable signs of a salsa boom. One salsa magazine here has a
              4
circulation of about 40,000. Its pages list 200 salsa-related events per month nationwide. Music stores
offer large collections of CDs with salsa _____, and salsa-based fitness classes are now
                                                      5
standard at Japanese gyms.

The salsa rebellion was in full swing on a recent weekend in Tokyo, when 3,400 people came together in the sixth annual Japan Salsa Congress—a three-day dance party.

| a natural process | accurate | criticism | firm | prejudiced |

For some Japanese fans, learning salsa involves lots of hard work. It's not _____. At
                                                                                        6
the salsa congress, for instance, some beginners took notes and others recorded moves with video cameras so that they could study and master the moves at home.

As with other hobbies in Japan, Japanese dancers are willing to pay a lot of money for the right acces-
sories with all the _____ details. Dancers can spend as much as 25,000 yen for a pair of must-
                          7
have salsa shoes. Female fans drop tens of thousands of yen at tanning salons to achieve a "sexy Latina" look.

Salsa's popularity in Japan coincides with a worldwide Latin boom over the last decade fueled by films like Wim Wenders's 1999 documentary *The Buena Vista Social Club* and the success of stars like Ricky Martin.

Many say salsa has a special popularity in Japan precisely because it is so different from the formal culture, in which people often keep _____ control over their emotions. Six years ago,
8
salsa received _____ from traditional Japanese people. They were _____
9 10
against the music because it seemed too passionate. Now, however, salsa is very popular in Tokyo.

"The Japanese have really embraced it," says Albert Torres, a major producer of salsa events worldwide. "It's like night and day. There's no comparison to six years ago. It's not the same city."

*(Based on information in Natalie Obiko Pearson, "Salsa Fanatics Defy Rigid Japan." The Japan Times, December 21, 2004.)*

## ▌WORDS IN DISCUSSION

*Apply the key words to your own life. Read and discuss each question in small groups. Try to use the key words.*

**EXAMPLE**

Someone who is very **critical**: ___My cousin Wendy___

**A:** *Wendy **criticizes** everyone around her. It's really annoying.*

**B:** *Why do you think she's so **critical**?*

**A:** *She's a perfectionist, so she **criticizes** anyone who isn't perfect.*

1. How often I am **tempted** to drive very fast: _____

2. What is written on the **label** of the shirt I am wearing: _____

3. What I know about the **process** of learning how to drive: _____

4. What I would do if a **prejudiced** person told me a racial joke: _____

5. How I would feel if I went to a modern art **exhibit**: _____

6. Something someone once said about me that was not **accurate**: _____

7. My opinion of working as a professional food **critic**: _____

8. A **classic** meal in my native country: _____

9. The last time I gave a **firm** answer: _____

10. A person who **encourages** me to follow my dreams: _____

## ▌WORDS IN WRITING

*Choose two topics and write a short paragraph on each. Try to use the key words.*

1. If one of your friends always **criticized** people, would you tell her to stop?

**EXAMPLE**

*I don't like it when people are always **criticizing** others, so I would talk with my friend. Of course, a **critic** can be helpful sometimes. For example, when I took piano lessons, I needed my teacher to explain when I'd made a mistake so that I could improve . . .*

2. How much **prejudice** do you see in the town where you live? Explain.

3. Would you rather visit an **exhibit** of Leonardo da Vinci's inventions or an **exhibit** of inventions by children in your town? Explain.

4. Have you ever **tempted** a friend to do something bad? Tell your story, and explain whether or not you would do so again.

5. Who has **encouraged** you to follow your dreams? Describe this person and the **encouragement** he or she gave you.

## PART A

*Choose the word that best completes each item and write it in the space provided.*

1. The *SS Great Britain* was ____constructed____ of iron, and in 1843 it became the first ship of its kind to cross an ocean.
   - a. exhibited
   - b. assisted
   - c. intended
   - d. constructed

2. Growing up, my brother and I were _____; we made everything a competition.
   - a. critics
   - b. rivals
   - c. masters
   - d. consultants

3. I read the _____ on the bottle to find out how often I could take the medicine.
   - a. label
   - b. process
   - c. issue
   - d. term

4. They did a poor job _____ the movie. Some parts should have been left out.
   - a. analyzing
   - b. editing
   - c. distributing
   - d. exhibiting

5. Our team was losing, but the clapping and cheers from our fans _____ us.
   - a. encouraged
   - b. tempted
   - c. intended
   - d. reflected

6. The company needed advice about foreign markets, so it hired a _____.
   - a. critic
   - b. rival
   - c. master
   - d. consultant

7. Learning a language is a _____; many steps must be taken towards improving your communication.
   - a. label
   - b. process
   - c. trial
   - d. term

8. The teacher asked us not to look at the test until she had finished _____ copies to the class.
   - a. analyzing
   - b. editing
   - c. distributing
   - d. tempting

9. In the newspaper I read several reviews of the play by different _____.
   - a. critics
   - b. rivals
   - c. masters
   - d. consultants

10. You can't say you won't like chemistry just because you found out your teacher will be a woman. That's _____.
    - a. debt
    - b. prejudice
    - c. data
    - d. issue

## PART B

Read each statement and write **T** for true *or* **F** *for* false *in the space provided.*

_T_ 1. When someone **assists** you, it's polite to say "thank you."

_____ 2. A dancer's body should always be **stiff**.

_____ 3. When the answer to a question is **obvious**, you need to carefully explain it to others.

_____ 4. **Reflecting** on your past means trying to forget it.

_____ 5. Borrowing money and seldom paying your bills will put you in **debt**.

_____ 6. The mayor served two **terms**. He was elected twice.

_____ 7. Leaving your wallet on the seat of your unlocked car would likely **tempt** a thief.

_____ 8. A computer is good for storing a lot of **data**.

_____ 9. If rare paintings are in an **exhibit**, only the owners can view them.

_____ 10. If Matt **intends** to travel the world, he should have a passport.

## PART C

Complete each item with a word from the box. Use each word once.

| accurate | available | concentrate | issue | trial |
|----------|-----------|-------------|-------|-------|
| analyze | classic | firm | master | ~~witnesses~~ |

1. Hoping to get a good description of the robbers, the police talked to several ____witnesses____.

2. You need to _____ when you're driving, so talking on the phone and eating aren't helpful activities behind the wheel.

3. With a record of eighteen wins at the professional level, Jack Nicklaus is a golf _____ .

4. The lawyer met with his client weeks before the _____ so that they could prepare their case.

5. The house was very old, and the stairs didn't feel _____ under my feet. I was afraid the old boards wouldn't hold my weight.

6. The prime minister needs to make _____ statements. That's why he keeps himself well informed and thinks before answering questions.

7. In history class we always discuss a(n) _____ from different viewpoints.

8. Scientists _____ test results before making conclusions.

9. I wanted to buy the boots in black, but only brown was _____.

10. My parents had a difficult time decorating the house because my father likes unusual modern pieces and my mother prefers _____ designs.

## ▎WORDS IN CONTEXT

*Use the sentences to guess what each key word means. Choose the meaning that is closest to that of the key word in **bold**.*

**1. benefit**
/'bɛnəfɪt/
*-noun*

- Rashid got a new job with good **benefits**, including three weeks of paid vacation each year.
- My grandmother now pays less for her medication. It's a **benefit** the government gives to the elderly.

*Benefit* means . . .    a. a promise    (b.) money or advantage    c. a prize

**2. contrast**
/'kɑntræst/
*-noun*

- We walked out of the dark movie theater and into the bright light. The **contrast** hurt my eyes.
- Vincent is very tall, and his wife is very petite. You can't help but notice the **contrast**.

*Contrast* means . . .    a. similarity    b. a difference    c. a surprise

**3. convenience**
/kən'vinyəns/
*-noun*

- Lalana enjoys the **convenience** of having the bus stop right in front of her building.
- Elevators and escalators offer **convenience**, but I prefer to walk up the stairs for exercise.

*Convenience* means . . .    a. movement    b. usefulness; ease    c. a rest

**4. insure**
/ɪn'ʃʊr/
*-verb*

- I'm a careful driver, but I still plan to **insure** my car. I don't want to pay for an accident caused by another.
- Matthew **insures** all the artwork he buys in case any of it is stolen. Each piece is very valuable.

*Insure* means . . .    a. to buy protection    b. to own    c. to make like new

**5. lessen**
/'lɛsən/
*-verb*

- Jonas hurt his leg while skiing. We did what we could to **lessen** the pain until medical help arrived.
- Angelita tried to **lessen** the shock of her news, but her parents were still very surprised to learn that she was going to move to another city.

*Lessen* means . . .    a. to help through laughter    b. to increase    c. to make smaller

**6. locate**
/'loʊkeɪt/
*-verb*

- Can you help me **locate** Washington Street on this map? I don't see it.
- The police are trying to **locate** the stolen car.

*Locate* means . . .    a. to replace    b. to find the position    c. to draw

**7. logic**
/'lɑdʒɪk/
-noun

- I don't understand your **logic**. Why do you wash the dishes before you put them in the dishwasher?
- You treat problems with the **logic** of a small child: you believe that if you can't see it, it must not exist.

*Logic* means . . .    a. a hope          b. a daily routine          c. a way of thinking

**8. rate**
/reɪt/
-noun

- I prefer to live in a small town. Large cities have a higher crime **rate**.
- They say the **rate** of accidents in the air is much lower than the rate on land.

*Rate* means . . .    a. seriousness    b. how often an          c. the degree of difficulty
                                         activity occurs

**9. require**
/rɪ'kwaɪɚ/
-verb

- Dogs **require** more care than cats. You have to walk a dog often.
- The contract **requires** two signatures: the employer's and the employee's.

*Require* means . . .    a. to need          b. to want          c. to show

**10. scale**
/skeɪl/
-noun

- My girlfriend dreams of a huge wedding, but I'd prefer something on a small **scale**.
- Even as a child I loved science, so while my classmates tried to do the simplest science projects, I created projects on a large **scale**.

*Scale* means . . .    a. a piece of land    b. a size or level    c. an amount of money

## ▌WORDS AND DEFINITIONS

*Match each key word to its definition.*

1. _____benefit_____ money or other advantages that you get from the government or as part of your job

2. _____ to buy protection for you or something you own in case of illness, accident, or theft

3. _____ the number of times something happens over a period of time

4. _____ the quality of being good or useful for a particular purpose, especially because it makes something easier

5. _____ to need something

6. _____ a large difference between two people or things

7. _____ the size or level of something when compared to what is normal

8. _____ to become smaller in size, amount, importance or value, or to make something do this

9. _____ a way of thinking; a set of sensible and correct reasons

10. _____ to find the exact position of something

# COMPREHENSION CHECK

*Choose the best answer.*

1. Plants **require** all of the following EXCEPT
   a. sunshine.
   b. water.
   c. meat.
   d. soil.

2. Linh created a colorful **contrast** in the room
   a. by placing red pillows on her white sofa.
   b. by painting the walls in a soft blue.
   c. by painting the walls bright orange.
   d. by matching the pillows, sofa, carpet, and walls.

3. I'm trying to **locate** the school office.
   a. Do you have the key?
   b. Can you point me in the right direction?
   c. I'm the school secretary.
   d. It needs a complete cleaning.

4. I felt that the teacher **lessened** the importance of my question
   a. by adding information from the Internet and two other textbooks.
   b. by taking the time to answer in detail.
   c. by writing key names and dates on the board.
   d. by making a joke and not really giving an answer.

5. The employment **rate** for people who want to work in the comfort of their own homes
   a. has increased thanks to computers.
   b. costs a lot of money.
   c. is more efficient for companies.
   d. has already stopped.

6. If the **scale** of a project is big, a company
   a. can use fewer workers than usual.
   b. requires more time than usual to complete it.
   c. may complete it sooner than everyone expects.
   d. should spend less money on it than other projects.

7. Which of the following is a common **benefit** that companies offer?
   a. use of a company uniform
   b. help paying medical costs
   c. driving lessons
   d. housecleaning

8. How might a supermarket offer **convenience**?
   a. by staying open seven days a week from 8 A.M. till midnight
   b. by closing its doors at 5 P.M. every day
   c. by lowering the prices on meat and fish
   d. by changing the look of the store with paint and new lights

9. Which of the following activities needs more emotion than **logic**?
   a. making a business decision
   b. singing a song
   c. playing a game of chess
   d. presenting an argument in an essay

10. What do people NOT **insure** their property against?
    a. fire
    b. theft
    c. flood water
    d. visitors

# WORD FAMILIES

Now that you have studied the ten key words and their basic definitions, you are ready to learn words that belong to the same family as some of the key words. A word family includes words that look alike but have different functions (noun, verb, adjective, or adverb). Their meanings are related but different.

**A.** *Look at each model phrase and decide whether the word in **bold** is used as a noun, verb, adjective, or adverb.*

|  | NOUN | VERB | ADJECTIVE | ADVERB |
|---|:---:|:---:|:---:|:---:|
| 1. **benefit** | | | | |
| • receive **benefits** | ✓ | | | |
| • to **benefit** workers | | ✓ | | |
| 2. **contrast** | | | | |
| • a strong **contrast** | | | | |
| • **contrast** two artists | | | | |
| 3. **convenience** | | | | |
| • the **convenience** of taxis | | | | |
| • a **convenient** time | | | | |
| 4. **insure** | | | | |
| • **insure** your home | | | | |
| • buy **insurance** | | | | |
| 5. **locate** | | | | |
| • **locate** a person | | | | |
| • the school's **location** | | | | |
| 6. **logic** | | | | |
| • use **logic** | | | | |
| • a **logical** conclusion | | | | |
| 7. **require** | | | | |
| • **require** a visa | | | | |
| • state the **requirements** | | | | |

**B.** *Read each sentence and match the word in **bold** with the correct definition from page 34.*

___g___ 1. All drivers in this state must have **insurance**.

_____ 2. Our history teacher asked us to write a paper in which we **contrast** two kings.

_____ 3. The new library will greatly **benefit** the students.

_____ 4. What are the **requirements** for becoming a fitness instructor?

_____ 5. The café next to the subway entrance is a **convenient** meeting place.

_____ 6. When we chose our apartment, a good **location** was most important.

_____ 7. Living at home after college was the most **logical** thing to do; I needed to find a job before I could rent an apartment.

a. to help someone, or to be useful to him or her

b. something needed or asked for

c. seeming reasonable and sensible

d. a particular place or position

e. to compare two people or things to show how they are different from each other

f. near and easy to get to

g. an arrangement with a company in which you regularly pay money to the company and the company pays the costs if anything bad happens to you or your property

## ▌ SAME WORD, DIFFERENT MEANING

*Most words have more than one meaning. Study the additional meanings of **benefit**, **insure**, and **rate**. Then read each sentence and decide which meaning is used.*

| | | |
|---|---|---|
| a. | **benefit** *n.* | money or other advantages that you get from the government or as part of your job |
| b. | **benefit** *n.* | an advantage or help that you get from something |
| c. | **insure** *v.* | to buy insurance for you or something you own |
| d. | **insure** *v.* | to make something certain to happen |
| e. | **rate** *n.* | the number of times something happens over a period of time |
| f. | **rate** *n.* | the speed at which something happens over a period of time |

___d___ 1. Everyone in my family gets a flu shot. We do what we can to **insure** our good health.

_____ 2. The professor spoke at such a fast **rate** that the students had trouble taking notes.

_____ 3. The restaurant owner was smart to **insure** the building. If he lost his business, he'd have nothing.

_____ 4. I believe that learning to play an instrument gives a child many **benefits**. Among them are a love of music, a sense of rhythm, and a better understanding of math.

_____ 5. The Philippines has a higher birth **rate** than Vietnam.

_____ 6. My job doesn't pay a lot, but it has great **benefits**—all my health expenses are covered, and I get four weeks of paid vacation each year.

## ▌ WORDS IN SENTENCES

*Complete each sentence on page 35 with one of the words from the box.*

| | | | | |
|---|---|---|---|---|
| benefit | ~~convenient~~ | lessen | logical | required |
| contrasts | insure | location | rate | scale |

1. Some hotels offer guests _____convenient_____ items such as bathrobes, slippers, hangers, shampoo, soap, coffee, pens, and paper free of charge.

2. One way Arabic _____ with English is that it's read from right to left.

3. When gas prices go up, car owners suffer, but oil companies _____.

4. The _____ of the office is not ideal, but the job itself interests me. Maybe in the future I'll find my dream job in the ideal place.

5. Teresa's apologies and sincere explanation did little to _____ Shani's anger.

6. The architect knew he could design the building rather quickly; this was a small-_____ project.

7. Technology changes our everyday lives at a fast _____.

8. What can parents do to _____ their children's success in school?

9. Two recent photographs are _____ to process the passport.

10. Renata is the kind of person who always wants a _____ explanation. Her nature didn't let her enjoy the fun of the magic show.

## WORDS IN COLLOCATIONS AND EXPRESSIONS

*Following are common collocations (word partners) and expressions with some of the key words. Read the definitions and then complete the conversations with the correct form of the collocations and expressions.*

| 1. benefit | |
|---|---|
| • benefit from | to get help from something |
| • for (someone's) benefit | in order to help someone |
| **2. contrast** | |
| • a contrast between | a difference between two people or things |
| • in (sharp) contrast to | used to compare two people or things |
| **3. insure** | |
| • insure that | to protect yourself against something bad happening |
| **4. scale** | |
| • on a grand scale | used to describe a large size or level of something when compared to what is normal |

1.    KEVIN:    Mom, this is my new friend Anatoly from Belorussia.

      MOTHER:    Hello, Anatoly. Would. . .you. . .like. . .to. . .stay. . .for. . .dinner?

      ANATOLY:    Dinner would be wonderful. Thank you.

           And you don't need to speak slowly _____*for my benefit*_____.

           I understand well enough.

2.    ACTOR:    Well, looks like we're ready for tonight, right?

      DIRECTOR:    Let's do a final check of all the lights, sound, and costumes. We need to _____ the performance goes well.

3.  CARSON:  You have a younger sister, don't you? Tell me about her.

    DAPHNE:  Well, Maggie is three years younger. _____ me, she's adventurous and fun-loving. As you know, I'm a calm person who likes quiet activities.

4.  WORKER 1:  What did you do over the weekend?

    WORKER 2:  Our friends threw a birthday party for their two-year-old _____. Clowns, a magician, everything . . .

    WORKER 1:  Sounds great, but will the child even remember all that?

5.  MRS. SHAW:  If we buy the house in Houston, we'll have to sell this one soon. Do you think we can sell it within two months?

    MR. SHAW:  This is a fine house, but it would _____ a good cleaning and a new paint job.

6.  TED:  You've been dating Kirsti for over two months. Sounds serious. Is it?

    STEVE:  I don't think so. . . . Kirsti and I talked over dinner last night, and I discovered a pretty big _____ her views on marriage and my own.

## ▌WORDS IN A READING

*Read this article about a new business practice. Complete it with words and expressions from the boxes.*

| ~~insure~~ | lessen | logical | rate |
|---|---|---|---|

### SETTING UP OPERATIONS IN SUNNY SPAIN

How can employers hold on to workers? For one thing, they can make sure that their employees have an adequate quality of life. But how can employers _____*insure*_____ their workers' all-around
<sub>1</sub>
happiness? Well, letting them work near sunny beaches would definitely help. In fact, a desire for an enjoyable lifestyle is why thousands of young Europeans go job hunting in Spain every year.

Many companies face the problem of high employee turnover, that is, workers too frequently joining and leaving the business. Companies like Avis, Hewlett-Packard, Nestle, and Citigroup, though, have come up with a new, _____ idea: sitting in ten inches of warm sand in Barcelona is
<sub>2</sub>
better than sitting in ten inches of cold snow in Poland. More and more companies, American and European alike, are starting to share this line of thinking in order to _____ employee
<sub>3</sub>
turnover. As a result, new jobs are being created where it is more pleasant to live, namely, Spain.

At present, about 50,000 people from all over Europe work in more than 2,000 Spanish call centers and service centers. Workers there handle technical support, accounting, and other "back-office" operations for large companies with main offices elsewhere. This practice is called "outsourcing." The
_____ of growth of such centers is expected to remain strong. According to London-
<sub>4</sub>
based Datamonitor PLC, the outsourcing industry will grow by 30,000 jobs in the next two years.

| benefits | in contrast to | location | require |
|----------|---------------|----------|---------|
| convenience | insures that | on a grand scale | |

Sunny beaches, though, are not the only reason why companies choose Spain as the
_____ for back-office operations. Having free time near the sand and sea
5
_____ employees; the employer's advantage is that wages in Spanish call and service
6
centers are thirty percent lower than in northern Europe. Also, there is the _____ of the
7
European Union (EU): it is easy and practical to hire people from anywhere in the EU to work in Spain
because they do not _____ visas or permits. Not having to waste time on getting docu-
8
ments means that companies save money. And _____ places like India and Eastern Europe,
9
Spain can handle sensitive banking and medical matters that must be addressed inside the EU. Last but
not least, the Spanish culture of warmth, friendship, and leisure _____ young Europeans
10
will continue to arrive in Spain _____ every year for sun, fun—and jobs.
11

*(Based on information in Andy Reinhardt and Carita Vitzthum, "Spain: Cafes, Beaches, and Call Centers." BusinessWeek, September 5, 2005.)*

## ▌WORDS IN DISCUSSION

*Apply the key words to your own life. Read and discuss each question in small groups. Try to use the key words.*

1. Tell about something that makes your life more **convenient**.

   **EXAMPLE**

   *My cell phone makes my life more **convenient**. I don't even have a regular phone in my home. Cell phones offer **convenience**. I can talk with friends and family from almost anywhere.*

2. Is your behavior usually ruled by **logic** or emotion?

3. Is there a strong **contrast between** your parents' taste in music and your own?

4. Has anyone ever **required** you to do something you didn't want to do or didn't see the importance of doing?

5. Do you believe that a person can **benefit** from watching TV? Why or why not?

6. How much do you understand when you listen to the radio or watch TV in English? How often is the **rate** of speech too fast?

7. When you cannot find the **location** of a place, do you look at a map or ask for directions?

8. Do you usually make plans on a small or large **scale**? Give an example.

9. What do you do to **insure** your success in school?

10. When you have a difficult day, what do you do to **lessen** the stress?

# WORDS IN WRITING

*Choose two topics and write a short paragraph on each. Try to use the key words.*

1. In your opinion, what is the ideal **location** to live in?

   **EXAMPLE**

   > Right now I'm a student, so I must live near the university. Later, when I have a job, I'll have to live in the city. But my ideal **location** is the beach. I want to spend time near the water. My dream house would be on the beach.

2. Share your knowledge about a process in your country (applying for car **insurance**, getting a library card, making a doctor's appointment, etc.). What are the **requirements** for completing this process?

3. Is there something you'd love to do **on a grand scale**? Explain.

4. Imagine you and another passenger are the only people left from a terrible plane crash. Your plane landed in the mountains. It's snowing, and it's still daylight. What would be the **logical** thing to do?

5. No two people are exactly alike. Describe your best friend's personality **in contrast to** yours.

## WORDS IN CONTEXT

*Use the sentences to guess what each key word means. Choose the meaning that is closest to that of the key word in **bold**.*

1. **attitude**
/ˈætəˌtud/
-noun

- Even though George is very intelligent, we don't want to give him the job; he has a negative **attitude**, always finding the bad in every situation.
- Some psychologists believe that you need to have a positive **attitude** toward your job to be successful at it.

*Attitude* means . . .  (a.) opinions and feelings  b. intelligence    c. appearance

2. **contribute**
/kanˈtrɪbyut/
-verb

- Albert Einstein **contributed** a lot to scientific development.
- When Annie was collecting money to help a classmate who was sick, she asked her parents' friends to **contribute**.

*Contribute* means . . .  a. to take away    b. to be intelligent    c. to give

3. **establish**
/ɪˈstæblɪʃ/
-verb

- Boston, Massachusetts was **established** in 1630.
- It's important to **establish** trust with a new pet.

*Establish* means . . .  a. to start something    b. to forget    c. to buy

4. **fade**
/feɪd/
-verb

- Daylight **fades** from the sky when the sun sets every evening.
- Fernando's memories of childhood had not **faded**; even after seventy-five years, he could still remember it clearly.

*Fade* means . . .    a. to shine    b. to gradually disappear  c. to become strong

5. **identify**
/aɪˈdɛntəˌfaɪ/
-verb

- If I showed you a picture of your grandfather's high school class, could you **identify** him?
- Astronomers can look at the sky and **identify** different stars and constellations.

*Identify* means . . .    a. to describe    b. to have little    c. to recognize and name
                                                       knowledge

6. **pressure**
/ˈprɛʃɚ/
-noun

- If a sales clerk tries to put **pressure** on you to buy something you don't want, it's a good idea to leave the store.
- Andrew is thirty six, so he is facing **pressure** from his family to get married.

*Pressure* means . . .    a. attempt to make    b. rejection of    c. commitment to
                                      someone do         someone's idea         something or someone
                                      something

**7. quote**
/kwoʊt/
-verb

• Our drama teacher stood up and **quoted** Shakespeare, saying, "To be or not to be?"

• You like to **quote** famous people, but I prefer to use my own words.

*Quote* means . . .
   a. to speak in old English
   b. to study acting
   c. to repeat someone's words exactly

**8. reputation**
/repyəˈteɪʃən/
-noun

• Jillian's mom told her that she couldn't date Will because of his **reputation** as a troublemaker; everyone in town said he was dangerous.

• High school juniors often search college guides to find out about the **reputations** of different universities.

*Reputation* means . . .
   a. opinion that people have of someone or something
   b. facts about someone or something
   c. problems that someone or something has

**9. spare**
/sper/
-adjective

• Paulo keeps a **spare** tire in the back of his jeep; this way, if he has a flat tire, he can take it off and put on the **spare** tire.

• We keep a **spare** key hidden under the doormat in case we lose our other keys.

*Spare* means . . .
   a. empty
   b. extra
   c. old

**10. wander**
/ˈwɑndɚ/
-verb

• The Dawsons' horse **wandered** far from home before it was found.

• When Lance had a free day in Paris, he decided not to take a guided tour, choosing instead to **wander** on foot and discover cafés and shops on his own.

*Wander* means . . .
   a. to follow a schedule
   b. to dream
   c. to walk slowly without a plan

## ▌WORDS AND DEFINITIONS

*Match each key word with its definition.*

1. _____spare_____ an extra thing that you keep so that it will be available if needed

2. _____ the opinion that people have of someone or something because of what has happened in the past

3. _____ to gradually disappear

4. _____ an attempt to make someone do something by using influence, arguments, threats, etc.

5. _____ to give money, help, or ideas to something that other people are also giving to

6. _____ to start something such as a company, system, situation, etc., especially one that will exist for a long time

7. _____ to repeat exactly what someone else has said or written

8. _____ to walk slowly across or around an area, usually without having a clear direction or purpose

9. _____ the opinions and feelings that people usually have about a particular thing, idea, or person

10. _____ to recognize and name someone or something

## COMPREHENSION CHECK

*Choose the best answer.*

1. In which sentence is the writer NOT **quoting** someone?
   a. "Truth is beauty."—John Keats
   b. "No man is an island."—John Donne
   c. My dad told me not to play with fire when I was a kid.
   d. "I cannot tell a lie."—George Washington

2. If Mark's hopes are **fading**,
   a. he is very optimistic
   b. he feels fine
   c. he is losing hope
   d. he has no opinion

3. Which comment could have been made by a student who has a good **attitude** toward studying?
   a. "I enjoy learning."
   b. "I hate homework."
   c. "Why do I have to go to school?"
   d. "I am too stupid to learn anything."

4. Which **spare** item do people usually NOT have in their cars?
   a. tire
   b. map
   c. radio
   d. key

5. If Juan **contributed** a lot to the group project, he probably
   a. did nothing.
   b. worked hard and suggested many good ideas.
   c. forgot the group meeting.
   d. skipped the presentation.

6. Sara's father was putting **pressure** on her to study medicine. What did her father say?
   a. "Relax. You don't need to think about your future now."
   b. "What you study is your decision."
   c. "I'm a doctor, so you have to become a doctor, too!"
   d. "You can go to art school, if that's what you want."

7. Hawaii has a **reputation** as a great place to go for vacation. This means
   a. it is very sunny and beautiful.
   b. people say wonderful things about Hawaii.
   c. Hawaii is expensive.
   d. Hawaiians dance beautifully.

8. Where has a major city NOT been **established**?
   a. California
   b. Saudi Arabia
   c. the Moon
   d. Russia

9. Who is likely to **wander**?
   a. an elementary school teacher
   b. a pilot
   c. a receptionist
   d. an explorer

10. A professional musician can probably **identify**
    a. the names of plants.
    b. a mathematical proof written by Descartes.
    c. a symphony written by Beethoven.
    d. the ingredients used in a delicious chocolate cake.

# ▌WORD FAMILIES

Now that you have studied the ten key words and their basic definitions, you are ready to learn words that belong to the same family as some of the key words. A word family includes words that look alike but have different functions (noun, verb, adjective, or adverb). Their meanings are related but different.

**A.** *Look at each model phrase and decide whether the word in **bold** is used as a noun, verb, adjective, or adverb.*

| | NOUN | VERB | ADJECTIVE | ADVERB |
|---|---|---|---|---|
| **1. contribute** | | | | |
| • **contribute** some money | | ✓ | | |
| • a generous **contribution** | ✓ | | | |
| **2. establish** | | | | |
| • **establish** a connection | | | | |
| • the **establishment** of this city | | | | |
| **3. identify** | | | | |
| • **identify** the problem | | | | |
| • Show **identification** | | | | |
| **4. pressure** | | | | |
| • feel a lot of **pressure** | | | | |
| • to **pressure** people | | | | |
| **5. quote** | | | | |
| • to **quote** someone famous | | | | |
| • a famous **quote** / **quotation** | | | | |
| **6. spare** | | | | |
| • a **spare** toothbrush | | | | |
| • no time to **spare** | | | | |

**B.** *Match each of the following sentences with the definition of the word in **bold**.*

_b_ 1. You need to show us **identification** before entering this building.

____ 2. We couldn't have succeeded without your **contribution**.

____ 3. Arnold never **pressures** his customers to buy something.

____ 4. My history teacher wants me to use **quotes** in my report.

____ 5. If you can **spare** a few minutes, please help me.

a. words from a book, poem, etc. that you repeat in your own speech or piece of writing

b. official documents that prove who you are

c. something that is given or done to help something else be successful

d. to make something such as time, money, or workers available for someone, especially when this is difficult

e. to try to make someone do something by using influence, arguments, or threats

# SAME WORD, DIFFERENT MEANING

Most words have more than one meaning. Study the additional meanings of **establish**, **establishment**, and **pressure**. Then read each sentence and decide which meaning is used.

| | | |
|---|---|---|
| a. | **establish** *v.* | to start something |
| b. | **establish** *v.* | to find out facts that will prove that something is true |
| c. | **establishment** *n.* | the act of starting something |
| d. | **establishment** *n.* | (*formal*) an institution, especially a business, store, or hotel |
| e. | **pressure** *n.* | an attempt to make someone do something by using influence, arguments, or threats |
| f. | **pressure** *n.* | the force produced by pressing on someone or something |

___f___  1. If you cut your hand, you should put **pressure** on the wound to stop the blood.

_____  2. The **establishment** of a unified system of spelling for the English language as spoken in the United States occurred when Daniel Webster published his dictionary in 1806.

_____  3. If we want to open a new department store downtown, we must first **establish** that people usually do their shopping in this area.

_____  4. Kyung Sun is under a lot of **pressure** from his parents now; they expect him to get a high score on the TOEFL this month.

_____  5. Smoking is not allowed in this **establishment**.

_____  6. Colombia was **established** in 1855.

# WORDS IN SENTENCES

Complete each sentence with one of the words from the box.

| | | | | |
|---|---|---|---|---|
| attitude | establish | identify | quotes | ~~spare~~ |
| contribution | faded | pressure | reputation | wander |

1. Sometimes homeless people ask if you can _____spare_____ some change, hoping you'll give them a little money.

2. Jenna's memories of her childhood have _____.

3. My uncle broke his leg, but he has a positive _____ and isn't depressed.

4. Oxford University has an excellent _____.

5. If you swim deep under the surface of the ocean, you can feel _____ in your ears.

6. At a potluck party, each guest is supposed to bring a(n) _____ to the dinner.

7. Before you can go on the Internet, you have to _____ a connection with a service provider.

8. After school, Ashish and his friends like to _____ downtown.

9. Mr. Jackson, our literature professor, asked us to include _____ in our essay tests.

10. Let's try to _____ the reason why you haven't been sleeping well.

# WORDS IN COLLOCATIONS AND EXPRESSIONS

*Following are common collocations (word partners) and expressions with some of the key words. Read the definitions and then complete the conversations with the correct form of the collocations and expressions.*

| | |
|---|---|
| 1. **attitude** | |
| • **have an attitude problem** | to be unhelpful and unpleasant to be with |
| 2. **identify** | |
| • **identify with (sb)** | to be able to share or understand the feelings of someone else |
| 3. **pressure** | |
| • **peer pressure** | the strong feeling that young people have that they should do the same things that their peers are doing |
| • **be under pressure** | to feel anxious because of the conditions of your work, family, or way of living |
| 4. **reputation** | |
| • **a good / bad reputation** | a positive/negative opinion that people have about someone or something |
| 5. **spare** | |
| • **spare time** | free time when you are not busy working |

1.    INTERVIEWER:    Why do you want to go to this university?

       LILIA:    Because it has a very _____*good reputation*_____ . If I go to a school that has a _____, I won't be able to find a job when I return to my home country.

2.    JESSICA:    Why did you start smoking?

       NATHAN:    I didn't want to, but my friends kept telling me I should try it. Finally, I gave in to _____ and started smoking with them. Now I wish I could quit.

       JESSICA:    You know, I _____ you. I also started smoking because of my friends. I quit last summer, so I know you can, too.

3.    STUDENT:    Do you have some time this afternoon, Professor? I'd like to show you my latest results.

       PROFESSOR:    Actually, I have some _____ right now. Let's talk.

4.    TRUCK DRIVER 1:    I know Joe works hard, but he _____. He's always complaining about his life, and it makes him a terrible boss.

       TRUCK DRIVER 2:    Yeah, he has a really bad attitude. I understand that he's _____ at home, but a lot of us have family problems, and we don't yell at everyone. I'm glad we're on the road most of the time and don't have to see him!

## ■ WORDS IN A READING

*Read this passage about psychology. Complete it with words and expressions from the boxes.*

| attitude | ~~contributes~~ | established | identifies | peer pressure | quote |
|---|---|---|---|---|---|

### FAMILY DINNERS: A SURPRISING ANTI-DRUG

Eating meals together turns out to be one of the best things we can do for our children. Enjoyable conversation at mealtime _____*contributes*_____ to children feeling good about themselves and their
<br>1
family. With any luck, it will draw them to the table for years to come.

To _____ the author Miriam Weinstein, family dining is "a simple ritual, but it
<br>2
has so many benefits." When families eat five or more meals together a week, twelve- to seventeen-year-olds are less likely to drink, smoke, or use drugs and more likely to have a positive _____,
<br>3
good grades, and a sense of well-being, according to a report released by the National Center on Addiction and Substance Abuse at Columbia University (CASA). In contrast, the study
_____ teens whose families eat fewer than three meals a week together as being more
<br>4
likely to fall to _____, engage in substance abuse, and have low grades and low self-
<br>5
esteem. CASA _____ national Family Day Monday to encourage families to eat together.
<br>6

| fades | reputation | spare time | wander |
|---|---|---|---|

Between working parents' schedules and children's activities, many families have a difficult time finding _____ to eat together. By the teen years, parents' effort to create family dinners
<br>7
_____ because they think teens don't care.
<br>8

That's not true, according to a study similar to CASA's, which mirrored its results but also found that teens who eat more meals with their families have healthier diets and are less likely to have unhealthy eating habits.

Although teenagers often have the _____ of not wanting to spend time at home,
<br>9
many teens don't want the freedom to _____ the city or hang out with their friends at
<br>10
mealtime. As one seventeen-year-old said, "I like that my parents expect me to be home for Friday night dinner. It makes me feel important."

*(Adapted from Barbara F. Meltz, "A Surprising Anti-drug: Dining as a Family." The Boston Globe, October 3, 2005.)*

## WORDS IN DISCUSSION

Apply the key words to your own life. Complete the questionnaire. Then discuss your answers with a classmate. Try to use the key words.

**EXAMPLE**

My favorite **quote**: _____"To be or not to be: that is the question."— Shakespeare_____

**A:** *Is that really your favorite **quote**?*

**B:** *It is.*

**A:** *I don't believe you. I think you're **quoting** Shakespeare because you want to sound intelligent.*

1. A famous **quote** from my country: _____

2. The **reputation** I had/have in high school: _____

3. What I will do when I next have **spare** time: _____

4. A person I know who has a good **attitude**: _____

5. A time when I was under a lot of **pressure**: _____

6. One of my dreams which I hope will never **fade**: _____

7. What I can **contribute** to a party: _____

8. Someone I could easily **identify** across a crowded room: _____

9. A club I would like to be **established** in my town: _____

10. A city I would like to spend an afternoon **wandering** in: _____

## WORDS IN WRITING

Choose two topics and write a short paragraph on each. Try to use the key words.

1. Describe a person you know who has a great **attitude**.

   **EXAMPLE**

   *My best friend has a great **attitude** because she is always positive. Even when we were camping in the rain last summer, she didn't have a negative **attitude** like the rest of us. Instead, she kept smiling and had fun.*

2. What is one great **contribution** that your country made to the world? Describe it.

3. If you were **wandering** down a romantic street in Spain on vacation, and the police stopped you and asked to see your **identification**, would you feel irritated, or would you happily show your ID? Explain.

4. Do you think that the **establishment** of English as a world language is good for the world or not? Explain.

5. What, if anything, do you think teachers should do to stop the **peer pressure** they witness in their classrooms?

| appoint | calculate | concept | extend | mere |
|---------|-----------|---------|--------|------|
| astonished | challenge | drag | extreme | passage |

## ▎WORDS IN CONTEXT

*Use the sentences to guess what each key word means. Choose the meaning that is closest to that of the key word in **bold**.*

**1. appoint**
/əˈpɔɪnt/
*-verb*

- We all agreed that Ray had the most experience, so we **appointed** him as our group leader.
- After only three years, Isabela was **appointed** program director.

*Appoint* means . . .   a. to prepare someone for a job   (b.) to choose someone for a job   c. to remove someone from a position

**2. astonished**
/əˈstɑnɪʃt/
*-verb*

- Samir's progress **astonished** all his teachers. He learned so much in one year.
- It **astonished** us to learn that Diana's father is a millionaire. She certainly doesn't dress or act as if she's rich.

*Astonish* means . . .   a. to surprise very much   b. to be strong   c. to confuse

**3. calculate**
/ˈkælkyəˌleɪt/
*-verb*

- As the mechanic listed the problems with my car and the cost to fix each one, I quickly **calculated** in my head how much repairs would cost. Would I have enough money?
- The computer **calculated** the distance from my house to the airport and also told me how much time it would take to get there.

*Calculate* means . . .   a. to write   b. to explain   c. to find out or measure

**4. challenge**
/ˈtʃæləndʒ/
*-noun*

- Ron finds his new job interesting; every day there is a new **challenge**.
- I enjoy a good **challenge**. Maybe that's why I get bored easily with routines.

*Challenge* means . . .   a. something that's scary   b. something that tests your skills   c. something that's mysterious

**5. concept**
/ˈkɑnsɛpt/
*-noun*

- Until Lisa spent a year in Italy, she had no **concept** of life in other countries.
- In general, I liked the **concept** that the architect had for our new home, but I explained that the rooms had to be larger, especially the kitchen.

*Concept* means . . .   a. a plan   b. a suggestion   c. an idea

**6. drag**
/dræg/
*-verb*

- My bag was so heavy that I couldn't carry it anymore. I had to **drag** it through the airport.
- Frank **dragged** the last piece of large furniture into his new apartment and then sat down to rest.

*Drag* means . . .   a. to pull   b. to wheel   c. to kick

7. **extend**
/ik'stɛnd/
-verb

- Taipei 101 is the world's tallest skyscraper. It **extends** 1,671 feet into the air.
- Boston's Freedom Trail **extends** for 2.5 miles and takes curious walkers to see important historical sites around the city.

*Extend means . . .*    a. to build or be built    b. to continue for a distance    c. to make use of

8. **extreme**
/ik'strim/
-adjective

- One danger of a volcano is its **extreme** heat.
- Charity's disappearance caused her parents **extreme** worry.

*Extreme means . . .*    a. moderate    b. immediate    c. very great

9. **mere**
/mir/
-adjective

- I was second at the finish line, but I was a **mere** second behind the winner.
- All I expected was a **mere** thank you. Is that too much to ask for?

*Mere means . . .*    a. important    b. small    c. clear

10. **passage**
/'pæsɪdʒ/
-noun

- I walked down the **passage** that led from the older building of the library to the newer one.
- In the story, the old house had a secret **passage**. The family used it to escape the house in times of trouble.

*Passage means . . .*    a. a narrow path    b. a reading room    c. a kind of transportation

## WORDS AND DEFINITIONS

*Match each key word with its definition.*

1. ___astonish___ to surprise someone very much

2. _____ an idea of how something is or how something should be done

3. _____ used to emphasize how small or unimportant someone or something is

4. _____ to find out or measure something using numbers

5. _____ very great in degree

6. _____ to continue for a particular distance, to cover a particular area

7. _____ something that tests your skill or ability, especially in a way that is interesting

8. _____ to choose someone for a job, position, etc.

9. _____ a narrow path with walls on each side that connects one room or place to another

10. _____ to pull someone or something heavy along the ground or away from somewhere

# COMPREHENSION CHECK

*Choose the best answer.*

1. Theresa **dragged** the chair across the room;
   a. it was light enough to carry.
   b. it moved easily on its wheels.
   c. it weighed nearly as much as she did.
   d. her angry throw created a loud crash against the wall.

2. The Great Pyramid of Giza in Egypt has a secret **passage**, and
   a. no one knows what it leads to.
   b. no one knows how to read it.
   c. no one knows his true name.
   d. no one knows how to turn it on.

3. In order to have a better **concept** of Spanish family life, you can do all of the following EXCEPT
   a. take out some books from the library on the subject.
   b. watch movies that take place in Tokyo.
   c. take part in an exchange program and live with a Spanish host family.
   d. talk to your classmate from Madrid about her family.

4. In planning our vacation, we should try to **calculate** all of the following EXCEPT
   a. how much money we can spend on the hotel.
   b. how many miles we'll drive in order to get there.
   c. how many business meetings we'll have.
   d. how much time we'll have for sightseeing.

5. Which of the following activities does NOT offer much of a **challenge**?
   a. washing dishes
   b. rock climbing
   c. starting your own business
   d. learning a new language

6. Greg is excited by **extreme** speeds. He probably likes
   a. to stroll in the park.
   b. to watch golf.
   c. to drive fast.
   d. to paint pictures.

7. Which of the following people can we **appoint**?
   a. a friend
   b. a club secretary
   c. a brother-in-law
   d. the king or queen of a country

8. My mother has a garden at our back door. It **extends**
   a. for many years already.
   b. near a large oak tree.
   c. for several yards along a narrow footpath.
   d. many different kinds of flowers.

9. Sung Hee said that her purse cost a **mere** $40. That means
   a. she got the purse on sale.
   b. she paid for the purse with a credit card.
   c. she has probably spent much more on purses in the past.
   d. she has probably spent much less on purses in the past.

10. The news of the divorce **astonished** us.
    a. After all, they just got married two months ago.
    b. There was much crying.
    c. Everyone knew the couple was having problems.
    d. It was a great relief.

Now that you have studied the ten key words and their basic definitions, you are ready to learn words that belong to the same family as some of the key words. A word family includes words that look alike but have different functions (noun, verb, adjective, or adverb). Their meanings are related but different.

**A.** *Look at each model phrase and decide whether the word in **bold** is used as a noun, verb, adjective, or adverb.*

| | NOUN | VERB | ADJECTIVE | ADVERB |
|---|---|---|---|---|
| 1. **appoint** | | | | |
| • **appoint** a task | | ✓ | | |
| • a surprising **appointment** | ✓ | | | |
| 2. **astonish** | | | | |
| • **astonish** me | | | | |
| • an **astonishing** idea | | | | |
| 3. **calculate** | | | | |
| • to **calculate** the distance | | | | |
| • use a **calculator** | | | | |
| 4. **challenge** | | | | |
| • the **challenge** of the job | | | | |
| • **challenge** someone | | | | |
| • a **challenging** game | | | | |
| 5. **extreme** | | | | |
| • **extreme** temperatures | | | | |
| • **extremely** thin | | | | |

**B.** *Read the first half of each sentence and match it with the appropriate ending.*

__c__ 1. I want my classes to

_____ 2. The dark circles under your eyes tell me that you're

_____ 3. Shelly was both excited and nervous about her

_____ 4. Of course, I can do simple addition and subtraction in my head. But to be certain, I

_____ 5. Their generosity

_____ 6. The last question on the test

a. **appointment** as department head.

b. was **challenging**. I hope I got it right.

c. **challenge** me. They shouldn't be too easy.

d. is **astonishing**. They're very kind.

e. **extremely** tired.

f. use a **calculator**.

## SAME WORD, DIFFERENT MEANING

*Most words have more than one meaning. Study the additional meanings of **appointment**, **extend**, and **passage**. Then read each sentence and decide which meaning is used.*

| | | |
|---|---|---|
| a. **appointment** *n.* | the act of choosing someone for a job, position, task, etc. |
| b. **appointment** *n.* | a meeting that has been arranged for a particular time and place |
| c. **extend** *v.* | to continue for a particular distance, to cover a particular area |
| d. **extend** *v.* | to increase something in size or amount of time |
| e. **passage** *n.* | a narrow area with walls on each side that connects one room or place to another |
| f. **passage** *n.* | a trip on a ship, or the cost of this |

___a___ 1. The president offered Maia the job of department head, but she chose not to accept the **appointment**. She's happy in her present position.

_____ 2. My plans have changed, and I want to stay here longer. May I **extend** my visa?

_____ 3. I wonder if there was a person who had paid for **passage** on the *Titanic* but didn't sail.

_____ 4. I'm in a bit of a hurry. I have an important **appointment** at 2:00 on the other side of town.

_____ 5. The path behind the house **extended** all the way down to the lake.

_____ 6. No one had used the **passage** for many years, so it was poorly lit and full of dust and dirt.

## WORDS IN SENTENCES

*Complete each sentence with one of the words from the box.*

| | | | | |
|---|---|---|---|---|
| appointment | calculate | concept | extend | mere |
| astonishing | challenging | drag | extremely | ~~passage~~ |

1. Opened in 1914, the Panama Canal is a ____passage____ between the Pacific and Atlantic Oceans.

2. Weather conditions near the ocean grew _____ violent, so we had to cancel our travel plans and stay closer to home for our vacation.

3. Noel has no _____ of time. He doesn't own a watch. He's always late.

4. _____ curiosity made me take another quick look at the TV star before we left the restaurant.

5. My little sister is funny. She says that her math homework is difficult, but when she wants to know how many days till her birthday or how much two DVDs will cost, she's quick to _____ the answer.

6. It was simply _____ to hear Sirirat sing so loudly in music class. She's usually so quiet.

7. I was having so much fun at my cousin's that I decided to _____ my stay.

8. I asked the movers to lift all the furniture and not _____ anything across the hardwood floor.

9. "Are you looking for _____ work?" read the job advertisement. "Call us today. We've been looking for *you*."

10. When is your hair _____? I can give you a ride if it's before 4:00 P.M.

## ■ WORDS IN COLLOCATIONS AND EXPRESSIONS

*Following are common collocations (word partners) and expressions with some of the key words. Read the definitions and then complete the conversations with the correct form of the collocations and expressions.*

| | | |
|---|---|---|
| 1. **challenge** | | |
| | • **face a challenge** | to be presented with something new, exciting, or difficult |
| | • **meet a challenge** | to successfully deal with something that requires a lot of skill and effort |
| 2. **drag** | | |
| | • **drag oneself away from** | to stop doing something, although you do not want to |
| | • **drag (sb) into (sth)** | to make someone participate in an activity or event even though he or she doesn't want to |
| 3. **extend** | | |
| | • **extended family** | family that includes parents, children, grandparents, aunts, uncles, etc. |
| 4. **passage** | | |
| | • **book passage** | to make a reservation for a trip (usually on a ship) |

1. DARYL: Mom, how long have Aunt Carrie and Uncle Elton been married?

   MOTHER: Let's see. I remember for their fifteenth anniversary they ___*booked passage*___ on the Queen Mary 2. That was two years ago. So they've been married for seventeen years already.

2. JAKE: Are you ready for the biology test today?

   SUE: Yeah. I feel ready to _____. I reviewed all week, and I got a good night's sleep last night.

3. NICK: What are you reading?

   COLE: A science fiction novel. It's so good that I can't _____ myself _____ it. I've been reading a few pages between classes all day.

4. TOM: Do you think our little sister will ever grow up?

   BILL: Jessica's nineteen already, but she's still very much like a child. She turns to Mom and Dad or even us every time life gets difficult. She has yet to _____ on her own.

5. BRUNO: Did you grow up here in Seattle?

   WESLEY: No. I was born in Chicago. In fact, most of our _____ still live there.

6. CATHLEEN: Can you believe that Martina refuses to apologize for what she did?!

   SONYA: Please don't _____ me _____ your argument with Martina. This is between you two, and I don't want to take sides.

## WORDS IN A READING

*Read this article about a future form of transportation. Complete it with words and expressions from the boxes.*

| | | |
|---|---|---|
| astonishing | drag | extreme |
| ~~concept~~ | extend | face the challenge |

### SPACE ELEVATOR

The _____concept_____ of an elevator to space was introduced in the 1978 novel *The Fountains of*
                 1
*Paradise* by Arthur C. Clarke. But is the idea really too _____ to be considered realistic?
                                                            2
Being able to take an elevator to the stars may sound surprising, but according to the U.K. newspaper
*Telegraph,* the trip may be possible by the year 2020.

   To create such an elevator, engineers first had to _____ of finding a strong enough
                                                      3
cable to _____ hundreds of tons of material out of the Earth and into space. However,
         4
the heavy load would be only one source of pressure on the elevator's cable; _____
                                                                            5
temperatures would put additional stress on any material used to carry the elevator up and down.
Finally, the cable itself would have to be long enough to reach a satellite 22,000 miles away! Many
questioned if it was possible for a cable to _____ that far into space and not break.
                                             6

| | | | |
|---|---|---|---|
| appointed | book passage | calculated | mere |

   The answer to the question came in the discovery of what is called "carbon nanotubes." This
material has been tested, and it is _____ that a string of carbon nanotubes measuring a
                                    7
_____ one-thousandth the diameter of a human hair can support 50,000 times its
        8
own weight.

   Now that engineers know what to use, they must decide how to use it. In a competition held by the
Spaceward Foundation, ten teams have been _____ to the task of creating the space elevator.
                                           9
Each team hopes to put together the winning design for a solar-powered cable car to outer space. With
engineers predicting a ride to the stars within the next fifteen years, are you ready to _____?
                                                                                        10

*(Based on information in "Elevator to the Stars." The Week, October 28, 2005.)*

## WORDS IN DISCUSSION

*Apply the key words to your own life. Read and discuss each question in small groups. Try to use the key words.*

1. Your school has just **appointed** you the leader of a group that will remodel the entire building. What changes will you recommend?

   **EXAMPLE**

   *I'd be happy to have this **appointment**. I'd add an Internet lounge and exercise room.*

2. Have you ever **extended** your stay while on vacation? If yes, for what reason? If no, was there a time you wanted to **extend** your stay but couldn't?

3. Would you rather have a boring job that paid well or a **challenging** job that paid much less?

4. How often do you use a **calculator**? Is it a **mere** convenience, or do you really need help **calculating**?

5. Have you ever spent time in **extremely** hot or cold temperatures? Explain.

6. If you won free **passage** for two on a ship to a place of your choice, where would you go and who would you take?

7. Are you close to your **extended family**? Explain.

8. What is your **concept** of a good education?

9. Imagine that you see your neighbor **dragging** a heavy bag toward her car. This neighbor never says hello in return to your greeting. Do you offer help or let her continue **dragging** the bag?

10. Is there something about you that others in your class may find **astonishing**?

## WORDS IN WRITING

*Choose two topics and write a short paragraph on each one. Try to use the key words.*

1. Have you ever been **astonished** by the behavior of someone from a different culture? What was so **astonishing**?

   **EXAMPLE**

   *I remember going to a Brazilian birthday party. I showed up exactly on time, but most of the other guests came an hour late. I learned that this was normal. It's funny how something so natural for one person can be so **astonishing** for another.*

2. Describe one of the greatest **challenges** you have ever **faced**.

3. Do you keep an **appointment** book, or do you remember important events in another way?

4. What is something that is hard to **drag yourself away** from?

5. Consider this situation: Derek borrowed $250 from his friend Seth and explained that the money was for car repairs. The following week Derek had a few new CDs and a new leather jacket. Seth got angry and ended the friendship. Was Seth's reaction too **extreme**? Explain why or why not.

# QUIZ 2

## PART A

*Choose the word that best completes each item and write it in the space provided.*

1. Many jobs _____*require*_____ a college education.
   - a. require
   - b. contribute
   - c. extend
   - d. establish

2. The Allegheny Mountain Tunnel _____ for over 6,000 feet.
   - a. drags
   - b. calculates
   - c. extends
   - d. fades

3. Unlike humans, computers will always make decisions based on _____ rather than emotion.
   - a. reputation
   - b. convenience
   - c. logic
   - d. pressure

4. Allan felt _____ from his friends to join the soccer team. He didn't want to disappoint them.
   - a. reputation
   - b. attitude
   - c. logic
   - d. pressure

5. We made a good group presentation; each student _____ an idea.
   - a. located
   - b. contributed
   - c. extended
   - d. established

6. Microwave ovens don't always make tasty meals, but they offer _____.
   - a. reputation
   - b. convenience
   - c. logic
   - d. pressure

7. We _____ Rafael as our treasurer because he's responsible and honest.
   - a. established
   - b. appointed
   - c. dragged
   - d. contributed

8. Some cars today have computers to help you _____ a place and keep you from getting lost.
   - a. establish
   - b. calculate
   - c. extend
   - d. locate

9. For my father's 50th birthday we're planning a party on a large _____.
   - a. concept
   - b. reputation
   - c. scale
   - d. rate

10. Daniel got only fourth place in the contest, but he has a good _____ about losing; he believes the whole experience taught him more about the game.
    - a. concept
    - b. reputation
    - c. attitude
    - d. logic

## PART B

*Read each statement and write **T** for true or **F** for false in the space provided.*

__F__ 1. In a race runners try to **wander** in order to win.

_____ 2. Medicine can **lessen** pain.

_____ 3. Sharing your secret with a friend is an example of **gossip**.

_____ 4. Wearing red shoes with white pants creates a **contrast**.

_____ 5. Asking you to clean all ten rooms in my family's house can be considered a **mere** favor.

_____ 6. The sound of a train **fades** as it comes closer to where you are.

_____ 7. If a country has a high birth **rate**, it means that many babies are being born there.

_____ 8. The game of chess offers a **challenge** for our minds but not our bodies.

_____ 9. It's common for parents to **drag** their babies because children at that age cannot walk yet.

_____ 10. Most people would be **astonished** to see their best friends at their birthday parties.

| benefits | concept | extreme | insured | reputation |
|----------|---------|---------|---------|------------|
| calculate | established | identify | ~~passage~~ | spare |

## PART C

*Complete each item with a word from the box. Use each word once.*

1. The heavy snow closed the only _____*passage*_____ from one side of the mountain to the other.

2. It was hard to _____ my luggage when I arrived at JKF Airport. Many other passengers had black suitcases like mine.

3. Rochelle doesn't work full-time, so her company can't offer her _____.

4. You can _____ the area of a room by multiplying the width by the length.

5. I realized my young niece did not have a good _____ of money when she asked me if $100 was enough to buy a car.

6. Arsenio always keeps _____ batteries and light bulbs in his house.

7. The research team faced _____ cold in Antarctica.

8. Alexander Graham Bell _____ the Bell Telephone Company in 1877.

9. The other driver never _____ his car, so Dana will have to pay for all the damage with her own money.

10. My grandfather worked hard to build a good _____ for our family business; my father has worked hard to keep it.

## WORDS IN CONTEXT

*Use the sentences to guess what each key word means. Choose the meaning that is closest to that of the key word in **bold**.*

**1. aim**
/eɪm/
-verb

- Nina **aims** to become a pilot, so she is applying to flight school.
- If this company **aims** to grow, we should hire a marketing director.

*Aim* means . . .  (a.) to plan    b. to discuss    c. to know

**2. approach**
/əˈproʊtʃ/
-verb

- When Cassie put down the bowl of milk, the little cat **approached** her.
- As the train **approaches** each station, the conductor announces its name.

*Approach* means . . . a. to move closer to someone or something    b. to remain still    c. to go away from

**3. current**
/ˈkɚənt/
-adjective

- Anita always manages to meet interesting men. Her **current** boyfriend is a famous explorer.
- Jessie likes to read the newspaper, but her sister surfs the Internet to learn about **current** events.

*Current* means . . .    a. present    b. past    c. old-fashioned

**4. custom**
/ˈkʌstəm/
-noun

- It is the **custom** in China for women to wear red wedding dresses.
- Is it the **custom** for people in many countries to celebrate the first day of the new year?

*Custom* means . . .    a. something unusual    b. something traditional    c. something funny

**5. generation**
/ˌdʒɛnəˈreɪʃən/
-noun

- My grandparents' **generation** listened to big band music, my parents' **generation** listened to folk music, and my **generation** listens to rock music.
- If you could go back in time and live in another **generation**, which time would you choose: the 1900s, the 1920s, or the 1950s?

*Generation* means . . . a. fashion group    b. music group    c. age group

**6. influence**
/ˈɪnfluəns/
-noun

- By discussing life with his grandson on their walks in the Czech countryside, Hansa had a great **influence** on the boy's thinking.
- Orson Welles's movie *Citizen Kane* had a strong **influence** on filmmaking in the twentieth century.

*Influence* means . . .    a. talk    b. change    c. effect

**7. moral**
/ˈmɔrəl/
-adjective

- My grandfather is a wise man who always acts in a correct and kind way; for this reason, when his grandchildren have difficult personal decisions to make, they often ask him for **moral** guidance.
- Even though Robin Hood, who stole from the rich and gave to the poor, was a criminal, many people agree with his **moral** standards.

*Moral* means . . .   a. relating to beliefs of what is right and wrong    b. relating to beliefs about crime    c. relating to beliefs about personal relationships

**8. preserve**
/prɪˈzɚv/
-verb

- In order to **preserve** the dinosaur bones, the museum carefully controls the temperature in exhibit rooms.
- My aunt carefully **preserves** family photographs in photo albums.

*Preserve* means . . .   a. to be careless with    b. to show    c. to protect and keep

**9. regard**
/rɪˈgard/
-noun

- When Eric rudely started to smoke in the nonsmoking section of the restaurant, the waitress complained, "You have no **regard** for the rules here."
- I really admire teachers; I have high **regard** for the important work that they do.

*Regard* means . . .   a. respect    b. interest    c. friendship

**10. style**
/staɪl/
-noun

- Even though Darren and Paulo are brothers, they have completely different driving **styles**; Darren drives slowly and carefully, but Paulo is a fast and dangerous driver.
- Most of John's friends dress in a casual way, but he prefers a more elegant **style** of dressing.

*Style* means . . .   a. skill    b. way of doing something    c. clothing

## ▌WORDS AND DEFINITIONS

*Match each key word with its definition.*

1. _____aim_____ to plan to achieve something

2. _____ something that people in a particular society do because it is traditional

3. _____ all the people in a society or family who are about the same age

4. _____ the particular way that someone does something

5. _____ to keep something or someone from being harmed, destroyed, or changed too much

6. _____ present; happening, existing, or being used now

7. _____ relating to beliefs of what is right and wrong behavior

8. _____ the power to have an effect on the way someone or something develops, behaves, or thinks

9. _____ respect for someone or something

10. _____ to move closer to someone or something

# ∎ COMPREHENSION CHECK

*Choose the best answer.*

1. Who has **regard** for Mozart?
   a. Razi, who rarely listens to classical music.
   b. Ellen, who wants to visit Mozart's birthplace in Vienna, Austria.
   c. Harry, who thinks that Mozart was not very talented.
   d. Annie, who falls asleep when she listens to Mozart's music.

2. Which person **aims** to save money?
   a. Yuri, who buys $500 sunglasses.
   b. Wanda, who goes shopping when she gets her paycheck.
   c. Isabelle, who has a savings account at the bank.
   d. Frank, who eats in expensive restaurants every night.

3. Who is NOT trying to **preserve** something?
   a. "We want to protect the pandas in our zoo."
   b. "You can wear your white shoes in the mud."
   c. "Please use a coaster so that the hot mug won't damage the table."
   d. "Let's take care of your grandmother's photograph by putting it in a picture frame with glass."

4. What does a dog happily **approach**?
   a. a bath
   b. a cage
   c. an angry lion
   d. a bowl of food

5. Richard was born in 1910. What did the teenagers of his **generation** do for fun?
   a. listen to the radio
   b. listen to CDs
   c. watch TV
   d. play computer games

6. Sara takes good care of her little sister when their parents are away. She also gives her a lot of excellent advice. How does Sara **influence** her sister?
   a. Sara does not influence her sister.
   b. Sara influences her sister in a positive way.
   c. Sara influences her sister in a negative way.
   d. Sara rarely influences her sister.

7. What's a **current** world problem?
   a. too much food
   b. global warming
   c. decreasing population
   d. general peace

8. What question relates to a **moral** decision?
   a. How many hours should I sleep tonight?
   b. Should I watch TV when I finish my homework?
   c. How much respect should I give to my parents?
   d. Where can I buy a new computer?

9. Which of the following is an example of a **custom**?
   a. Grace went to Disney World last fall.
   b. Every winter, Grace decorates her windows with candles.
   c. Grace is shopping today.
   d. Grace has swum in the Pacific Ocean.

10. What do you think is the best description of the **style** in which Buckingham Palace, the home of Queen Elizabeth II, is decorated?
    a. relaxed
    b. simple
    c. fancy
    d. cheap

## WORD FAMILIES

Now that you have studied the ten key words and their basic definitions, you are ready to learn words that belong to the same family as some of the key words. A word family includes words that look alike but have different functions (noun, verb, adjective, or adverb). Their meanings are related but different.

**A.** *Look at each model phrase and decide whether the word in **bold** is used as a noun, verb, adjective, or adverb.*

|  | NOUN | VERB | ADJECTIVE | ADVERB |
|---|:---:|:---:|:---:|:---:|
| **1. aim** |  |  |  |  |
| • **aim** to succeed |  | ✓ |  |  |
| • explain our **aim** | ✓ |  |  |  |
| **2. approach** |  |  |  |  |
| • slowly **approach** Denver |  |  |  |  |
| • interrupt our **approach** |  |  |  |  |
| **3. current** |  |  |  |  |
| • **current** events |  |  |  |  |
| • **currently** busy |  |  |  |  |
| **4. influence** |  |  |  |  |
| • a strong **influence** |  |  |  |  |
| • **influence** friends |  |  |  |  |
| • an **influential** person |  |  |  |  |
| **5. preserve** |  |  |  |  |
| • **preserve** the documents |  |  |  |  |
| • the **preservation** department |  |  |  |  |
| **6. style** |  |  |  |  |
| • a unique **style** |  |  |  |  |
| • a **stylish** woman |  |  |  |  |

**B.** *Match each of the following sentences with the definition of the word in **bold**.*

__c__ 1. Ghandi was an **influential** person; he changed the lives of many people.

_____ 2. **Currently**, I am working in Germany, but I plan to move to Argentina soon.

_____ 3. The museum will hire a specialist who knows about the **preservation** of dinosaur bones.

_____ 4. Eric's **aim** is to start his own business before his 30th birthday.

_____ 5. Mothers strongly **influence** their children.

_____ 6. My Italian teacher is really **stylish**; she always wears the latest fashions.

_____ 7. The **approach** of the thunderstorm made us hurry inside.

a. attractive in a fashionable way

b. the act of keeping something unharmed or unchanged

c. having a lot of influence

d. the act of coming closer in time or distance

e. have an effect on the way someone or something develops, behaves, or thinks

f. at the present time

g. something that you are trying to achieve

## ▌SAME WORD, DIFFERENT MEANING

*Most words have more than one meaning. Study the additional meanings of **approach**, **moral**, and **style**. Then read each sentence and decide which meaning is used.*

| | | |
|---|---|---|
| a. | **approach** *v.* | to move closer to someone or something |
| b. | **approach** *v.* | to ask someone for something when you are not sure if he or she will do what you want |
| c. | **moral** *adj.* | relating to beliefs of what is right and wrong behavior |
| d. | **moral** *adj.* | always behaving in a way that is based on strong beliefs about what is right and wrong |
| e. | **style** *n.* | the particular way that someone does something |
| f. | **style** *n.* | a particular design or fashion for something such as clothes, hair, furniture, music, etc. |

___a___ 1. As the train was **approaching** the station, we hugged and said goodbye.

_____ 2. I can't imagine my brother stealing that money. He's always been such a **moral** person.

_____ 3. Sylvia has an unusual dancing **style**.

_____ 4. A homeless man **approached** us on the street and asked us for money.

_____ 5. The death penalty is a **moral** issue; its supporters believe it is correct for the government to kill a terrible criminal, while its opponents feel it is wrong for a person to kill another person under any circumstances.

_____ 6. Vince told the salesman, "I don't like this **style**. Do you have any modern bikes?"

## ▌WORDS IN SENTENCES

*Complete each sentence with one of the words from the box.*

| | | | | |
|---|---|---|---|---|
| aim | currently | generation | moral | regard |
| approaches | ~~custom~~ | influence | preservation | style |

1. It is the _____custom_____ in much of South America for a girl to have a big party on her fifteenth birthday.

2. As our boat _____ Niagara Falls, please put on your raincoats so that you won't get wet.

3. If your _____ is to work in Paris, you'd better learn French.

4. Willa trusts June to baby-sit for her children because June is a(n) _____ person.

5. When shopping for a new shirt, it's important to consider price, fit, and _____.

6. To show your _____ for the other passengers on the subway, please do not speak loudly on your cell phone.

7. In Jen's grandmother's _____, women did all the cooking, but life has changed; Jen's husband often makes dinner.

8. We know that the ancient Egyptians were experts at _____ because we still have their mummies today.

9. Salvador Dali had a great _____ on modern art.

10. Anita used to only run, but she is _____ training for a triathalon, in which she will run, swim, and bike.

## ▌WORDS IN COLLOCATIONS AND EXPRESSIONS

*Following are common collocations (word partners) and expressions with some of the key words. Read the definitions and then complete the conversations with the correct form of the collocations and expressions.*

| | |
|---|---|
| 1. **aim** | |
| • **aim (sth) at (sb)** | to point something at a person or thing you want to hit |
| 2. **approach** | |
| • **an interesting approach** | an interesting way of doing something or solving a problem |
| 3. **current** | |
| • **current events** | topics that are in the news now |
| 4. **generation** | |
| • **generation gap** | a lack of understanding between older and younger people |
| 5. **influence** | |
| • **be/have a good/bad influence on (sb)** | to affect someone in a positive/negative way |
| 6. **regard** | |
| • **regard (sb/sth) as** | to think about someone or something in a particular way |

1. SAM: Why doesn't my grandson like to listen to country music with me? What's his problem?

   JOHN: I don't think there's a problem, Sam. There's just a _____ *generation gap* _____ . Young people like different music from the kind we like.

2. TV ANCHOR 1: Good evening, and welcome to *The World Today*.

   TV ANCHOR 2: In this hour we will be discussing _____. We'll begin by looking at the week's top news in Africa.

3. STUDENT 1: Wasn't Dostoyevsky an amazing writer?

   STUDENT 2: I'm sorry, but his books are not my style. They're too long and complicated!

   STUDENT 1: Are you crazy? I _____ Dostoyevsky _____ a genius!

4.   MOTHER:   You can't go out with Tom tonight.

DAUGHTER:   Why not?

MOTHER:   He's a _____ on you. Ever since you started spending time with him, you've been staying out late and forgetting to do your homework. Why can't you be friends with Peter again? He was such a _____ on you. You got great grades when you dated him.

DAUGHTER:   Peter was boring.

5.   COACH:   Scoring is easy. You just need to _____ the ball _____ the hoop.

STUDENT:   (*throws the ball unsuccessfully*)
Oops. I missed! Sorry, I don't have good aim.

6. BEN FRANKLIN:   I am going to fly a kite in the sky during a thunderstorm to see if I can prove that lightning is electrical.

FRIEND:   That's an _____, but it sounds strange. I don't think it will work.

## ▍WORDS IN A READING

*Read this article about community service. Complete it with words and expressions from the boxes.*

| aims | bad influence | generations | moral | regards . . . as |
|------|---------------|-------------|-------|------------------|

### PROFESSOR AND STUDENTS HELP ANCIENT CULTURE LIVE ON

English Associate Professor Troi Carleton _____aims_____ to save Zapotec, a language native to
                                              1
Mexico—and to do it before it is lost to new _____ transformed by technology and social
                                             2
change. She _____ the language _____ part of a culture and feels that when
           3
a language dies, its culture also dies. Carleton is just one of many linguists who now believe that saving

dying languages is a _____ duty.
                    4

This summer Carleton took eight student volunteers from San Francisco State University to

Oaxaca, Mexico, where twenty-three dialects of Zapotec are spoken. The Zapotecs called Mexico their

home for thousands of years before Spain colonized Mexico and made Spanish—a completely foreign

tongue—the country's official language. Spanish has had a _____ on the local language,
                                                          5
causing it to disappear slowly.

This was the second year Carleton's students worked on _____ the Zapotec language.
6
The field experience provides a rare opportunity for students to learn about linguistics and language documentation.

The students, who must take linguistics classes and speak Spanish to participate in the ongoing project, focused on Zapotec Teotitlan del Valle, a dialect from a small town named Teotitlan in the Oaxaca valley. Joining Teotitlan officials, community elders, and local university students, they worked toward three goals: developing a Spanish/Zapotec dictionary, developing a grammar that all Zapotec community members could use, and taking down an oral history for the town museum.

Carleton wanted to involve the SFSU students in a first-hand language preservation project, so she _____ Teotitlan, a town known for its textile production and successful international
7
market for rugs. She knew the people of Teotitlan were eager to preserve their language and _____, and they welcomed SFSU into their community.
8
Carleton began the Zapotec preservation project after working for seven years to help preserve Chatino, another Zapotec dialect. She produced the first Chatino/Spanish/English dictionary and published several articles on Chatino. Earlier in her career, she worked in Malawi, Africa.

The professor plans to continue to bring students each summer to gather more language and cultural information and to contribute to the Teotitlan museum, which includes sections on the town's history, individual stories, and cultural life and details about the _____ of their traditional
9
storytelling, myths, and legends.

Carleton's students, who are _____ preparing for next year's trip, are working on
10
developing a Spanish/Zapotec dictionary of at least 5,000 words.

*(Adapted from Lisa Rau with Matt Itelson, "Professor and Students Help Ancient Culture Live On." The San Francisco State News, Fall 2005.)*

## ▌ WORDS IN DISCUSSION

*Apply the key words to your own life. Complete the questionnaire. Then discuss your answers with a classmate. Try to use the key words.*

**EXAMPLE**

My **approach** to getting in shape: _____*swim every day*_____

*A: I have a different **approach**. I stopped taking the bus to work, and I bike instead.*

*B: How long does it take you to get to work now?*

*A: A long time . . . That's the downside of this **approach**: I'm late to work. But I'm in great shape!*

1. Something I **aim** to do in the next ten years: _____

2. What people say about my clothing **style**: _____

3. How I feel about following the **customs** of my native culture: _____

4. A photograph that I want to **preserve** forever: _____

5. How much I know about **current** world news: _____

6. What life was like for my parents' **generation**, when they were young: _____

7. The academic subject that I **regard** as the most interesting: _____

8. The person who has had the greatest **influence** on me: _____

9. What I would do if a dangerous person **approached** me on the street: _____

10. How much I agree with my parents about what is **moral**: _____

## WORDS IN WRITING

*Choose two topics and write a short paragraph on each. Try to use the key words.*

1. Do you think it is important to **preserve** old buildings, or would you rather spend money on constructing new buildings?

    **EXAMPLE**

    *I love history, so the **preservation** of old buildings is important to me. In particular, I think it's important to **preserve** some old homes so that we can understand how people used to live a long time ago.*

2. Describe a **custom** from your grandparents' **generation** that is rarely practiced now. What was the **custom**? Why isn't it popular with your **generation**? Explain.

3. What **styles** of music do you enjoy? Explain.

4. What **current** news story interests you? Explain.

5. If you had to follow a famous and **influential** person's **approach** to life, whose would you choose? Why?

**Key Words**

| | | | | |
|---|---|---|---|---|
| broad | effective | goal | neglect | scene |
| comment | focus | mercy | otherwise | tear |

## ▌WORDS IN CONTEXT

*Use the sentences to guess what each key word means. Choose the meaning that is closest to that of the key word in **bold**.*

**1. broad**
/brɔd/
-*adjective*

- The wrestler had strong legs, big arms, and a **broad** chest.
- **Broad** streets fill the city of Moscow. They are busy with traffic and pedestrians.

*Broad* means . . .     a. unusual     (b.) very wide     c. very narrow

**2. comment**
/ˈkɑmɛnt/
-*noun*

- At the end of the lecture, the speaker asked the students if they had any questions or **comments**.
- Dina was upset by her boyfriend's **comments** about her new hairstyle.

*Comment* means . . .     a. a complaint     b. an opinion     c. a question

**3. effective**
/ɪˈfɛktɪv/
-*adjective*

- For many, yoga is an **effective** way to lower stress and improve physical health.
- The medicine is very **effective**. I took some an hour ago, and I feel better already.

*Effective* means . . .     a. producing a desired result     b. physically tiring     c. causing happiness

**4. focus**
/ˈfoʊkəs/
-*verb*

- During the Olympic Games, the whole world **focuses** on sports.
- This week, students are **focusing** more on preparing for the big dance than on studying for their exams.

*Focus* means . . .     a. to study     b. to give all your attention     c. to plan

**5. goal**
/goʊl/
-*noun*

- My **goal** is to learn German well enough to have a basic conversation.
- The company met its **goal**: it increased production and lowered costs.

*Goal* means . . .     a. something you aim to do     b. a talent or skill     c. the future

**6. mercy**
/ˈmɚsi/
-*noun*

- The criminal asked for **mercy**. She explained that she had to steal to feed her children.
- The stronger team showed no **mercy**; they gave the other players no chance to score, and they won the game.

*Mercy* means . . .     a. freedom     b. weakness     c. kindness and pity

7. **neglect**
/nɪˈglɛkt/
-verb

- The dentist warned me not to **neglect** my teeth or else I'd lose them all by old age.
- Having a party is a great idea, but you're **neglecting** an important fact: Saturday is a holiday, and most people will want to be with their families.

*Neglect* means . . .   a. to express a worry      b. to complain about      c. to give little attention

8. **otherwise**
/ˈʌðɚˌwaɪz/
-adverb

- I must finish my paper by Friday; **otherwise**, the teacher will give me a lower grade.
- You need to pay first. **Otherwise**, they won't serve you.

*Otherwise* means . . . a. if so                b. if not                c. but

9. **scene**
/sin/
-noun

- I love watching DVDs because I can watch my favorite **scenes** over and over again.
- The director asked the actors to remain on the stage to prepare for the fight **scene**.

*Scene* means . . .     a. a joke               b. part of a play        c. a song
                                                        or movie

10. **tear**
/tɛr/
-verb

- Be careful not to **tear** the letter. It was written by your great-grandfather, so it's very old.
- I **tore** my shirt when I pulled it on too quickly.

*Tear* means . . .      a. damage              b. to lose              c. to get dirty

## WORDS AND DEFINITIONS

*Match each key word with its definition.*

1. ___otherwise___ if not (used when there will be a bad result if something does not happen)

2. _____ something you hope to do in the future

3. _____ to give all your attention to a particular thing

4. _____ very wide

5. _____ to damage a piece of paper, cloth, etc. by pulling it too hard or by letting it touch something sharp

6. _____ a part of a play, movie, or other dramatic art form during which the action all happens in one place over a short period of time

7. _____ kindness, pity, and a willingness to forgive

8. _____ producing the result that was wanted

9. _____ to not pay enough attention to someone or something, or to not take care of someone or something very well

10. _____ an opinion that you give about someone or something

# COMPREHENSION CHECK

*Choose the best answer.*

1. One might expect a hockey player to have (a) **broad**
   a. forehead.
   b. nose.
   c. smile.
   (d.) shoulders.

2. An **effective** way of stopping curious neighbors from bothering you is
   a. to put up a fence and some curtains.
   b. to exchange secrets with them.
   c. to tell them a story from your childhood.
   d. to ask them to call you on the phone only once a day.

3. Marek needs to pass this exam. **Otherwise**,
   a. he will pass the course.
   b. he will have to take the course again.
   c. he should have studied harder.
   d. he will be the strongest student in his class.

4. An example of a rude **comment** would be
   a. "He dances like a gorilla."
   b. "He's a talented dancer."
   c. "I'm sorry he isn't coming to the dance tonight."
   d. "Did you dance with him?"

5. If a student often **neglects** his studies, which would he most likely do?
   a. prepare for a test
   b. ask the teacher for help
   c. help another student with homework
   d. forget to do a homework assignment

6. The court system can show **mercy** by
   a. refusing to let lawyers speak.
   b. sending a criminal to prison for life.
   c. giving a light punishment for a serious crime.
   d. finding everyone guilty.

7. Which of these things can easily **tear**?
   a. a glass dish
   b. a tall tree
   c. an old pair of pants
   d. a new mobile phone

8. A romantic **scene** CANNOT be found in
   a. a play.
   b. a ballet.
   c. a film.
   d. a bouquet of flowers.

9. I didn't **focus** on one main idea, so my essay
   a. was very clear.
   b. was hard to understand.
   c. had an interesting title.
   d. used good examples.

10. Yoon studies karate and is very serious about it. Her **goal** is
    a. to quit.
    b. to find a new hobby.
    c. to reach the highest level–a black belt.
    d. to be safe.

# ▍WORD FAMILIES

Now that you have studied the ten key words and their basic definitions, you are ready to learn words that belong to the same family as some of the key words. A word family includes words that look alike but have different functions (noun, verb, adjective, or adverb). Their meanings are related but different.

**A.** *Look at each model phrase and decide whether the word in **bold** is used as a noun, verb, adjective, or adverb.*

| | NOUN | VERB | ADJECTIVE | ADVERB |
|---|:---:|:---:|:---:|:---:|
| **1. comment** | | | | |
| • write a **comment** | ✓ | | | |
| • **comment** loudly | | ✓ | | |
| **2. effective** | | | | |
| • **effective** medicine | | | | |
| • work **effectively** | | | | |
| **3. focus** | | | | |
| • **focus** clearly | | | | |
| • be the **focus** | | | | |
| **4. neglect** | | | | |
| • **neglect** your health | | | | |
| • suffer from **neglect** | | | | |
| • a **neglected** pet | | | | |
| **5. tear** | | | | |
| • **tear** the paper | | | | |
| • a **torn** pair of jeans | | | | |

**B.** *Read the first half of each sentence and match it with the appropriate ending.*

_b_ 1. The parents were guilty of

___ 2. The teacher invited me to

___ 3. The sweater was

___ 4. Sometimes letters can communicate more

___ 5. That actor is very popular, and he loves being the

___ 6. The garden looked

a. **comment** once we finished the reading.

b. **neglect**; their children were poorly taken care of at home.

c. **focus** of everybody's attention wherever he goes.

d. **torn**, but I didn't care. It kept me warm.

e. **effectively** than a phone conversation.

f. **neglected**. Most of the flowers had already died.

## ■ SAME WORD, DIFFERENT MEANING

*Most words have more than one meaning. Study the additional meanings of **focus**, **otherwise**, and **scene**. Then read each sentence and decide which meaning is used.*

| | | |
|---|---|---|
| a. **focus** *n.* | the thing, person, situation, etc. that people pay special attention to |
| b. **focus** *n.* | special attention that you give to a particular person or subject |
| c. **otherwise** *adv.* | if not (used when there will be a bad result if something does not happen) |
| d. **otherwise** *adv.* | in a different way |
| e. **scene** *n.* | a part of a play, movie, or other dramatic art form during which the action all happens in one place over a short period of time |
| f. **scene** *n.* | a view of a place as you see it, or as it appears in a picture |

  _b_  1. Thato's main **focus** now is her career. She gives little time to anything else.

_____ 2. The balcony **scene** is the most famous part of Shakespeare's play *Romeo and Juliet*.

_____ 3. I want to finish all my homework today. **Otherwise**, I'll have to find time on the weekend to do it, and I won't enjoy my cousin's visit as much.

_____ 4. The personal lives of famous people are often the **focus** in certain magazines.

_____ 5. The mother watched the **scene** in the kitchen with disbelief: her children were washing the dishes together instead of fighting or making a mess.

_____ 6. Everyone thought Dana would move back home after quitting college, but she decided **otherwise**. She's now living in the city and working full-time at a café.

## ■ WORDS IN SENTENCES

*Complete each item with a word from the box.*

| | | | | |
|---|---|---|---|---|
| broad | effectively | goal | ~~neglect~~ | scene |
| comment | focus | mercy | otherwise | torn |

1. My grandmother cared so much for others that she would often _____*neglect*_____ her own needs.

2. Marianne's _____ was to graduate from college in three years instead of four.

3. Sermin's parents asked her to _____ more in school. Her teachers had complained that she wasn't paying attention in classes.

4. When I was little, I had a favorite blanket. Even when it was old and _____, I still wanted to hold it at night while I slept.

5. My sister believes that toothpaste _____ removes stains.

6. After the president's speech, reporters asked people in the audience to _____.

7. Unlike my father, whose nose is long and narrow, I have a _____ nose.

8. "_____!" cried the crowd outside the courthouse. They believed that the man didn't deserve the death sentence.

9. The artist painted a _____ of a couple walking in a park on a summer day.

10. Don't forget to take your cell phone; _____, I won't be able to reach you.

## WORDS IN COLLOCATIONS AND EXPRESSIONS

*Following are common collocations (word partners) and expressions with some of the key words. Read the definitions and then complete the conversations with the correct form of the collocations and expressions.*

| 1. **comment** | |
|---|---|
| • **comment on (sb/sth)** | to give an opinion about someone or something |
| • **make a comment about (sb/sth)** | to state an opinion about someone or something |
| 2. **focus** | |
| • **focus on (sb/sth)** | to pay special attention to a particular person or thing |
| • **the focus of attention** | the subject that people are interested in |
| 3. **tear** | |
| • **tear (sth) apart** | separating something into pieces |
| • **tear (sth) open** | to open something very quickly by tearing it |

1. SIDONIE: Look. You got a letter from Spain. And what beautiful stamps!

   THOMAS: Let me see.

   SIDONIE: Can you try not to _____ *tear* _____ the envelope
   _____ *open* _____ ? I'd like to save the stamps for my collection.

2. ACTOR: I'd like to have some idea about the questions you'll be asking on the show.

   HOST: Well, after the opening greetings and usual conversation, I'll ask you to
   _____ briefly _____ your
   decision to act on stage rather than in films.

3. FATHER: Is Jill over at Katlyn's again?

   MOTHER: Does that surprise you? Jill and Katlyn are best friends. They're always together.
   You can't _____ them _____.

   FATHER: Well, at least ask our daughter to come home for dinner.

4. TEACHER: Has your group decided on a topic?

   STUDENT: Yes, our project will _____ homeless animals and ways to
   help them.

5. DELORES: Have you seen Rhea's outfit today?

   DANILO: Yeah. So?

DELORES: Isn't it awful? I don't know anyone who wears so many colors at one time.

DANILO: Look, Rhea's a nice person. I don't think you should _____ unkind _____ about her clothes. If she hears you, she'll be hurt.

6. HUSBAND: What took you so long in that store?

WIFE: Sorry. Two customers in line began to yell at one another. Their argument became _____. One had gone out on a date with the other's ex-boyfriend. I couldn't help but listen!

## WORDS IN A READING

*Read this article about a Canadian photographer. Complete it with words and expressions from the boxes.*

| effective | ~~focus...on~~ | neglected | otherwise | scenes |
|---|---|---|---|---|

### THE PHOTOGRAPHY OF EDWARD BURTYNSKY

In the 19th century, painters like Thomas Cole and Albert Bierstadt chose deep canyons and tall mountains as the subjects of their work. They framed nature and let viewers see beauty untouched by human hands. But the world is different now, and the land no longer looks the same. The story of how the land changed since Cole and Bierstadt's time can be learned through photography.

In his exhibit "Manufactured Landscapes," Canadian artist Edward Burtynsky shows twenty years of history in pictures. His theme: nature under attack. The photographer brilliantly uses his art to ___*focus*___ people's attention ___*on*___ how land has been greatly changed by
           1                              2
industry. He forces our eyes to see _____ we would _____ turn away from.
                                         2                        3
*The Los Angeles Times* calls the pictures "frightening and inviting."

The talent of the photographer lies in his ability to find beauty in the _____ remains
                                                                              4
of the industrial world. The combination is _____: Burtynsky succeeds in creating a
                                                    5
strange feeling of wonder. Parts of nature were destroyed and left behind, but Burtynsky's camera takes society back to see the land in a new light.

| broad | comment | goal | mercy | torn apart |
|---|---|---|---|---|

In one picture, Burtynsky used his camera to catch the bright orange of a polluted river. In another, a huge ship lies _____ on a beach in Bangladesh. Each of the large-scale photographs
                            6
shows a _____ piece of land ruined without _____ by human need: these
              7                                            8
are the places where natural resources were turned into things for our use—buildings, cars, boats.

Was it Burtynsky's _____ to call attention to an environmental problem? Should
                          9
each photograph be seen as a _____ on humans' cruel relationship with nature?
                                   10

Most critics say no. The photographs are there only to record a period of human history; they serve as documents. The photographer neither lets us look away nor tells us that what we see is our wrongdoing. We must simply look and decide for ourselves.

*(Based on information in "Edward Burtynsky: Manufactured Landscapes." The Week, August 5, 2005.)*

## ▎ WORDS IN DISCUSSION

*Apply the words to your own life. Read and discuss each question in small groups. Try to use the key words.*

1. Do you ever **neglect** to do something you know you should do?

   ### EXAMPLE

   *Sometimes I don't brush my teeth before bed. I don't want to **neglect** my teeth, but sometimes it's really late, and I feel too tired to brush them.*

2. What is an **effective** way for you to remember people's names?

3. What is one **goal** you have in life?

4. When someone hurts your feelings and then apologizes, do you show any **mercy**, or do you stay angry?

5. When you get your picture taken, do you usually have a **broad** smile on your face? Why or why not?

6. What is the main **focus** of your life at present?

7. You're on the bus, and you just realized your notebook is at home. You need to look at your notes: otherwise, you won't be able to make an important presentation today. What do you do?

8. Choose an interesting movie and describe your favorite **scene**.

9. How do you protect important pictures and documents from **tearing**?

10. When you are watching a movie in a movie theater, do you ever make loud **comments** about the movie to the people sitting next to you?

## ▎ WORDS IN WRITING

*Choose two topics and write a short paragraph on each. Try to use the key words.*

1. Do you **tear open** presents, or do you take your time opening them?

   ### EXAMPLE

   *Why wait? I love to **tear open** a gift and find out what's inside. Some people open things carefully because they want to save the paper. I'm not one of those people.*

2. What do you need to **focus on** doing to improve your English?

3. How can **neglected** pets be helped? Should the owners be punished?

4. Do you wear **torn** jeans? Why or why not?

5. Is there a way to fight a cold **effectively**? Explain.

# WORDS IN CONTEXT

*Use the sentences to guess what each key word means. Choose the meaning that is closest to that of the key word in **bold**.*

1. **accuse**
   /əˈkyuz/
   -verb

   - Because Jackson was driving a silver car that looked exactly like the car that had been stolen, the police **accused** Jackson of stealing it.
   - Our science teacher **accused** Nell of cheating when he saw her looking at someone else's test.

   *Accuse* means . . .  a. to punish someone  b. to yell at someone  c. to say that someone has done something wrong

2. **authority**
   /əˈθɔrəti/
   -noun

   - The president has the **authority** to pass or veto a bill.
   - Parents have the **authority** to send their children to bed at a reasonable hour.

   *Authority* means . . .  a. power  b. weakness  c. intelligence

3. **bribe**
   /braɪb/
   -noun

   - When the police stopped Mike for speeding on the highway, he offered them a **bribe**, saying that he would give them $50 if they would not give him a speeding ticket.
   - When Rosie told her Spanish teacher, "I'll give you two front-row basketball tickets if you give me an A," he said, "Sorry, I do not take **bribes**."

   *Bribe* means . . .  a. an honest gift  b. a dishonest offer of money or gifts  c. money

4. **brief**
   /brif/
   -adjective

   - I have a **brief** conversation with my boss every Wednesday; it lasts for only ten minutes.
   - If you don't feel like spending a long time with my relatives, we can have a **brief** visit.

   *Brief* means . . .  a. long  b. detailed  c. short

5. **graceful**
   /ˈgreɪsfəl/
   -adjective

   - Because Sophie took ballet lessons for five years, she is a **graceful** dancer.
   - If you had to perform in front of a large group of people, would you have a difficult time, or would you be **graceful**?

   *Graceful* means . . .  a. moving in an attractive way  b. moving in a clumsy way  c. athletic and energetic

**6. immense**
/ɪˈmɛns/
-adjective

- The Sahara is an **immense** desert extending over thousands of miles.
- *Titanic* is a good movie, but it cost an **immense** amount of money to make—more than $200 million!

*Immense* means . . .   a. extremely large       b. average       c. very small

**7. involve**
/ɪnˈvalv/
-verb

- Educating children **involves** many people: learners, teachers, and parents.
- Building the youth center will **involve** many volunteers, including the architect and the construction workers.

*Involve* means . . .   a. to include       b. to know about       c. to have no interest in

**8. root**
/rut/
-noun

- The **roots** of a tree drink water from the earth.
- You need to pull a weed's **roots** out of the ground to get rid of it.

*Root* means . . .   a. top of a plant       b. middle of a plant       c. part of a plant that grows underground

**9. seek**
/sik/
-verb

- When Hugh **seeks** advice, he talks to his brother.
- If you are **seeking** help with your spelling, you should use a dictionary.

*Seek* means . . .   a. to play       b. to try to find or get       c. to find

**10. visible**
/ˈvɪzəbəl/
-adjective

- The Great Wall of China is the only manmade structure **visible** from space.
- If you look out the window during a big snowstorm, you will only see ice and snow; the road will not be **visible**.

*Visible* means . . .   a. impossible to see       b. you can see it       c. cloudy

## WORDS AND DEFINITIONS

*Match each key word with its definition.*

1. ____seek____ to try to find or get something

2. _____ can be seen

3. _____ the power someone has because of his/her official position

4. _____ to say that someone has done something wrong or illegal

5. _____ extremely large

6. _____ to include or affect someone or something

7. _____ moving in a smooth and attractive way

8. _____ the part of a plant or tree that grows under the ground

9. _____ money or gifts that you use to persuade someone to do something

10. _____ continuing for a short time

# COMPREHENSION CHECK

*Choose the best answer.*

1. A **brief** conversation may last
   a. for four hours.
   b. all morning.
   c. for ten minutes.
   d. for eleven hours.

2. Which of the following is **immense**?
   a. an ant
   b. the Grand Canyon
   c. a piece of paper
   d. a puddle

3. In which of the following quotes is a person **accusing** someone?
   a. "You are wonderful."
   b. "Let's have a picnic."
   c. "Do you like to play beach volleyball?"
   d. "You ate my sandwich!"

4. Where are the **roots** of a flower that is growing in a sunny field?
   a. in the sunshine
   b. inside the flower
   c. in the ground under the flower
   d. a flower does not have roots.

5. Which of the following is NOT **graceful**?
   a. a swan
   b. a professional dancer
   c. a pig
   d. a concert pianist

6. In which quote is a person offering a **bribe** to someone else?
   a. "You can tell everyone about it."
   b. "If I give you this candy bar, will you promise to keep quiet?"
   c. "Happy birthday! Here's ten dollars."
   d. "Please don't make me do my homework!"

7. Who has **authority** when the parents are away?
   a. the eight-year-old boy
   b. the ten-year-old girl
   c. the dog
   d. the baby-sitter

8. Ming **involves** many people in his art projects. This means he
   a. works alone.
   b. sells a lot of art.
   c. creates art with other people.
   d. buys a lot of art.

9. If a flower is **visible** to you, you can
   a. see it.
   b. smell it.
   c. hear it.
   d. touch it.

10. Which of the following can you NOT **seek**?
    a. truth
    b. a person
    c. help
    d. anger

# WORD FAMILIES

Now that you have studied the ten key words and their basic definitions, you are ready to learn words that belong to the same family as some of the key words. A word family includes words that look alike but have different functions (noun, verb, adjective, or adverb). Their meanings are related but different.

**A.** *Look at each model phrase and decide whether the word in **bold** is used as a noun, verb, adjective, or adverb.*

| | NOUN | VERB | ADJECTIVE | ADVERB |
|---|:---:|:---:|:---:|:---:|
| **1. accuse** | | | | |
| • **accuse** of murder | | ✓ | | |
| • a shocking **accusation** | ✓ | | | |
| **2. bribe** | | | | |
| • accept a **bribe** | | | | |
| • to **bribe** someone | | | | |
| • guilty of **bribery** | | | | |
| **3. brief** | | | | |
| • a **brief** discussion | | | | |
| • **briefly** interested | | | | |
| **4. graceful** | | | | |
| • a **graceful** athlete | | | | |
| • dance **gracefully** | | | | |
| • said with **grace** | | | | |
| **5. involve** | | | | |
| • **involve** many people | | | | |
| • his **involvement** | | | | |
| **6. visible** | | | | |
| • a **visible** problem | | | | |
| • **visibly** relieved | | | | |

**B.** *Read the first half of each sentence and match it with the appropriate ending.*

___g___ 1. The government is trying to stop

_____ 2. I'm an honest person, so you can't

_____ 3. When he saw the storm clouds, Aaron was

_____ 4. When we were sure who was guilty, we made a(n)

_____ 5. We could talk only

_____ 6. A deer walks

_____ 7. The students were proud of their

_____ 8. A dancer must move with

a. **accusation**.

b. **grace**.

c. **gracefully**.

f. **visibly** worried.

g. **bribery**.

h. **involvement** in the team.

i. **bribe** me.

j. **briefly**.

## SAME WORD, DIFFERENT MEANING

Most words have more than one meaning. Study the additional meanings of **authority**, **brief**, and **root**. Then read each sentence and decide which meaning is used.

| | | |
|---|---|---|
| a. **authority** *n.* | the power someone has because of his/her official position |
| b. **authorities** *n. pl.* | the people or organization that are in charge of a particular place |
| c. **brief** *adj.* | continuing for a short time |
| d. **brief** *adj.* | using only a few words and not describing things in detail |
| e. **root** *n.* | the part of a plant or tree that grows under the ground |
| f. **root** *n.* | the main cause of a problem |

__e__ 1. If we dig in the ground around the tree, we'll find its **roots**.

_____ 2. I will send you a **brief** report on what happened.

_____ 3. We need to find the **root** of the problem.

_____ 4. Greg and Allison had a **brief** conversation while they were walking to their next class.

_____ 5. When the **authorities** arrived, the bank robber had already run away.

_____ 6. Who has **authority** in this office?

## WORDS IN SENTENCES

Complete each sentence with one of the words from the box.

| | | | | |
|---|---|---|---|---|
| accusation | bribe | gracefully | involvement | seeking |
| authority | briefly | immense | ~~roots~~ | visible |

1. The _____ roots _____ of a plant are under the ground.

2. If you are _____ help with your math homework, why not call the math tutor?

3. Jairo was surprised by his brother's _____ in filming a Hollywood movie.

4. "Sorry, Bob. You don't have the _____ to tell me not to play my guitar here. It's my porch!"

5. Jessie was _____ interested in learning how to make sushi, but after a lesson she decided that she would rather buy sushi in a restaurant.

6. In a Japanese tea ceremony, the tea must be poured _____.

7. "We have a good reason for making this _____, Ms. Jones. We found your fingerprints on the stolen pearls."

8. The pilot told the passengers to look to the right, where the Andes Mountains were _____ through the clouds.

9. An honest person will never try to _____ you.

10. Russia is a(n) _____ country, measuring 17 million square kilometers.

# WORDS IN COLLOCATIONS AND EXPRESSIONS

*Following are common collocations (word partners) and expressions with some of the key words. Read the definitions and then complete the conversations with the correct form of the collocations and expressions.*

1. **accuse**
   - **accuse (sb) of (doing sth)**      to say that someone has done something wrong or illegal

2. **brief**
   - **a brief meeting**      a short meeting

3. **involve**
   - **be/get involved in (sth)**      to take part in an activity or event

4. **root**
   - **have its roots in (sth)**      have its origin in something
   - **a person's roots**      a person's connection with a place because his/her ancestors or family lived there

5. **seek**
   - **hide and seek**      a game in which children hide and search for each other

1. RECEPTIONIST: When can you meet with Mr. Jackson?

   GEORGIA: I have _____ *a brief meeting* _____ at one o'clock, so I'll be free by two.

2. ANN: Why did Margaret break up with Tommy?

   BECKY: He was _____ some bad business, pressuring old people into buying insurance that was much too expensive.

   ANN: Wow! I'm glad she got out of that relationship.

3. MOTHER: Did you eat the last chocolate chip cookie?

   LITTLE BOY: Who, me? Mom, how could you _____ me _____ doing that? Maybe the dog ate it.

   MOTHER: I don't think so. I see chocolate on your face!

4. DAD: Why is Jeff in the hall closet?

   MOM: The kids are playing _____.

5. PETE: Where are you from?

   VLADIMIR: Well, my _____ are in Russia because I grew up there, but I'm married to an American and I've been living in Texas for two years now.

6. STUDENT: Where did salsa dancing begin?

   INSTRUCTOR: Salsa _____ Latin America and Africa.

# WORDS IN A READING

*Read this article about politics. Complete it with words and expressions from the boxes.*

| bribes | brief | involved in | ~~seeking~~ | visibly |
|--------|-------|-------------|-------------|---------|

## HOW COMMON IS BRIBERY AROUND THE WORLD?

In 2005, the Gallop International survey group telephoned ordinary people in countries around the world. Close to 55,000 people in sixty-nine countries were polled. The survey group was

_____seeking_____ information about bribes. Respondents were asked _____ questions
   1                                                                             2

about their governments. Did they feel that their political systems were honest or corrupt?

The survey showed that many people worry that bribery is common in their governments. It suggests that poor families are most hurt by corruption. In addition, citizens of low-income countries usually pay a significantly larger percentage of their income in _____ than do citizens in
                                                                                          3

higher income countries.

Asked about change over the past three years, the overall view of citizens in forty-eight countries out of sixty-nine is that corruption has increased _____. However, the amount of bribery
                                                                              4

depends on the country and the social class of the people. At one end, a very low percentage of families in a group of mostly high-income countries were _____ bribing over the course of the
                                                                            5

past year. At the other end, a relatively high proportion of families in a group of central and eastern European, African, and Latin American countries paid a bribe in the previous twelve months.

| accused | authorities | immense | roots |
|---------|-------------|---------|-------|

The _____ of bribery depend on the country; people pay bribes for different reasons
        6

in different countries. An illegal payment may be understood to be required to get a free service or to speed up delivery of a business permit or license or to resolve a problem, even when a bribe is not demanded. Among the sixty-nine countries surveyed, a majority of respondents in Bolivia, the Dominican Republic, Ethiopia, India, Mexico, Nigeria, Paraguay, and Peru who paid a bribe say they did so because the money was directly asked for by the _____. Approximately half of
                                                                              7

those who paid a bribe in Ghana, Moldova, and Pakistan say the same.

Bribes are often thought to be common in political parties. At 4.0 on a scale of 1 to 5, with 5 considered "extremely corrupt," political corruption is a(n) _____ concern of respondents.
                                                                   8

Internationally, people _____ political leaders of accepting bribes. Three quarters of all
                           9

respondents believe that the political life of their country is affected by corruption to a moderate or large extent. This view of corruption in political parties is shared by rich and poor in many countries. This suggests that people around the world do not expect that there will be a quick end to bribery in the near future.

*(Based on "Transparency International Poll Shows Widespread Public Alarm About Corruption." allafrica.com, December 9, 2005.)*

# WORDS IN DISCUSSION

*Apply the key words to your own life. Read and discuss each question in small groups. Try to use the key words.*

### EXAMPLE

The number of times I have offered someone a **bribe** in my life: ___10___

**A:** *Ten? Why have you offered so many **bribes**?*

**B:** *I always tried to **bribe** my little sister when we were kids. I didn't want her to tell my mom about the trouble I got into. Don't worry. I've never tried to **bribe** anyone else.*

1. Something **immense** that I would love to see: _____

2. Something that is **visible** from my window: _____

3. The place where my family has its **roots**: _____

4. Something or someone that I only loved **briefly**: _____

5. A person who is **involved** in my life: _____

6. A time when I **accused** someone of doing something bad: _____

7. Something I can do **gracefully**: _____

8. My opinion of the **authorities** in my home town: _____

9. Something that I will **seek** this year: _____

10. What I would say if someone tried to **bribe** me: _____

# WORDS IN WRITING

*Choose two topics and write a short paragraph on each. Try to use the key words.*

1. Do you think that parents should have the **authority** to tell a teenager which career he or she should **seek**? Explain.

### EXAMPLE

*I believe that parents should help their teenagers make important decisions, but I don't think they have the **authority** to tell them what careers they should have. This is pressuring them! People need to follow their own dreams.*

2. If you could be **involved** in decision making at a high level in your government, would you want to? Why or why not?

3. What is something that you would love to do **gracefully**? Explain.

4. What are the **roots** of your favorite kind of music? Describe how this music began.

5. Would you rather be really excellent at one sport for a **brief** amount of time or good at this sport for many years? Explain.

# QUIZ 3

## PART A

*Choose the word that best completes each item and write it in the space provided.*

1. "Hi, Cara. It's Nalin. Please call me back tonight." is an example of a(n) _____*brief*_____ message.
   - a. immense
   - b. brief
   - c. graceful
   - d. broad

2. Hannah wants to improve her vocabulary this summer. Her _____ is to read two new books every month.
   - a. custom
   - b. comment
   - c. goal
   - d. style

3. It's a _____ in more than one country to take off your shoes when you enter a home.
   - a. style
   - b. scene
   - c. custom
   - d. bribe

4. Gavin was so happy; he had a _____ smile on his face all day long.
   - a. brief
   - b. current
   - c. broad
   - d. effective

5. Jazz had a strong _____ on rock music.
   - a. influence
   - b. style
   - c. regard
   - d. comment

6. Views of marriage and family life change with each new _____. Children don't always follow the practices of their parents.
   - a. style
   - b. generation
   - c. scene
   - d. comment

7. Using water and soap is a(n) _____ way to clean your hands.
   - a. effective
   - b. visible
   - c. broad
   - d. graceful

8. The Independence Day celebration _____ the whole town. Everyone contributes, and everyone has fun.
   - a. involves
   - b. seeks
   - c. focuses
   - d. preserves

9. Because our supervisor is rather lazy, we have little _____ for him.
   - a. influence
   - b. authority
   - c. regard
   - d. comment

10. Mark Twain's relaxed writing _____ made his stories seem more real to many readers of the time.
    - a. style
    - b. generation
    - c. scene
    - d. authority

## PART B

*Read each statement and write **T** for true or **F** for false in the space provided.*

__T__  1. You need to follow traffic laws; **otherwise** you may cause an accident.

_____  2. A court of law must always show **mercy** to those who are guilty.

_____  3. The completion of Chicago's Sears Tower in May of 1973 is an example of a **current** event.

_____  4. Glass can easily **tear.**

_____  5. Wrinkles and gray hair are **visible** signs of aging.

_____  6. Drivers should slow down as they **approach** a stop sign.

_____  7. If you have a pet, you should **neglect** it every day.

_____  8. Police officers are allowed to accept **bribes** much like waiters accept tips.

_____  9. When you watch a comedy, you expect to see some funny **scenes.**

_____ 10. Someone with an **immense** fortune cannot pay his or her bills.

## PART C

*Complete each item with a word from the box. Use each word once.*

| | | | | |
|---|---|---|---|---|
| accusing | authority | focuses | moral | roots |
| aims | ~~comment~~ | graceful | preserve | seeking |

1. During the interview, the actress chose not to make any _____comment_____ on her recent divorce.

2. The company _____ to increase its business by twenty-five percent within two years.

3. Teachers have the _____ to ask a student to leave the classroom if he or she is behaving poorly.

4. I watched the eagle's _____ flight across the sky.

5. American news _____ more on national news than world news.

6. Museums carefully control temperatures and the amount of sunlight in order to _____ priceless works of art.

7. Paige was careful not to harm the _____ of the plant as she moved it to a bigger pot.

8. Kyra is _____ me of spreading gossip about her, but I've said only good things about her.

9. For many, churches and temples are not only places of worship, but also places of _____ instruction.

10. If you're _____ guidance, you should talk to Cole. He's been working here for nine years, and he's done this kind of project many times in the past.

Key Words

| affect | declare | instant | publish | severe |
|--------|---------|---------|---------|--------|
| crush | export | precious | scatter | wound |

## WORDS IN CONTEXT

*Use the sentences to guess what each key word means. Choose the meaning that is closest to that of the key word in **bold**.*

**1. affect**
/əˈfɛkt/
-verb

- Winter weather **affects** the way I feel. When it's cold and dark outside, I have less energy and I become very quiet.
- His kind words **affected** me. I forgot why I had been angry, and I smiled.

*Affect* means . . .     a. to bring to an end     b. to weaken     (c.) to produce a change

**2. crush**
/krʌʃ/
-verb

- Let's **crush** the empty boxes before throwing them into the garbage can.
- As the new passenger sat down, she **crushed** my bouquet of flowers before I could move them.

*Crush* means . . .     a. to damage by pressing     b. to fold in two     c. to lift up high

**3. declare**
/dɪˈklɛr/
-verb

- In 1836, Alabama became the first state to **declare** Christmas a holiday.
- The mayor's voice was loud and strong as he **declared** the new town library open.

*Declare* means . . .     a. to state officially     b. to speak with anger     c. to plan

**4. export**
/ˈɛkspɔrt/
-noun

- Taiwanese **exports** to the United States include metals like iron and steel.
- Furniture **exports** are important to the Italian economy. Among the top buyers are the United States, Germany, France, the United Kingdom, Russia, and Spain.

*Export* means . . .     a. a product sold to another country     b. a product bought from another country     c. a product made and sold in same country

**5. instant**
/ˈɪnstənt/
-adjective

- Thankfully the medicine gave me **instant** relief.
- The movie was loved by all, and it brought the director **instant** fame.

*Instant* means . . .     a. happening as a surprise     b. happening immediately     c. happening over a long period of time

**6. precious**
/ˈprɛʃəs/
-adjective

- Because I couldn't visit for more than a few days with my friends, our time together was **precious**.
- In the days after the flood, the government sent in a **precious** supply of drinking water.

*Precious* means . . .     a. valuable or important     b. generous     c. adorable

**7. publish**
/ˈpʌblɪʃ/
-verb

- American author Mark Twain had been writing since the 1860s, but his most famous novel, *The Adventures of Huckleberry Finn*, wasn't **published** until 1885.
- I wonder what people read for entertainment before magazines were **published**.

*Publish* means . . .    a. to create          b. to put into print          c. to increase

**8. scatter**
/ˈskætɚ/
-verb

- Mia's efforts to brush the flour off the table only caused it to **scatter** everywhere.
- When the mouse ran into the classroom, the students jumped up and **scattered**.

*Scatter* means . . .    a. to move in different directions     b. to push hard          c. to make noise

**9. severe**
/səˈvɪr/
-adjective

- Many schools and businesses closed during the **severe** winter storm.
- The damage to the car was **severe**. I wonder if the driver got hurt.

*Severe* means . . .    a. very bad or serious     b. funny          c. difficult

**10. wound**
/wund/
-noun

- When little Richie fell, I ran over to him to see if any of his **wounds** were serious.
- It's important to keep a **wound** clean for it to heal well.

*Wound* means . . .    a. pain          b. an injury like a cut     c. a dirty piece of clothing

## ▌WORDS AND DEFINITIONS

*Match each key word with its definition.*

1. _____publish_____ to arrange for something to be written, printed, and sold

2. _____ to produce a change in someone or something

3. _____ to state officially and publicly that something is happening or that something is true

4. _____ a product that is sold to another country

5. _____ to press something or someone so hard that it is damaged or injured

6. _____ very bad or serious

7. _____ happening or produced immediately

8. _____ to move or be made to move in many different directions

9. _____ an injury, especially a deep cut made in the skin by a knife or bullet

10. _____ valuable or important and not to be wasted

*Choose the best answer.*

1. All of the following may be called **precious** EXCEPT
   a. time spent with loved ones.
   b. water when you travel across a desert.
   c. an extra pair of jeans.
   d. food taken with you on a camping trip.

2. The book was an **instant** bestseller;
   a. it took many years for people to appreciate it.
   b. the author was sad that the success lasted so briefly.
   c. it was read only by a small circle of people.
   d. the author didn't expect success so soon.

3. The bad mood of another person easily **affects** me;
   a. I pay no attention and continue my activities.
   b. I become just as sad or just as upset.
   c. I don't mind seeing tears or listening to complaints.
   d. I remain calm no matter what.

4. All of the following things may be **declared** EXCEPT
   a. war on another country.
   b. independence.
   c. the closing of a company.
   d. a joke.

5. Which of the following CANNOT **scatter**?
   a. a group of children in a park
   b. a phone message on a table
   c. clouds in the sky
   d. dust on the floor

6. Which of the following could easily cause a **wound**?
   a. a plastic bowl
   b. a rubber glove
   c. a cold drink
   d. a sharp piece of glass

7. My headache was so **severe** that
   a. I was able to think clearly and continue to study.
   b. I didn't need any medicine.
   c. I slept easily.
   d. I spent the rest of the day on the couch with my eyes closed.

8. Which of the following shows the act of **crushing** something?
   a. a politician giving a speech
   b. artists performing a dance
   c. a woman folding a letter
   d. another person stepping heavily on your foot

9. George is going to have his work **published** this year;
   a. I wonder when he'll start writing.
   b. I'll be sure to buy a copy and read it.
   c. I look forward to listening to it.
   d. I expect to receive a letter soon.

10. Which of the following is NOT an example of an **export**?
    a. Indian tea to Russia
    b. Finnish wood to Japan
    c. California wine to New York
    d. Egyptian cotton to Switzerland

# WORD FAMILIES

Now that you have studied the ten key words and their basic definitions, you are ready to learn words that belong to the same family as some of the key words. A word family includes words that look alike but have different functions (noun, verb, adjective, or adverb). Their meanings are related but different.

**A.** *Look at each model phrase and decide whether the word in **bold** is used as a noun, verb, adjective, or adverb.*

| | NOUN | VERB | ADJECTIVE | ADVERB |
|---|---|---|---|---|
| 1. **declare** | | | | |
| • to **declare** a holiday | | ✓ | | |
| • a **declaration** of independence | ✓ | | | |
| 2. **export** | | | | |
| • Brazilian **exports** | | | | |
| • **export** soybeans | | | | |
| 3. **instant** | | | | |
| • **instant** success | | | | |
| • in an **instant** | | | | |
| 4. **scatter** | | | | |
| • **scatter** seeds | | | | |
| • **scattered** villages | | | | |
| 5. **severe** | | | | |
| • **severe** damage | | | | |
| • suffer **severely** | | | | |
| 6. **wound** | | | | |
| • a gunshot **wound** | | | | |
| • **wound** someone severely | | | | |

**B.** *Read each sentence and match the word in **bold** with the correct definition.*

_b_ 1. Theodore says he fell in love with Kelly the **instant** he first saw her.

___ 2. China **exports** heavily to help its economy.

___ 3. The thief seriously **wounded** the police officer with a single shot from his gun.

___ 4. The colonies in the New World fought to be independent from Britain. In 1776 they all signed a **declaration** of independence and became the United States of America.

___ 5. Industry has **severely** hurt forests around the world.

___ 6. There were **scattered** rainstorms all along the coast.

a. to sell products to another country

b. a moment in time

c. spread over a wide area

d. an official or important statement about something

e. very badly or to a great degree

f. to injure someone, especially with a knife or gun

# SAME WORD, DIFFERENT MEANING

Most words have more than one meaning. Study the additional meanings of **precious**, **publish**, and **scatter**. Then read each sentence and decide which meaning is used.

| | | |
|---|---|---|
| a. | **precious** *adj.* | valuable or important and should not be wasted |
| b. | **precious** *adj.* | important to you because you are reminded of people or events in your life |
| c. | **publish** *v.* | to arrange for something to be written, printed, and sold |
| d. | **publish** *v.* | to make official information available for people to use |
| e. | **scatter** *v.* | to move or be made to move in many different directions |
| f. | **scatter** *v.* | to throw or drop a lot of things over a wide area |

___a___ 1. Life is **precious** and our time is limited, so learn to make each day special.

_____ 2. When was the first dictionary of American English **published**?

_____ 3. My neighbor **scattered** birdseed on the grass to attract birds.

_____ 4. New guidelines for nutritional standards were **published** last year.

_____ 5. As soon as the president finished his announcement, the reporters **scattered** to make phone calls and start spreading the news.

_____ 6. My grandmother died when I was young, so the few memories I have of her are very **precious**.

# WORDS IN SENTENCES

Complete each sentence with a word from the box.

| | | | | |
|---|---|---|---|---|
| affected | declaration | instant | published | severely |
| crushed | exports | precious | scatter | ~~wound~~ |

1. Luckily, Eduardo wasn't too badly hurt in the accident. He has only a small _____*wound*_____ on his forehead.

2. The cold weather _____ hurt the orange and lemon trees.

3. The President's visit to our city _____ many businesses positively. Many visitors meant that more money was being spent in hotels, restaurants, and stores.

4. The local newspaper _____ a list of the ten best places in town to eat and put us at number one, so we've been getting a lot of new customers.

5. The family's _____ that they had no money left surprised everyone. They had always been one of the richest families in the state.

6. I felt like I was being _____ under the weight of the box, but I held it for another minute till my friend returned to help me.

7. This watch is a(n) _____ gift from my grandparents. I don't have much else to remember them by.

8. Australia _____ coal, meat, and metals.

9. I bought a lottery ticket and in a(n) _____ won $50. I spent the money that very afternoon.

10. In the winter, people _____ salt and sand on the roads and sidewalks to help prevent accidents.

## ▌WORDS IN COLLOCATIONS AND EXPRESSIONS

*Following are common collocations (word partners) and expressions with some of the key words. Read the definitions and then complete the conversations with the correct collocations and expressions.*

| | |
|---|---|
| **1. affect** | |
| • **affect (sb) deeply/ be deeply affected (by)** | to make someone feel strong emotions |
| **2. crush** | |
| • **be crushed to death** | to die by being crushed |
| **3. declare** | |
| • **declare war (on)** | to officially state the start of a war |
| • **declare that** | to state something officially and publicly |
| **4. precious** | |
| • **precious to (sb/sth)** | valuable or important to someone or something |
| • **precious metal** | a rare and valuable metal such as gold or silver |

1. STUDENT: When did England enter World War I?

   TEACHER: England _____*declared war on*_____ Germany on August 4, 1914.

2. SHAYLA: The watch is beautiful, but why did you spend so much money?

   KIM: Well, it's your eighteenth birthday. That's special. And since we're going off to different colleges in the fall, I wanted you to remember that our friendship will always be very _____ me.

3. MEMBER 1: Why do you think the president called for this meeting?

   MEMBER 2: I think this year's projects require more money, so my guess is that he'll _____ our club fees will have to be raised.

4. TINA: Did Meg tell you that Cory asked her to marry him?

   GLORIA: Yes. And Meg said Cory even wrote a poem for her. She was _____ his words. She couldn't speak at first. Then she said yes.

5. SON: Mom, what's platinum? I heard the word on TV today.

   MOTHER: Platinum is a _____, like silver or gold. It's often used in jewelry.

6. BROTHER: I think I'll try rock climbing one day.

   SISTER: And I think you should stick to hockey. That's dangerous enough. In rock climbing, there's not only the danger of falling, but you can also be _____ by falling rocks.

## ▌WORDS IN A READING

*Read this article about the Amazon rainforest. Complete it with words and expressions from the boxes.*

| affected . . . deeply | instant | severely |
|---|---|---|
| exported | ~~published~~ | wound |

### SAVING THE AMAZON

Kenko Minami and singer/songwriter Sting have a common love—the Amazon rainforest, and since the late 1980s they have worked to save it. Sting first visited the Amazon in 1987, and two years later he _____published_____ a book called *Jungle Stories: The Fight for the Amazon.* In it, he wrote that

**1**

one visit to the forest is enough to understand its mysterious beauty as well as its importance to the planet. For Kenko Minami, it was one visit with an Amazon chief that _____ her so

**2**

_____. Minami met Sting and Chief Raoni of the Kayapo tribe in February of 1989. The two men made a stop in Japan as part of their world tour, which was organized to make people aware of the rainforest's _____ damaged state. Minami, a concert promoter, was asked to help

**3**

with the tour. When she met Chief Raoni and shook his hand, she felt a(n) _____

**4**

connection to his home in the Amazon.

Three months after her first meeting with Raoni, Minami created the Rainforest Foundation of Japan (RFJ). To date, she has made twenty trips to Brazil and has spent much time with the Kayapo and Xingu tribes.

Sadly, industries like land development and gold mining continue to _____ the

**5**

Amazon. Minami adds that every year land is taken and made into farms, many of which grow soybeans that are then _____ to Japan.

**6**

| crushed | declared that | precious . . . to | scattered |
|---|---|---|---|

But the hurt does not end there. Rare animals and special trees like mahogany are being stolen from the Amazon. As for the tribes, they suffer, too. Not only is their land being _____,

**7**

but diseases are being brought in by outsiders. Five hundred years ago there were about 10 million Indians, or *Indios*, living in the Amazon; today 200 tribes are _____ across the same
8
area, and they total only several hundred thousand. The low numbers are serious: it is these very people, the Amazon Indians, who best know and care most for the forest, which is believed to have plants that can cure serious diseases like cancer.

Many understand very well how _____ the rainforest is _____ the
9
environment, but little action has been taken to save it. At the United Nations Earth Summit in Rio de Janeiro, the Brazilian president at the time _____ ten percent of the country's land
10
would be given to the Amazon tribes for their use alone. That promise was made in 1992; however, to date only four percent has been officially set aside.

Minami warns that the world must think hard and act now: "This planet is all one body. If we cut off one part of that body, the rest of the body will suffer."

*(Based on information from Stephen Hesse, "Amazon's Best Defense Is Its People." The Japan Times, October 26, 2005.)*

## ▌WORDS IN DISCUSSION

*Apply the key words to your own life. Read and discuss each question in small groups. Try to use the key words.*

1. What can you make to eat in an **instant**?

   **EXAMPLE**

   > *I can make a cheese sandwich in an **instant**. It only takes a few seconds to put a slice of cheese on bread.*

2. Name an example of **severe** weather that you've experienced. How **severe** was it?

3. What kinds of products does your country **export**? Do you know which countries these **exports** go to?

4. What is commonly found **scattered** across the floor in your home? What about your friend's home?

5. What information that a newspaper **publishes** daily are you most interested in?

6. How has the weather **affected** you today? Explain.

7. Why do you think people like jewelry made of **precious metals**?

8. If you could **declare** any day of the year to be a national holiday in your country, what day would you choose and what holiday would you create?

9. Do you know how to care for different kinds of **wounds**? Explain.

10. What kinds of foods are **crushed** before eating them? How can you **crush** them?

# ▌ WORDS IN WRITING

*Choose two topics and write a short paragraph on each one. Try to use the key words.*

1. What is the most **precious** thing you own?

   **EXAMPLE**

   > *My dog Fred is **precious to** me. He's like family. I couldn't find another dog like him. I wouldn't sell him for any money . . .*

2. What kind of music **deeply affects** you? Why?

3. Have you ever been seriously **wounded**? What's the most serious **wound** you've ever received?

4. Do you know your country's history well? Explain about a time when your country **declared** war on another country or when another country **declared** war on your country.

5. Describe a book that was **published** within the past five years that you enjoyed reading.

## ▌WORDS IN CONTEXT

*Use the sentences to guess what each key word means. Choose the meaning that is closest to that of the key word in **bold**.*

**1. acquire**
/əˈkwaɪɚ/
*-verb*

- After our company **acquired** an office in Framingham, we decided to hire more workers.
- Megan would rather **acquire** a nice apartment in the city than a big house in the suburbs.

*Acquire* means . . .   a. to do business   (b.) to buy   c. to move

**2. bitter**
/ˈbɪtɚ/
*-adjective*

- After her husband left her for a younger woman, Molly felt **bitter**.
- It's understandable that Wjotek feels **bitter**; he was fired from his job for no reason.

*Bitter* means . . .   a. relaxed   b. slightly worried   c. angry and upset

**3. consume**
/kənˈsum/
*-verb*

- America **consumes** more electricity than any other nation.
- SUVs **consume** a lot more gas than other cars.

*Consume* means . . .   a. to use   b. to find   c. to give

**4. dare**
/dɛr/
*-verb*

- When Juliana **dared** Pedro to open the door to the scary old house, he did, despite his fear.
- Kenji **dared** his friend to climb to the top of the thirty-foot tree.

*Dare* means . . .   a. to discourage   b. to talk about   c. to tell someone to do something dangerous

**5. discipline**
/ˈdɪsəplɪn/
*-noun*

- A good teacher must be able to keep **discipline** in the classroom; if students are wild and don't follow the rules, they can't learn.
- In the military, **discipline** is important; soldiers must follow rules and orders.

*Discipline* means . . .   a. intelligent way of doing things   b. controlled way of doing things   c. uncontrolled way of doing things

**6. humble**
/ˈhʌmbəl/
*-adjective*

- Zeke is a **humble** man; even though he is the president of a successful company, he is never arrogant.
- Alexia is so **humble** that, after running 26.2 miles in the marathon, she said, "I didn't do anything special. You should praise the winners instead of me."

*Humble* means . . .   a. arrogant   b. modest   c. sophisticated

**7. inspect**
/ɪnˈspɛkt/
-verb

- Every purse that is made in this factory is **inspected** twice before it is sent to the shops; because of this, you can see that the bags are of a very high quality.
- Before you buy a new home, it is a good idea to **inspect** the bathroom and the kitchen to make sure that the water works properly.

*Inspect* means . . .    a. to have a quick look at    b. to examine carefully    c. to not pay attention

**8. participate**
/parˈtɪsəˌpeɪt/
-verb

- Leaders from around the world will **participate** in a conference on the environment.
- When you are a student, do you simply sit quietly in class, or do you **participate**, asking questions and contributing your ideas?

*Participate* means . . .    a. to take part in    b. to skip    c. to visit

**9. remedy**
/ˈrɛmədi/
-noun

- Aspirin is a **remedy** for a headache.
- Education is a **remedy** for many social problems.

*Remedy* means . . .    a. an idea about a problem    b. something you pay for    c. a successful way to deal with a problem

**10. yield**
/yild/
-verb

- What kind of vegetables do the farms in your native country **yield**?
- Our teamwork **yielded** great results.

*Yield* means . . .    a. to produce    b. to go first    c. to plant

## ▌WORDS AND DEFINITIONS

*Match each key word with its definition.*

1. _*participate*_    to take part in an activity or event

2. _____    to tell or persuade someone to do something dangerous as a way of proving that they are brave

3. _____    to examine something carefully

4. _____    modest; not considering yourself or your ideas to be as important as other people's

5. _____    a successful way of dealing with a problem

6. _____    controlled way of doing things in which people obey rules and orders

7. _____    to buy a company or property

8. _____    to produce something

9. _____    angry and upset because you feel something bad or unfair has happened to you

10. _____    to completely use time, energy, goods, etc.

# COMPREHENSION CHECK

*Choose the best answer.*

1. What is a **remedy** for a sore throat?
   a. talking a lot
   b. taking a long walk in the cold
   c. drinking hot tea with honey
   d. singing loudly

2. Which person is **bitter**?
   a. Victoria is happy about her life.
   b. When someone stole Sam's watch, he did not feel sad for long.
   c. Every day Nadia angrily thinks about how her husband lost his job.
   d. Min feels peaceful.

3. In which place is there usually a lot of **discipline**?
   a. a disco
   b. a picnic
   c. a birthday party
   d. a military school

4. Which of the following people is **daring** someone?
   a. "You don't have to try bungee jumping if you don't want to."
   b. "No pressure. Only join the game if you feel like it."
   c. "I don't care what you do."
   d. "Are you too scared to jump into the cold lake? Jump! Jump! Jump!"

5. Which sentence is about something being **consumed**?
   a. Plants produce oxygen.
   b. No one is eating the apple pie.
   c. The truck uses several gallons of gasoline.
   d. The sun gives heat to our planet.

6. Which statement would a **humble** person make?
   a. "I'm the most beautiful girl in my class."
   b. "I'm a very important person, so put me on the VIP list for this restaurant."
   c. "I'm a simple and ordinary person. He's more important than I am."
   d. "I'm amazing, aren't I?"

7. If a company **yields** a profit, it
   a. makes money.
   b. remains the same.
   c. loses money.
   d. has no profit.

8. Who CANNOT **participate** in a discussion?
   a. a man
   b. a woman
   c. a child
   d. a baby

9. Where do people usually NOT look to **acquire** knowledge?
   a. a library
   b. a book
   c. the beach
   d. a university

10. If a detective **inspects** a room, he
    a. cleans it.
    b. examines it, searching for clues.
    c. relaxes in it.
    d. decorates it.

# WORD FAMILIES

Now that you have studied the ten key words and their basic definitions, you are ready to learn words that belong to the same family as some of the key words. A word family includes words that look alike but have different functions (noun, verb, adjective, or adverb). Their meanings are related but different.

**A.** *Look at each model phrase and decide whether the word in* **bold** *is used as a noun, verb, adjective, or adverb.*

|  | NOUN | VERB | ADJECTIVE | ADVERB |
|---|---|---|---|---|
| 1. **acquire** |  |  |  |  |
| • **acquire** a building |  | ✓ |  |  |
| • a new **acquisition** | ✓ |  |  |  |
| 2. **bitter** |  |  |  |  |
| • a **bitter** enemy |  |  |  |  |
| • **bitterly** rejected |  |  |  |  |
| 3. **dare** |  |  |  |  |
| • **dare** someone |  |  |  |  |
| • accept a **dare** |  |  |  |  |
| 4. **discipline** |  |  |  |  |
| • necessary **discipline** |  |  |  |  |
| • to **discipline** the students |  |  |  |  |
| 5. **inspect** |  |  |  |  |
| • **inspect** the room |  |  |  |  |
| • a long **inspection** |  |  |  |  |
| 6. **participate** |  |  |  |  |
| • **participate** in the games |  |  |  |  |
| • audience **participation** |  |  |  |  |

**B.** *Match the following sentences with the definition of the word in* **bold***.*

_b_ 1. When I heard the **dare**, I shook my head and said, "No way!"

_____ 2. The U.S. government requires every car to pass a yearly **inspection**.

_____ 3. "Why didn't you invite me to your party?" Fiona said **bitterly**.

_____ 4. Thirty percent of your grade will be based on class **participation**.

_____ 5. Marta **disciplines** her dog when he disobeys.

_____ 6. Let's talk about the company's latest **acquisition**.

a. with a lot of anger or sadness

b. something dangerous that a person is told to do

c. something that you have bought

d. the act of taking part in something

e. the act of carefully checking something to be sure that it is in good condition or that rules are being obeyed

f. to punish someone

## SAME WORD, DIFFERENT MEANING

*Most words have more than one meaning. Study the additional meanings of **acquire**, **consume**, and **discipline**. Then read each sentence and decide which meaning is used.*

| | | |
|---|---|---|
| a. | **acquire** *v.* | to buy a company or property |
| b. | **acquire** *v.* | to develop or learn a skill, or to become known for a particular quality |
| c. | **consume** *v.* | to completely use time, engery, goods, etc. |
| d. | **consume** *v.* | to eat or drink something |
| e. | **discipline** *n.* | controlled behavior in which people obey rules and orders |
| f. | **discipline** *n.* | the ability to control your own way of doing things and working |

___a___ 1. We have just **acquired** a small farm in Ukraine.

_____ 2. My 13-year-old cousin can **consume** an entire pizza.

_____ 3. If you want to become a successful athlete, you must have **discipline** and work out in the gym every day.

_____ 4. While living in Paris, I **acquired** basic knowledge of French.

_____ 5. There is a **discipline** problem in Mrs. Hill's class; she can't control the children.

_____ 6. Washing machines and driers **consume** a lot of energy.

## WORDS IN SENTENCES

*Complete each sentence with one of the words from the box.*

| | | | | |
|---|---|---|---|---|
| acquired | consumed | discipline | inspection | remedy |
| bitterly | dared | humble | ~~participation~~ | yielded |

1. The ___participation___ of many talented artists made the community art fair a success.

2. One _____ for stress is watching a funny movie.

3. Becoming a doctor requires intelligence, hard work, and _____.

4. I can't believe that our family _____ five boxes of cereal in one week!

5. The United States _____ Alaska in 1867.

6. The _____ old man was embarrassed when we praised him; he insisted that he was a simple person who did not deserve special attention.

7. When George's friends _____ him to eat the worm, he swallowed it.

8. When Joan's husband left her, she cried _____; she felt she had wasted many years with him.

9. After a careful _____ of the vase, the archeologist decided that it was from the Fourth century A.D.

10. The chemistry class's science experiment _____ some interesting results.

# WORDS IN COLLOCATIONS AND EXPRESSIONS

*Following are common collocations (word partners) and expressions with some of the key words. Read the definitions and then complete the conversations with the correct form of the collocations and expressions.*

1. **bitter**
   - **a bitter taste**      a very strong taste, like coffee without sugar
   - **bitterly cold**      extremely cold
   - **until the bitter end**      continuing to the end even though it is extremely difficult to do so

2. **dare**
   - **a daring person**      someone who is brave and willing to do dangerous things

3. **discipline**
   - **self-discipline**      the ability to make yourself do the things that you ought to do, without someone else making you do them

4. **remedy**
   - **remedy the problem**      to solve the problem

---

1. **TEACHER:** Can you give me an example of a place where it is _____*bitterly cold*_____?

   **STUDENT:** Sure. Antarctica.

2. **VIVIA:** I want to speak good English, but I'm too lazy to study.

   **LUCY:** You can't learn English by magic, Vivia. You need to have a lot of _____ and work hard if you want to learn a language.

3. **MOTHER:** My son Gregory is traveling through the Amazon next week.

   **FRIEND:** Wow, he's really _____.

4. **CHEF:** Yuck. This cake isn't sweet enough! It has _____.

   **ASSISTANT:** We can _____ by putting some powdered sugar on top.

5. **PLAYER 1:** This is painful! We're losing 5–0, and it's pouring rain. Should we quit?

   **PLAYER 2:** No. We are going to play _____.

# WORDS IN A READING

*Read this article about medicine. Complete it with words and expressions from the boxes.*

| acquire | ~~bitter~~ | consumes | inspection | participate | self-discipline |
|---------|-----------|----------|------------|-------------|-----------------|

## HEALING ART FOR CHILDREN IN HOSPITALS

For kids, the hospital can be a scary place. It can give them _____bitter_____ feelings. And, when
<sub>1</sub>
being there becomes a routine part of life, the hospital can also be a boring place. This is why teachers
and volunteers with Arts for Life offer children something special at Brenner Children's Hospital. Five
days a week—sometimes also on weekends—they give children staying in the hospital or being treated
as outpatients the chance to make art.

Now, children have something to look forward to when they come to the hospital. Making art there
_____ their time and energy in a positive way. They can have fun and _____
           2                                                                                    3
new skills.

On the day we visited, Emily Johnson, an Arts for Life teacher, had set up two long tables outside
the outpatient clinic. A quick _____ of the cart at the end of the tables revealed paints,
                          4
papers, markers, and other art supplies. Each day, Johnson suggests an activity in which kids can
_____. Children have made memory boxes, necklaces, bracelets, drawings, paintings. This
      5
particular morning, the children were making masks. Parents are welcome to join in, and some did.

The children are members of a club no one wishes to belong to. They speak casually about things that
adults would require a lot of _____ to talk about without emotion. Johnson once heard a
                          6
girl—delighted to make a connection with another girl—say, "Oh, we both have the same cancer!"

| a daring person | humble | remedy | yield |
|-----------------|--------|--------|-------|

Anna Vogler, 27, is the founder of Arts for Life. The nonprofit organization grew out of her
experiences when her younger sister, now a healthy high school sophomore, learned in 2001 that she
had bone cancer. At that time, Vogler moved back home to help.

Vogler, who had taught art in both rural Vermont and Guatemala, was both an art lover and
_____. Now, her brave attitude and her love of art motivated her to help sick children.
      7
Considering that Arts for Life has five staff members, six interns, four music teachers, fifteen
volunteers, and helps hundreds of children, Volger is very _____ about her achievements.
                                                         8
"Our organization is one of many," she said.

Nationally, close to 100 percent of children's hospitals and about sixty percent of hospitals overall
have some sort of formal arts program. Hospitals find that such programs _____ great
                                                                      9

benefits not only in patient satisfaction but also in staff satisfaction. For the children, the art is a

_____ for boredom. They are using their hearts, their minds, and their hands.
**10**

*(Based on Kim Underwood, "Volunteers Take Healing Art To Children In Hospitals—Let's Play." Journal Reporter, November 6, 2005.)*

## ▌WORDS IN DISCUSSION

*Apply the key words to your own life. Complete the questionnaire. Then discuss your answers with a classmate. Try to use the key words.*

### EXAMPLE

Something I felt **bitter** about: _____*losing the volleyball game last weekend*_____

*A: Why were you **bitter**?*

*B: My team should have won, but the referee made a bad call. It wasn't fair. I'm not usually a **bitter** person, but I felt really **bitter** then.*

1. If someone praised my intelligence, how **humble** I would be: _____

2. How much **self-discipline** I have: _____

3. Something **bitter** that I sometimes eat or drink: _____

4. Something I once **dared** my friend to do: _____

5. Someone who **inspects** my work: _____

6. The type of home I would like to **acquire**: _____

7. The number of sandwiches I can **consume** if I am very hungry: _____

8. A class in which I would like to **participate**: _____

9. A natural **remedy** I have tried: _____

10. If I try to grow a garden, the kind of vegetables it might **yield**: _____

## ▌WORDS IN WRITING

*Choose two topics and write a short paragraph on each. Try to use the key words.*

1. Describe the most **bitter** cold that you have experienced.

### EXAMPLE

*Without a doubt, the most **bitter** cold that I've experienced was in the Czech Republic in February. My friends and I took a bus from Prague to a little village in the countryside. When we got off the bus that night, we stepped into deep snow. The **bitter** wind stung our faces.*

2. Do you feel that people where you live **consume** too much energy (for example, electricity or gasoline)? Explain.

3. In your opinion, what is the best **remedy** for a bad mood?

4. Would you rather have a friend who is **humble** or proud? Explain.

5. Tell a true story from your life about a **dare**. Who **dared** you, or whom did you **dare**? What happened?

**CHAPTER**

# 12

**Key Words**

| alternative | boundary | liberty | network | variety |
|---|---|---|---|---|
| boast | community | media | tradition | weave |

## WORDS IN CONTEXT

*Use the sentences to guess what each key word means. Choose the meaning that is closest to that of the key word in **bold**.*

1. **alternative**
   /ɔl'tɚnətɪv/
   -noun

   - I have the **alternative** of walking to school. When the weather's nice and I'm not in a rush, I choose to walk rather than take the bus.
   - Two students in my group want to make a presentation on city crime, but I asked the group if we could discuss an **alternative**.

   *Alternative* means . . (a.) another choice     b. the best plan     c. a hard decision

2. **boast**
   /boʊst/
   -verb

   - When we were children, my older brother liked to **boast** that he was faster and stronger than I was. Now he is more modest about his abilities and talents.
   - Rafael **boasted** about his high score on the exam, but he didn't know that Mia got 100 percent. In contrast, Mia is very quiet about her success in school.

   *Boast* means . . .     a. to tell a lie     b. to talk with too much     c. to share a secret
   self-satisfaction

3. **boundary**
   /'baʊndəri/
   -noun

   - Rivers and mountains often serve as natural **boundaries**, separating one piece of land from another.
   - The tennis player hit the ball outside the **boundary** and lost the point.

   *Boundary* means . . .     a. a large piece of land     b. shelter     c. a line showing the
   edge of a space

4. **community**
   /kə'myunəti/
   -noun

   - I really enjoy the academic **community** at my college. The instructors are friendly and helpful, and the students share a love for learning.
   - There is a strong Chinese **community** in the city of Toronto. There are many language schools, dance groups, and small businesses run by Chinese-Canadians.

   *Community*     a. a group of buildings     b. a group of people     c. one's hometown
   means . . .                                         with something
                                                       in common

5. **liberty**
   /'lɪbɚti/
   -noun

   - Many countries have a holiday when they celebrate their **liberty**. For example, Brazil became free from Portugal in the 19th century, and today Brazilians celebrate this event on September 7. That's their Independence Day.
   - As the owner of the business, Chau has the **liberty** of taking a vacation whenever she wants.

   *Liberty* means . . .     a. freedom     b. strength     c. good luck

6. **media**
/'midiə/
-noun plural

- The **media** covered every detail of the royal wedding. Pictures, stories, and reports were in every newspaper and magazine.
- Some movie actors want attention from the **media** to help their careers.

*Media* means . . .   a. film directors   b. advertisements   c. TV, radio, newspapers, magazines

7. **network**
/'nɛtwɚk/
-noun

- Charmian is a weather reporter for a local TV station. Her dream is to get a job with a major **network**.
- My favorite radio show is on a national **network**; I can listen to it far from home.

*Network* means . . .   a. an institute of learning   b. a film company   c. a group of radio or TV stations

8. **tradition**
/trə'dɪʃən/
-noun

- In Belgium it's a **tradition** to kiss cheeks among family and friends.
- We have a **tradition** of planting a tree every spring.

*Tradition* means . . .   a. an old practice   b. a strict rule   c. a bad joke

9. **variety**
/və'raɪəti/
-noun

- For a small grocery store, this place has a good **variety** of products. There's plenty to choose from.
- This ice cream shop had such a large **variety** of flavors that it took me a long time to decide which one I wanted.

*Variety* means . . .   a. a lot of different things   b. a group of similar things   c. one or two choices

10. **weave**
/wiv/
-verb

- Today we have machines that **weave** thread into cloth.
- In the town of Torzhok, artists **weave** gold thread into small purses and handkerchiefs.

*Weave* means . . .   a. to wrap or cover   b. to cut cloth   c. to make threads into cloth

## ▌ WORDS AND DEFINITIONS

*Match each key word with its definition.*

1. ____tradition____ a practice or way of doing something that has existed for a long time

2. _____ to talk with too much self-satisfaction about your own abilities and achievements

3. _____ the line that marks the edge of a surface, space, or area of land

4. _____ people who live in the same area, or who have the same interests or background

5. _____ the freedom to do what you want without having to ask for permission

6. _____ to make cloth or carpets by crossing threads under and over each other

7. _____ all the organizations such as television, radio, and newspapers that provide news and information to the public

8. _____ a group of radio or television stations that broadcasts many of the same programs in different parts of the country

9. _____ something you can choose to do or use instead of something else

10. _____ a lot of things of the same type that are different from each other in some way

## COMPREHENSION CHECK

*Choose the best answer.*

1. You can **weave** a
   a. painting.
   b. tablecloth. *(circled)*
   c. pillow.
   d. garden.

2. If you don't want to take medicine for a headache, a good **alternative** might be
   a. listening to loud music.
   b. having a serious conversation.
   c. having a massage and taking a long nap.
   d. running a few miles.

3. Both parents and students want schools to offer some **variety** in
   a. test scores.
   b. rules.
   c. the cost of books.
   d. cafeteria food.

4. A person **boasts** because he or she is
   a. too proud of his or her own achievements.
   b. very humble.
   c. disappointed in himself or herself.
   d. jealous of other people's achievements.

5. An example of a family **tradition** is
   a. doing housework.
   b. a family picnic every year on Independence Day.
   c. each person having his or her own cell phone.
   d. having an argument.

6. A radio **network** broadcasts
   a. only within a certain area.
   b. only at a certain time.
   c. in every country.
   d. throughout a country.

7. Mass **media** include
   a. music CDs.
   b. a person's diary.
   c. a national radio program.
   d. school newspapers.

8. A **boundary** can
   a. join two towns together.
   b. separate one town from the other.
   c. make two towns equal.
   d. serve as protection for the people of both towns.

9. A high school teacher has the **liberty** of
   a. choosing what to give for homework.
   b. deciding what time to start and end class.
   c. choosing what language to speak in.
   d. not teaching if the students look tired.

10. You can help your **community** by doing all of the following EXCEPT
    a. offering food to the homeless.
    b. attending a party.
    c. cleaning up the neighborhood park.
    d. giving old books to the library.

# WORD FAMILIES

Now that you have studied the ten key words and their basic definitions, you are ready to learn words that belong to the same family as some of the key words. A word family includes words that look alike but have different functions (noun, verb, adjective, or adverb). Their meanings are related but different.

**A.** *Look at each model phrase and decide whether the word in **bold** is used as a noun, verb, adjective, or adverb.*

|  | NOUN | VERB | ADJECTIVE | ADVERB |
|---|---|---|---|---|
| 1. **alternative** |  |  |  |  |
| • find an **alternative** | ✓ |  |  |  |
| • an **alternative/alternate** way |  |  |  | ✓ |
| • **alternate** two things |  | ✓ |  |  |
| 2. **boast** |  |  |  |  |
| • loves to **boast** |  |  |  |  |
| • a **boast** about one's athletic skill |  |  |  |  |
| • a **boastful** person |  |  |  |  |
| 3. **tradition** |  |  |  |  |
| • start a **tradition** |  |  |  |  |
| • the **traditional** way |  |  |  |  |
| 4. **variety** |  |  |  |  |
| • a **variety** of sources |  |  |  |  |
| • **various** sources |  |  |  |  |

**B.** *Read the first half of each sentence and match it with the appropriate ending.*

___c___ 1. Eli was going to have his birthday party outside tomorrow, but it looks like it will rain. An outdoor party may not be a good choice; he needs

_____ 2. I don't care to listen to Wanda talk about all her success. I've heard too many of her

_____ 3. Some students study grammar by reading explanations quietly; others understand grammar through conversation. In short, students learn grammar in

_____ 4. In my opinion, modesty shows self-confidence, and self-doubt is what lies behind

_____ 5. We were surprised when the couple kissed at the beginning of the wedding; it is more

_____ 6. Mom, we're both tired in the evenings, so why don't we

a. **various** ways.

b. **boasts**.

c. an **alternative** plan.

d. **traditional** for the couple to kiss at the end of the ceremony.

e. **boastful** talk.

f. **alternate** who cooks? I'll make dinner tonight, okay?

## SAME WORD, DIFFERENT MEANING

*Most words have more than one meaning. Study the additional meanings of* **boast**, **boundary**, *and* **network**. *Then read each sentence and decide which meaning is used.*

| | | |
|---|---|---|
| a. | **boast** *v.* | to talk with too much self-satisfaction about your own abilities and achievements |
| b. | **boast** *v.* | if a place boasts something good, the place has it |
| c. | **boundary** *n.* | the line that marks the edge of a surface, space, or area of land |
| d. | **boundary** *n.* | the limit of what is acceptable or thought to be possible |
| e. | **network** *n.* | a group of radio or television stations that broadcasts many of the same programs in different parts of the country |
| f. | **network** *n.* | a group of people, organizations, etc. that are connected or work together |

___b___ 1. New York **boasts** some excellent restaurants. They are featured in magazines and on TV.

_____ 2. Politeness has its **boundaries**, and chewing gum loudly at a funeral goes beyond them.

_____ 3. The number of **networks** has grown over the years, and so have viewers' choices.

_____ 4. This row of trees marks the northern **boundary** of my family's land.

_____ 5. My roommate used the Internet to form a **network** of teachers who work in city schools.

_____ 6. Please don't think I'm **boasting**. I just want you to know what I can offer your company.

## WORDS IN SENTENCES

*Complete each sentence with one of the words from the box.*

| | | | | |
|---|---|---|---|---|
| alternated | boundaries | Liberty | network | various |
| boastful | ~~community~~ | media | traditional | wove |

1. Joaquin contacted the Filipino _____*community*_____ when he arrived in Philadelphia, and he received some good advice about finding work and a place to live.

2. I enjoy meeting other photographers. By having a _____ of people in the same profession, I learn about interesting jobs and new uses of technology.

3. The _____ report stories that will bring them a bigger audience.

4. Rachel appeared to be rather _____ when she told us how much money she earns.

5. Sending men to the moon tested the _____ of science and technology.

6. The cake had layers of chocolate cake _____ with layers of chocolate cream.

7. The Statue of _____ is a symbol of freedom to many.

8. It is _____ for the head of the family to sit at the head of the table.

9. When I was a little girl, my mother _____ ribbons into my hair.

10. I found _____ personal items in the closet of my new room, from a tie to a bar of soap. The person who rented the place before me must have left the things behind.

## WORDS IN COLLOCATIONS AND EXPRESSIONS

*Following are common collocations (word partners) and expressions with some of the key words. Read the definitions and then complete the conversations with the correct form of the collocations and expressions.*

| | | |
|---|---|---|
| 1. **alternative** | | |
| | • **alternative to** | something you can choose to do or use instead |
| 2. **boundary** | | |
| | • **boundary of** | the limit of |
| | • **set boundaries** | to mark or state a limit |
| 3. **liberty** | | |
| | • **take the liberty of (doing sth)** | to do something without asking permission because you do not think it will upset or offend anyone |
| 4. **tradition** | | |
| | • **break tradition** | to go against tradition, not following the way something has been done for a long time |
| 5. **variety** | | |
| | • **a wide variety of (sth)** | a lot of things of the same type that are different from each other in some way |

1. ASSISTANT: Have you reviewed the figures? Is business really bad?

   DIRECTOR: We're still having financial trouble, but I want to find a(n) _____*alternative to*_____ firing employees in order to save money.

2. NEIGHBOR: I saw your friend take a walk this morning. I think she was wearing your new raincoat.

   PAMELA: Well, she's an old college roommate. I'm not surprised she'd _____ going into my closet.

3. MOTHER: How is your baby-sitting job going?

   ROSE: Not bad, but I don't like all the rules Mrs. Fisher makes for her kids.

   MOTHER: Parents _____ because children need rules to guide their behavior. You know that.

4. QUINN: I heard you got a dog.

   STACEY: Yes. Just two days ago. We looked at _____ dogs before we chose Minnie, our new French poodle.

5.  **Marge:** Is Ocean Beach safe for young swimmers?

    **Jenny:** Absolutely. There are markers in the water that show the _____ safe water for swimming. No one is allowed to swim beyond the markers.

6.  **Uma:** Did Laura get accepted to Yale?

    **Janice:** She did, but that's not where she's going. She chose Princeton.

    **Uma:** I think everyone in Laura's family studied at Yale University. Her family is probably upset that she's going to _____.

## ▌WORDS IN A READING

*Read this article about a popular online news program. Complete it with words and expressions from the boxes.*

| | | |
|---|---|---|
| **a wide variety of** | **boasts** | **break tradition** |
| ~~alternative to~~ | **boundaries of** | **take the liberty** |

### ROCKETBOOM: A MODEL FOR VIDEO BLOGS

What is an ___alternative to___ TV news? Video blogs. These personal Web journals are testing the
                       1
_____ information technology. Video blogging is still in its early days, but Amanda
          2
Congdon and Andrew Michael Baron have already found an approach that viewers like. Congdon, an

actress by profession, is the face and voice of *Rocketboom*, a young video blog that already

_____ 50,000 viewers. Congdon writes news reports with Baron, the blog's creator.
          3
Together they cover _____ topics, from technology to pop culture.
                              4

What makes this online news program so successful? The news is delivered in a fresh manner:

Congdon and Baron _____ and use frank humor and silliness in their show. As they
                            5
report the news, they also _____ of making personal comments on everything from the
                                    6
U.S. presidential election to the use of human bones to create jewelry.

| | | |
|---|---|---|
| **community** | **media** | **network** |

New shows are presented Monday through Friday at 9 A.M. Earlier shows are saved on the web site

for viewers to enjoy. Each show takes about an hour and a half to record, but even more time is needed

to plan and write the script. The show uses comedy, but during pre-show discussions and production

Congdon and Baron are very serious.

While *Rocketboom* has a unique approach, it is like a typical blog in how it creates a

_____, a special group of people, through online dialogue. The three-minute daily show
          7
also includes videos sent in by viewers and has a _____ of correspondents, who are
                                                          8

connected throughout the U.S. and Europe. With the number of their viewers growing, Congdon and Baron plan to sell either subscriptions or advertisements and then create other shows on the same model. Many think that *Rocketboom* is the future of _____, changing how people define television.

9

*(Based on information in Heather Green, "Rocketboom's Powerful Lift-Off." BusinessWeek, September 5, 2005.)*

## WORDS IN DISCUSSION

*Apply the key words to your own life. Read and discuss each question in small groups. Try to use the key words.*

1. Have you ever **broken tradition**?

   **EXAMPLE**

   > *I don't like to **break tradition**, especially a family one. This year I don't have a choice. My family is always together for Christmas, but I'm studying in another country right now, and it's too far away to go home for the holiday.*

2. What can you see **a wide variety of** at the grocery store?

3. How do you go to work or to school? Do you have an **alternative**?

4. Can you name at least three popular TV programs shown by the same **network**?

5. Do you know many people in the **community** you are living in right now?

6. Can you recall what kinds of **boundaries** your parents **set** for you as you were growing up?

7. Do you believe everything the **media** report? Why or why not?

8. Have you ever **taken the liberty of** ordering food for someone else at a restaurant?

9. Where are you from? What does your hometown **boast**?

10. Name at least two things that one can **weave**.

## WORDS IN WRITING

*Choose two topics and write a short paragraph for each. Try to use the key words.*

1. What can you **boast** about?

   **EXAMPLE**

   > *I can **boast** about my Web site. It took a lot of time to build it. The pictures and the music work well together. I've seen my friends' homepages, and I can easily say that mine looks more professional.*

2. What's a good **alternative to** watching a movie on a rainy day?

3. What's a popular holiday in your native country? What's the **traditional** way to celebrate?

4. Think of the neighborhood you live in. Describe how **boundaries** are marked to show people's land.

5. Is there a job you share and **alternate** turns with another person (for example, taking out the trash or making dinner)? What happens if you or your partner forgets to take a turn?

# QUIZ 4

## PART A

*Choose the word that best completes each item and write it in the space provided.*

1. For a brief time in 1982, the Florida Keys _____*declared*_____ independence from the United States and called their land the Conch Republic.
   - a. declared
   - b. published
   - c. acquired
   - d. inspected

2. The children _____ flowers under their feet as they ran through the garden.
   - a. inspected
   - b. crushed
   - c. consumed
   - d. weaved

3. Jayden felt _____ when he was not chosen to be the new department head; he believed he was the best person for the job.
   - a. humble
   - b. instant
   - c. severe
   - d. bitter

4. At airports they must carefully _____ planes for ice during winter weather.
   - a. inspect
   - b. consume
   - c. acquire
   - d. dare

5. In the suburbs, people often use fences and bushes to mark _____.
   - a. communities
   - b. remedies
   - c. boundaries
   - d. networks

6. My poem will be _____ in the school magazine next month.
   - a. consumed
   - b. published
   - c. acquired
   - d. inspected

7. A college student has the _____ of choosing his or her main subject of study.
   - a. liberty
   - b. remedy
   - c. media
   - d. boundary

8. The _____ report the news twenty-four hours a day seven days a week.
   - a. communities
   - b. remedies
   - c. media
   - d. exports

9. The fans who had been fighting after the game _____ when the police arrived at the stadium.
   - a. boasted
   - b. participated
   - c. scattered
   - d. dared

10. This land has been in our family for several generations. We _____ it before World War I.
   - a. consumed
   - b. crushed
   - c. acquired
   - d. inspected

## PART B

Read each statement and write **T** for true or **F** for false in the space provided.

__F__ 1. A **humble** person likes to talk about his or her success in life.

_____ 2. When time is **precious**, you are careful about how you spend it.

_____ 3. The instructors and students at a school form a **community**.

_____ 4. If there isn't an **alternative** to walking, you'll easily find a bus or taxi.

_____ 5. The process of making a TV series is an example of a **network**.

_____ 6. When someone gets fame and fortune after many years of hard work, we say they experience **instant** success.

_____ 7. Farm lands **yield** grains and vegetables.

_____ 8. A store with a wide **variety** of products offers customers a choice.

_____ 9. If soldiers have little **discipline**; this helps create a strong army.

_____ 10. To help the environment, we should **consume** energy carefully and responsibly.

## PART C

Complete each item with a word from the box. Use each word once.

| | | | | |
|---|---|---|---|---|
| affects | dared | ~~participates~~ | severe | weave |
| boasts | exports | remedy | tradition | wounds |

1. When classroom discussion is particularly interesting, Geitha actively ____participates____.

2. Mining is very important to the South African economy, but the country's _____ also include fruit, wool, and grains, especially corn.

3. Whenever we go to a restaurant, Riley _____ about her own cooking and compares her food to what we're eating.

4. Music _____ me like nothing else; it's a powerful art form.

5. My grandfather believes that swallowing a raw egg is a(n) _____ for a stomach ache.

6. It's a(n) _____ at American weddings to throw rice at the happily married couple.

7. Our cat came home with a few small _____; it likely fought with another cat in the neighborhood.

8. At the Thai restaurant, my friends _____ me to order one of the spiciest dishes on the menu. I did, and after one bite my mouth was on fire.

9. The tornado caused _____ damage in this area.

10. When I took a closer look at the cloth, I had even more appreciation for the skill the artist used to _____ it.

## WORDS IN CONTEXT

*Use the sentences to guess what each key word means. Choose the meaning that is closest to that of the key word in **bold**.*

**1. assume**
/əˈsum/
*-verb*

- Even though April hasn't answered my invitation, I **assume** that she's coming to my party.
- Because I'm moving from Tokyo to London, I **assume** that my English will improve.

*Assume* means . . .    a. to know for sure    (b.) to think something is true without proof    c. to have no idea

**2. bar**
/bar/
*-verb*

- Security guards will **bar** you from entering the courthouse if they find that you are carrying a weapon.
- The thirteen-year-old was **barred** from entering the dance club because he was too young.

*Bar* means . . .    a. to prevent    b. to open    c. to allow

**3. conscience**
/ˈkanʃəns/
*-noun*

- After Maurizio stole his sister's money, his **conscience** made him feel guilty, so he returned the money before she could find out that it was missing.
- The witness didn't want to send the accused to prison, but she followed her **conscience** and told the truth.

*Conscience* means . . .    a. sense of humor    b. sense of right and wrong    c. bad way of thinking

**4. deceive**
/dɪˈsiv/
*-verb*

- Mr. Andrews **deceived** everyone in the town; he told them that he was a banker, and then he ran away with their money.
- If your friend **deceived** you, telling you he needed to borrow your car to go to the hospital when he really wanted it to go to the beach, would you ever trust him again?

*Deceive* means . . .    a. to be honest    b. to play a good joke on someone    c. to make someone believe something that is not true

**5. display**
/dɪˈspleɪ/
*-verb*

- My mother **displays** a special picture of my brothers and me in a frame on her desk.
- The British crown jewels are **displayed** in the Tower of London.

*Display* means . . .    a. to pay for    b. to put things in a place where people can see them easily    c. to photograph someone or something important

**6.** **omit**
/ouˈmɪt/
-verb

- If you are in a hurry at the grocery store, you might accidentally **omit** something important on your shopping list.
- Because the teacher did not like Exercise 5, she told the students to **omit** it from their homework.

*Omit* means . . .      a. to leave out          b. to include          c. to add

**7.** **qualify**
/ˈkwaləˌfaɪ/
-verb

- If your IQ is in the top two percent of the population, you **qualify** to enter Mensa, a club of highly intelligent people.
- Very few people can run fast enough to **qualify** for the Olympics.

*Qualify* means . . .      a. lack the          b. meet the          c. fail
                                   requirements       requirements

**8.** **solemn**
/ˈsaləm/
-adjective

- Both weddings and funerals are **solemn** occasions.
- Even though Christie is only six years old, she often has a **solemn** expression on her face.

*Solemn* means . . .      a. light-hearted          b. ordinary          c. very serious

**9.** **thorough**
/ˈθɚoʊ/
-adjective

- Jason is excellent at sweeping the floor; he is always very **thorough**, cleaning every corner and under all the furniture.
- When you do homework, do you do a **thorough** job, or do you work quickly and miss some questions?

*Thorough* means . . . a. quick          b. incomplete          c. careful

**10.** **volume**
/ˈvalyəm/
-noun

- Please turn down the **volume** of the TV; it's much too loud!
- The **volume** of traffic in Istanbul has increased a lot recently.

*Volume* means . . .      a. amount of sound          b. silence          c. cars
                                   or activity

## WORDS AND DEFINITIONS

*Match each key word with its definition.*

1. ___*display*___ to put things in a place where people can see them easily

2. _____ to leave out

3. _____ amount of sound or activity

4. _____ to make someone believe something that is not true

5. _____ careful to do everything that you should and avoid mistakes

6. _____ to prevent someone from doing something

7. _____ very serious

8. _____ to pass an examination or meet the requirements of knowledge or skill that you need in order to do something

9. _____ the feelings that tell you whether what you are doing is morally right or wrong

10. _____ to think that something is true although you have no proof

## COMPREHENSION CHECK

*Choose the best answer.*

1. If there is a large **volume** of traffic on the street, there
   a. is a lot of music.
   b. are a lot of cars.
   c. are few cars.
   d. are no cars.

2. If Alice listens to her **conscience**, she will
   a. yell at her mother.
   b. help someone she doesn't like.
   c. skip her history class.
   d. steal from her friend.

3. Which of the following people is **assuming** something?
   a. "I have no idea if it's going to rain tomorrow."
   b. "Maggie will bring ice cream to the party; she told me yesterday."
   c. "Even though I haven't seen my results, I'm sure that I passed the test."
   d. "Tomorrow is Tuesday."

4. Where does a shop usually NOT **display** new products?
   a. in a hard-to-find back corner
   b. in the front window
   c. in the front of the shop
   d. near the cash register

5. A construction worker who does **thorough** work building a house
   a. forgets to put a door on the bathroom.
   b. does not finish the roof.
   c. completes every part of the house.
   d. leaves a hole in one wall.

6. Who is **barring** someone from doing something?
   a. Mom says that Nadia can go to the party.
   b. The policeman will not let Ralph drive because he's had many beers.
   c. Li-chen gives her aunt opera tickets.
   d. The elderly woman gave the young couple directions to the volcano.

7. Which person is trying to **deceive** someone?
   a. a salesman who accurately describes the car he is selling
   b. a teenager who uses a fake ID to get into a nightclub
   c. a worker who gives honest answers during a job interview
   d. a trustworthy neighbor who tells true stories

8. Which event is NOT a **solemn** occasion?
   a. an important religious ceremony
   b. a wedding
   c. a comedy show
   d. a funeral

9. If a boy **qualifies** for a swimming race, he
   a. wins the race.
   b. loses the race.
   c. cannot enter the race.
   d. can enter the race.

10. If Oksana accidentally **omitted** flour when making a cake, how would the cake probably taste?
    a. delicious
    b. fantastic
    c. very strange
    d. perfect

# WORD FAMILIES

Now that you have studied the ten key words and their basic definitions, you are ready to learn words that belong to the same family as some of the key words. A word family includes words that look alike but have different functions (noun, verb, adjective, or adverb). Their meanings are related but different.

**A.** *Look at each model phrase and decide whether the word in **bold** is used as a noun, verb, adjective, or adverb.*

| | NOUN | VERB | ADJECTIVE | ADVERB |
|---|:---:|:---:|:---:|:---:|
| **1. assume** | | | | |
| • can't **assume** that | | ✓ | | |
| • my first **assumption** | ✓ | | | |
| **2. deceive** | | | | |
| • **deceive** people | | | | |
| • **deceptive** appearance | | | | |
| • clever **deception** | | | | |
| **3. display** | | | | |
| • **display** new books | | | | |
| • an interesting **display** | | | | |
| **4. omit** | | | | |
| • **omit** one detail | | | | |
| • an important **omission** | | | | |
| **5. qualify** | | | | |
| • **qualify** for the team | | | | |
| • a **qualified** job applicant | | | | |
| • job **qualifications** | | | | |
| **6. thorough** | | | | |
| • be very **thorough** | | | | |
| • read an essay **thoroughly** | | | | |

**B.** *Read the first half of each sentence and match it with the appropriate ending.*

_____*i*_____ 1. After working in the chemistry lab, you should

_____ 2. Don't trust the television commercial that promises you whiter teeth; it is

_____ 3. Everyone wanted to see the robot on

_____ 4. An excellent swimmer is

_____ 5. Quinn's lies and

_____ 6. Before applying to join the club, make sure you have the right

_____ 7. If Rico doesn't have proof to support his idea, he is making an

_____ 8. I was surprised by the

a. **display** at the technology fair.

b. **qualified** to be a lifeguard.

c. **deception** made his girlfriend cry.

e. **qualifications**.

f. **deceptive** advertising.

g. **assumption**.

h. **omission** of Jim's picture from the yearbook.

i. wash your hands **thoroughly**.

## SAME WORD, DIFFERENT MEANING

Most words have more than one meaning. Study the additional meanings of **bar**, **display**, and **thorough**. Then read each sentence and decide which meaning is used.

| | | |
|---|---|---|
| a. **bar** *v.* | to prevent someone from doing something |
| b. **bar** *n.* | a long narrow piece of metal or wood |
| c. **display** *v.* | to put things in a place where people can see them easily |
| d. **display** *v.* | to clearly show a feeling or quality |
| e. **thorough** *adj.* | careful to do everything that should be done and avoid mistakes |
| f. **thorough** *adj.* | including every possible detail |

__*b*__ 1. Because Julie's apartment was on a dangerous street, she had **bars** on her windows.

_____ 2. The newspaper gave a **thorough** report of the president's speech.

_____ 3. Zhang Wei **displayed** his love for his son when he smiled at the baby.

_____ 4. The gate **barred** the reporters from driving up the movie star's driveway.

_____ 5. Bookstores **display** new books in their windows.

_____ 6. Please be **thorough** when cleaning the bathroom; don't forget to wash the mirrors and empty the trash.

## WORDS IN SENTENCES

Complete each sentence with one of the words from the box.

| | | | | |
|---|---|---|---|---|
| assumption | conscience | display | ~~qualify~~ | thorough |
| bars | deception | omitted | solemn | volume |

1. You must be from California to _____*qualify*_____ for this scholarship.

2. Abdullah's _____ guides him.

3. Everyone at the party became _____ when they heard the sad news.

4. I was shocked by Jessica's _____; I had thought that she was a true friend.

5. Mrs. Stevens felt irritated, so she _____ Mrs. Jones from the party guest list.

6. Your report must be _____. Don't leave anything out.

7. Joe looked sadly through the _____ of his prison cell, and felt deep regret.

8. Some restaurants have a(n) _____ of some of their dishes in their front windows.

9. When Carina heard Sal's accent, she guessed that he was Irish; her _____ was correct.

10. Because of the _____ of letters that the president receives every day, he cannot write you a personal response.

# WORDS IN COLLOCATIONS AND EXPRESSIONS

*Following are common collocations (word partners) and expressions with some of the key words. Read the definitions and then complete the conversations with the correct form of the collocations and expressions.*

1. **bar**
   - **a bar of soap/candy**      a small block of soap or candy
   - **behind bars**      in prison

2. **conscience**
   - **listen to your conscience**      pay attention to your feelings of what is right and wrong

3. **display**
   - **on display**      arranged for people to look at

4. **qualify**
   - **highly qualified**      having the right knowledge, experience, and skills for a job

5. **thorough**
   - **do a thorough job**      do a job carefully and completely

1.     DIEGO:     When can I see your paintings, Molly?

       MOLLY:     Anytime this month. They are _____ *on display* _____ in Hill's Gallery.

2.   MAFIA MAN 1:     Why doesn't Jimmy eat dinner with us anymore?

    MAFIA MAN 2:     The police caught him a few months ago. Now he's _____.

    MAFIA MAN 1:     Poor Jimmy. I heard that the food is terrible in jail.

3.     MANAGER:     Thank you for coming to this job interview. I can see from your resume that you are _____ to be my assistant. Now I want to ask about the way you work. Do you work quickly?

   JOB APPLICANT:     Yes, but I don't like to race. When you work too fast, it's impossible to _____.

    MANAGER:     I agree completely. You're hired.

4. HOTEL WORKER:     Is there anything else you'd like for your room?

   HOTEL GUEST:     Yes, I'd like an extra _____ soap.

5.     JENNIFER:     Should I take the job that pays a lot of money or the job that helps people?

    MOTHER:     Don't ask me, honey. Just _____.

## WORDS IN A READING

*Read this article about fashion. Complete it with words and expressions from the boxes.*

| ~~assumes~~ | barred | omit | qualify | solemn |
|---|---|---|---|---|

### THE MODEL WHO BECAME A MONK

Everyone ___*assumes*___ that if a fashion model who has spent years in the business wants a
1
new job, she will become an actress, makeup artist, or photographer. Becoming a monk, however, is an

option that most people would _____ when considering a model's future. To be a monk,
2
a person must be serious and holy. Considering this, can a fashion model _____ to be a
3
monk? Shouldn't people like fashion models be _____ from entering the spiritual life?
4

In a move that created a great deal of shock, disbelief, and admiration in Nepal, one of the

Himalayan country's top models, Kohinoor Singh, recently decided to shave her head, throw out her

makeup, and put on the traditional clothing of a Buddhist monk. Now she is ready for the religious life

and its _____ ceremonies.
5

| deceived | displayed | listen to her conscience | thoroughly | volume |
|---|---|---|---|---|

Her years of photo shoots, bikinis, and glamour are over. Now this woman is simply a monk

smiling pleasantly at the thought of the future. She believes that people were _____ by
6
her modeling into thinking that she was not a spiritual person.

In a recent online interview, the former model explained that she has not changed at all. She has

always been a spiritual person. It is only because the media have always portrayed her according to her

looks, she believes, that people are now noticing a sudden change.

Kohinoor Singh, now Ani Lhosang Dolma, had a successful career in the small but quickly growing

modeling world of Nepal. Her beauty has been _____ in advertisements, on TV, and in
7
music video hits. It is the _____ of sales of her music videos that made her a star.
8

The *Kathmandu Post* rated her one of the "top 5 models in Nepal" in February this year, calling her

"sensational." But that has now all changed overnight. After _____ examining her beliefs,
9
this model has decided to _____.
10

"To be peaceful and happy," she says, "one needs to be content with whatever one has."

*(Based on information in "The Model Who Became A Monk." Asian Pacific Post, October 20, 2005.)*

## WORDS IN DISCUSSION

*Apply the key words to your own life. Complete the questionnaire. Then discuss your answers with a classmate. Try to use the key words.*

### EXAMPLE

Something I could never **qualify** for: <u>Manchester United soccer team</u>

**A:** *I agree with you. I couldn't **qualify** for any soccer team!*

**B:** *Actually, I'm a pretty good soccer player. I'm going to try out for our school's soccer team next month. I think I can **qualify** for that team!*

1. A job I am **qualified** for: _____

2. Something I think people should be **barred** from doing: _____

3. A terrible person whom I believe has no **conscience**: _____

4. A person whom I trust never to **deceive** me: _____

5. How **thorough** I am when I clean: _____

6. Something I do not want to **omit** when packing for a trip: _____

7. A place where I feel **solemn**: _____

8. What I like to see **displayed** in shop windows: _____

9. The **volume** at which I like to listen to music: _____

10. What I **assume** about my future: _____

## WORDS IN WRITING

*Choose two topics and write a short paragraph on each. Try to use the key words.*

1. Have you ever made an **assumption** about someone that was completely wrong? What did you **assume**, and how did you find out that you were mistaken?

### EXAMPLE

*Last year a new neighbor moved into my apartment building. The name on his mailbox sounded Turkish, so I **assumed** he was Turkish. One day, in the elevator, I decided to greet my new neighbor with the one word of Turkish I knew, and he looked at me in total confusion. Later, I learned he was Italian!*

2. Imagine that you are going to help select the next leader of your country. What **qualifications** do you believe this person should have? Explain.

3. Do you believe that it is okay to **omit** some stories about your life when you are talking with your family, or do you feel that such an **omission** is **deceptive**? Explain.

4. Do you feel that the government should **bar** any artists from **displaying** their work? Explain.

5. Describe a time when your **conscience** helped you make an important decision.

Key Words

| deserve | ensure | lack | method | task |
|---------|--------|------|--------|------|
| elect | essential | manage | purchase | unite |

## WORDS IN CONTEXT

*Use the sentences to guess what each key word means. Choose the meaning that is closest to that of the key word in **bold**.*

1. **deserve**
/dɪˈzɚv/
-*verb*

   - We took our mother out to dinner on her birthday. Truthfully, she **deserves** a lot more for all that she's done for us.
   - Your performance was the best. You **deserved** first place, not second.

   *Deserve* means . . .   a. to have earned something   b. you should rest   c. you should ask for something special

2. **elect**
/ɪˈlɛkt/
-*verb*

   - The students **elected** Norma to be their class president.
   - U.S. senators are **elected** to office every six years.

   *Elect* means . . .   a. to respect   b. to choose by voting   c. to prepare for a position

3. **ensure**
/ɪnˈʃʊr/
-*verb*

   - Leandra wants to **ensure** her consideration for the position of supervisor, so she works hard and shows an interest in learning new skills.
   - There will be additional police officers at the stadium to **ensure** the safety of the fans during and after the game.

   *Ensure* means . . .   a. to make certain   b. to get by cheating   c. to recommend

4. **essential**
/ɪˈsɛnʃəl/
-*adjective*

   - It's **essential** to eat well and drink enough water every day.
   - The flood came very quickly. Craig and Mayumi had only enough time to grab a few **essential** things before they had to rush out of their home.

   *Essential* means . . .   a. healthy   b. somewhat expensive   c. necessary

5. **lack**
/læk/
-*noun*

   - It was clear who the company would hire: Vivian had everything that the director was looking for; Mimi's **lack** of experience made her the weaker choice.
   - My brother's **lack** of humor makes him very sensitive. He needs to learn to laugh more, even at himself.

   *Lack* means . . .   a. not having something   b. a desire for something   c. the loss of something

6. **manage**
/ˈmænɪdʒ/
-*verb*

   - My legs were sore and my fingers were cold, but I still **managed** the climb.
   - Vince faced a lot of difficulties after his wife died and left him with two children. With some help from his parents, he somehow **managed**.

   *Manage* means . . .   a. to have confidence   b. to succeed   c. to continue

**7. method**
/ˈmɛθəd/
-noun

- The cashier instructed me to choose a payment **method**; I used my credit card.
- Do you have a **method** for learning grammar? What has helped you?

*Method* means . . .   a. a book     b. a secret     c. a planned way

**8. purchase**
/ˈpɚtʃəs/
-verb

- Many couples believe it's important to talk together before **purchasing** something expensive like a car or computer.
- I decided to take only one suitcase of clothes with me. If I needed more things, I'd **purchase** them after I arrived.

*Purchase* means . . .   a. to search for something     b. to buy     c. to clean

**9. task**
/tæsk/
-noun

- My sister sees cooking as a **task**; I see it as something fun to do.
- Jamal is very organized. He always makes a list of **tasks** he needs to do at the start of each work day.

*Task* means . . .   a. a job     b. a game     c. a test of skill

**10. unite**
/yuˈnaɪt/
-verb

- The workers **united** and faced their boss. As one voice, they made their complaints clearly heard.
- The school project was not only about collecting money for a new library; it helped **unite** the students and created a feeling of school spirit.

*Unite* means . . .   a. to start a discussion     b. to join together     c. to decide to do something suddenly

## WORDS AND DEFINITIONS

*Match each key word with its definition.*

1. _____ensure_____ to do something to be certain of a particular result

2. _____ the state of not having something or not having enough of something

3. _____ to buy something

4. _____ to have earned something by good or bad actions or behavior

5. _____ to choose someone for an official position by voting

6. _____ to succeed in doing something difficult

7. _____ to join together with other people and act as one group, or to make people join together this way

8. _____ a job or particular thing you have to do, especially a difficult or annoying one

9. _____ a planned way of doing something

10. _____ important and necessary

# ▌COMPREHENSION CHECK

*Choose the best answer.*

1. All of the following jobs are common office **tasks** EXCEPT
   a. filing reports.
   b. taking a coffee break.
   c. sending a fax.
   d. making photocopies.

2. A neighbor sees you with several grocery bags and asks, "Can you **manage**?" He wants to know if you are
   a. selling something.
   b. spending your money wisely.
   c. able to carry everything by yourself.
   d. willing to share your food with him.

3. Eric is a good student and often gets 100 percent on his tests. That's why he **deserves**
   a. a textbook.
   b. extra homework for review.
   c. a failing grade.
   d. a high grade this semester.

4. What is **essential** when making a sandwich?
   a. bread
   b. meat
   c. cheese
   d. tomatoes

5. Francine went into town and **purchased** a few things at the
   a. library and then the park.
   b. doctor's office and then her friend's home.
   c. grocery store and then the pharmacy.
   d. health club and then her son's school.

6. If you suffer from a **lack** of money, you
   a. would never ask for help paying school tuition.
   b. can open a couple of bank accounts and save money.
   c. can be generous and lend money.
   d. cannot buy everything you need.

7. All the following people would use a **method** in their activities EXCEPT
   a. an instructor teaching a language.
   b. an athlete training for the Olympics.
   c. a worker on break drinking tea.
   d. a parent raising a child.

8. People **elect**
   a. a restaurant owner.
   b. the Queen of England.
   c. the president of the United States.
   d. a champion boxer.

9. Mr. McGurrin wanted to **ensure** his child's safety, so he
   a. let his 13-year-old go to a night club.
   b. taught his 16-year-old to drive fast.
   c. taught his daughter how to dance the waltz.
   d. made his son wear a seatbelt while driving.

10. What would be a likely reason for a group of workers to **unite**?
    a. Each person has different vacation plans.
    b. Half of them want to work part-time; the other half want to work full-time.
    c. They all want more sick days and more vacation time.
    d. They disagree over which of them should be the new vice president.

## WORD FAMILIES

Now that you have studied the ten key words and their basic definitions, you are ready to learn words that belong to the same family as some of the key words. A word family includes words that look alike but have different functions (noun, verb, adjective, or adverb). Their meanings are related but different.

**A.** *Look at each model phrase and decide whether the word in* **bold** *is used as a noun, verb, adjective, or adverb.*

|  | NOUN | VERB | ADJECTIVE | ADVERB |
|---|:---:|:---:|:---:|:---:|
| 1. **elect** |  |  |  |  |
| • **elect** her president |  | ✓ |  |  |
| • hold an **election** | ✓ |  |  |  |
| 2. **lack** |  |  |  |  |
| • a **lack** of skills |  |  |  |  |
| • **lack** experience |  |  |  |  |
| 3. **manage** |  |  |  |  |
| • **manage** by oneself |  |  |  |  |
| • a **manageable** situation |  |  |  |  |
| 4. **method** |  |  |  |  |
| • try a new **method** |  |  |  |  |
| • be very **methodical** |  |  |  |  |
| 5. **purchase** |  |  |  |  |
| • **purchase** new furniture |  |  |  |  |
| • a large **purchase** |  |  |  |  |
| 6. **unite** |  |  |  |  |
| • **unite** the students |  |  |  |  |
| • a **united** community |  |  |  |  |

**B.** *Read the first half of each sentence and match it with the appropriate ending.*

___c___ 1. The tourists' bags were full of

_____ 2. My father takes care of his prized sports car; when he cleans it, he's

_____ 3. Upset over the loss of several good teachers, the parents formed a

_____ 4. There was a lot to do, but I didn't complain because I knew it was

_____ 5. Tolya doesn't like old movies. He thinks they're slow and says they

_____ 6. Some believe that a woman can win the next

a. very **methodical**.

b. **lack** fight scenes, car chases, and other excitement.

c. **purchases** when they returned to the bus.

d. **united** group to discuss their concerns with the principal.

e. U.S. presidential **election**.

f. **manageable**. I just had to think clearly and get organized.

## SAME WORD, DIFFERENT MEANING

Most words have more than one meaning. Study the additional meanings of **elect**, **manage**, and **united**. Then read each sentence and decide which meaning is used.

| | | |
|---|---|---|
| a. **elect** *v.* | to choose someone for an official position by voting |
| b. **elect** *v.* | to choose to do something |
| c. **manage** *v.* | to succeed in doing something difficult |
| d. **manage** *v.* | to direct or control a business and the people who work in it |
| e. **united** *adj.* | involving or done by everyone |
| f. **united** *adj.* | closely related by sharing feelings or goals |

___b___ 1. Tad has **elected** to take Spanish. All students at his school must study a language for two years.

_____ 2. Mr. Gharios has **managed** his family's Lebanese restaurant for the past fifteen years.

_____ 3. Angela Merkel was the first woman in Germany to be **elected** chancellor.

_____ 4. The film was a **united** production; two different movie companies worked together on it.

_____ 5. How will you **manage** in a new city without a job or a place to stay?

_____ 6. The students stood **united** in the decision to help the homeless in their town; they all shared the feeling that they could make a difference.

## WORDS IN SENTENCES

Complete each sentence with one of the words from the box.

| | | | | |
|---|---|---|---|---|
| deserves | ensure | lacks | method | tasks |
| elect | essential | ~~manageable~~ | purchases | united |

1. The baby-sitter looked at the noisy children and the food thrown on the floor; the situation was far from ___manageable___. What was she going to do?

2. I left the store and put my _____ down next to me to make a phone call.

3. The students made a(n) _____ effort to convince the teachers to give less homework over the holidays. They all wanted time to be with friends and family.

4. My dad, who loves spicy food, believes that hot sauce is a(n) _____ ingredient in nearly every dish he eats.

5. Your essay is good, but it _____ details. You need to explain more and give examples.

6. Politicians are always trying to _____ their good standing in politics, so they make promises, shake hands, hold babies, and smile whenever they're in public.

7. On holidays, our boss sometimes gives us the choice of working and getting paid more, or taking the day off. I always _____ to work for more money.

8. The book has a good _____ for teaching new vocabulary. It presents each new word in eight different contexts.

9. Sui Yang is really good about getting all of her _____ done on time, from small jobs to big ones.

10. Amy _____ a pay raise. She's worked hard and brought in a lot of new business.

## ▌WORDS IN COLLOCATIONS AND EXPRESSIONS

*Following are common collocations (word partners) and expressions with some of the key words. Read the definitions and then complete the conversations with the correct form of the collocations and expressions.*

| | |
|---|---|
| 1. **deserve** | |
| • **deserve to (do sth)** | to have earned the right to do something |
| 2. **ensure** | |
| • **ensure that** | to do something to be certain of a particular result |
| 3. **essential** | |
| • **the bare essentials** | the most basic and necessary things |
| 4. **manage** | |
| • **manage to (do sth)** | to succeed in doing something difficult |
| 5. **purchase** | |
| • **a major purchase** | something bought that is very expensive (like a house or car) |
| • **make a purchase** | to buy something |

1.     TROY:     Let me help you with your groceries.

      SAORI:     That's all right. I don't want to trouble you.

      TROY:     No trouble. We live on the same floor. Anyway, how will you _____*manage to*_____ open the door without dropping anything? You have three bags and an umbrella.

2.   MR. PALMER:     Buying a house is _____. It means we now need to watch our spending.

  MRS. PALMER:     Well, at least for a little while we can do without smaller things like trips to the movie theater and dinner at restaurants.

3.     DENISE:     I never see you with fewer than ten CDs in your bag. How will you fit everything into your backpack when we go camping?

      GLEN:     Don't worry. When we go camping, I won't carry anything extra. I'll leave the CDs at home and take only _____.

4.     LYNN:     Torey and Dallas didn't pass the course?

      RAY:     No. They failed because they cheated on the final exam. I don't feel sorry for them; they _____ be punished.

5.     KURT:     How was your cruise? Did you and Dad enjoy it?

    MOTHER:     Very much. They did everything to _____ we were comfortable and had everything we needed.

6.    NATALIE:    Thanks for remembering to get me a magnet from Dallas. I'll add it to my collection on the refrigerator.

CRAIG:    No problem. I had just enough time to _____ in the souvenir shop before my plane departed.

## WORDS IN A READING

*Read this article about a growing movement in education. Complete it with words and expressions from the boxes.*

| ensure that | essential | manage to do | purchased | task |
|---|---|---|---|---|

### HOME SCHOOLING

Many American children do not go to school. Instead, they stay at home and learn all they need to know from their parents. Of course, teaching children all the _____essential_____ subjects and skills is

1

not an easy _____. So how do parents _____ the job? It differs from

2                                              3

household to household.

Wanting to _____ their children make progress, some parents copy a typical school

4

schedule and make a day of study just as it would be at a regular school. To make certain that their home-schooled children's learning experience is no worse than a traditional one, parents can also buy standard textbooks and ready-made lesson plans. *Kingdom of Children*, a book on home schooling, tells about one

mother who even _____ school desks to create a traditional classroom in the basement.

5

| deserve to | elect | lack | method | unites |
|---|---|---|---|---|

But many other parents _____ not to copy from traditional school systems, choosing

6

real contexts over standard material. This group of parents believes that it is better to allow children to

experience a freer and more natural way of learning. Their _____ of teaching makes it

7

possible to have lessons during daily activities and field trips outside the home, for example, a lesson

on percentages at the grocery store or a history lesson at the museum.

Some argue that children taught at home do not develop in the same way as those taught in

school. They point out that such children _____ social skills, being at home with their

8

parents so much. This could happen in some households, but many parents of home-schooled

children create networks and form clubs, teams, and groups for outside activities. Studies have

shown that home-schooled children actually spend more time in social situations than regular

school students do.

Is that why home schooling has become so popular among American families? Not entirely. Today

forty-nine percent of parents teaching their children at home explain that children _____

9

have quality instruction and it cannot be found in regular schools. Other reasons to give an education at home include the wish to protect children from violent behavior and negative pressure from classmates. Whatever the reasons may be, the fact is that a large number of American parents have already made their decision: The National Home Education Network _____ millions of school-aged children from a variety of backgrounds in a special educational experience—where the classroom is found outside the school and inside the family.

*(Based on information in "When School Is at Home." The Week, September 9, 2005.)*

## ▌WORDS IN DISCUSSION

*Apply the key words to your own life. Read and discuss each question in small groups. Try to use the key words.*

1. Do you **manage to** get all your **tasks** done on time?

   **EXAMPLE**

   *I like to do things right, and this means I don't rush. I don't always **manage** to do things on time. But I think I know which **tasks** can wait.*

2. What can you do to **ensure** good health?

3. Have you ever voted in an **election** of any kind? Explain.

4. What do you think is the best **method** for learning English grammar?

5. Have you ever got a grade in school that you felt you didn't **deserve**? Explain.

6. Do you take time to think before making **a major purchase**? How much time do you take?

7. What causes the most stress in your life right now? A **lack** of time, money, or something else?

8. Name a reason for students to **unite**.

9. Think about what you have in your pockets and bags right now. Which items are essential?

10. How can you **ensure that** you'll have a good time on a trip?

## ▌WORDS IN WRITING

*Choose two topics and write a short paragraph on each. Try to use the key words.*

1. What is **essential for** your happiness?

   **EXAMPLE**

   *Family is important to me. I'm very close to my parents, brothers, and sister. They help me with everything. We also have fun together. I think it's **essential** to have people to love and to love you back.*

2. Some professional athletes make a lot of money. Do you think they **deserve** such high salaries?

3. Was there a time you ever **lacked** confidence? Explain.

4. What is the most expensive thing you've ever **purchased**?

5. What kind of person does it take to **manage** a business?

# CHAPTER 15

**Key Words**

| coarse | dust | march | rejoice | tremble |
|--------|------|-------|---------|---------|
| colony | empire | psychology | revenge | valley |

## WORDS IN CONTEXT

*Use the sentences to guess what each key word means. Choose the meaning that is closest to that of the key word in **bold**.*

**1. coarse**
/kɔrs/
*-adjective*

- Because Elina did not have money to buy fine or smooth cloth, she made her dress from **coarse** material.
- Fishermen often wear sweaters that are made from **coarse** wool.

*Coarse* means . . .    a. high quality    (b.) rough and thick    c. soft and fine

**2. colony**
/ˈkɑləni/
*-noun*

- In 1776, the thirteen English **colonies** in North America declared their independence from Great Britain and became the United States of America.
- Cape Verde was a Portuguese **colony** from 1463 to 1975, when it gained its independence.

*Colony* means . . .    a. a country or area that is ruled by another country    b. a country that is ruled by its own people    c. a new country

**3. dust**
/dʌst/
*-noun*

- The boxes in my grandmother's attic, which had not been touched for forty years, were covered with **dust**.
- When a truck drives down a dry dirt road, it creates a cloud of **dust**.

*Dust* means . . .    a. big pieces of dirt    b. tiny pieces of dirt that are like powder    c. large amounts of dirt

**4. empire**
/ˈɛmpaɪ⋅/
*-noun*

- When England was part of the Roman **Empire**, many Latin words entered the English language.
- In 1226, Genghis Khan ruled an **empire** that stretched from Southeast Asia to Central Europe.

*Empire* means . . .    a. a country that is controlled by one ruler    b. many countries that are controlled by many governments    c. a group of countries controlled by one ruler or government

**5. march**
/mɑrtʃ/
*-verb*

- When Yoon was doing his military service, he and the other soldiers in his troop did not walk in a relaxed way; they had to **march** together.
- During Mardi Gras, musicians in New Orleans **march** down the street playing jazz music.

*March* means . . .    a. to walk in a comfortable way    b. to walk with friends    c. to walk with firm, regular steps

**6. psychology**
/saɪˈkɑlədʒi/
-noun

- Hugo is studying **psychology** because he is interested in problems of the mind.
- Ed is interested in learning more about the **psychology** of animals because he wants to understand the way that his dog thinks.

*Psychology* means . . .    a. the study of the human body     b. the study of plants     c. the study of the mind

**7. rejoice**
/rɪˈdʒɔɪs/
-verb

- When Dominic and his friends heard that their favorite soccer team had won the World Cup, they **rejoiced**, dancing in the street.
- When Helen learned that the war was over, she **rejoiced**.

*Rejoice* means . . .    a. to play a game     b. to feel or show that you are very happy     c. to be mildly happy

**8. revenge**
/rɪˈvɛndʒ/
-noun

- After Sarah told an unkind joke about Isabel at the party, Isabel thought, "I will get **revenge**!" And she did; she spilled a cup of coffee on Sarah's new sweater.
- When Joe saw another man kiss his girlfriend, he wanted **revenge**.

*Revenge* means . . .    a. something you do as a joke     b. something you do to hurt someone who has harmed you     c. something you do because you are sad

**9. tremble**
/ˈtrɛmbəl/
-verb

- Clara's hands **trembled** as she opened the letter from her long, lost love.
- If you say hello to a ghost, your voice might **tremble**.

*Tremble* means . . .    a. to remain calm     b. to be strong     c. to shake

**10. valley**
/ˈvæli/
-noun

- When we reached the bottom of the mountain, we had a picnic in the sunny **valley**; then we started climbing the next mountain.
- Marta's aunt has a little farm in a **valley** surrounded by the Alps.

*Valley* means . . .    a. land near the ocean     b. land on top of a mountain     c. low land between mountains

## ▌ WORDS AND DEFINITIONS

*Match each key word with its definition.*

1. _____tremble_____ to shake because you are upset, afraid, or excited

2. _____ an area of lower land between two lines of hills or mountains

3. _____ something you do in order to punish someone who has harmed or offended you

4. _____ the study of the mind and how it works

5. _____ dry powder that consists of extremely small pieces of dirt, sand, etc.

6. _____ a country or area that is ruled by another country

7. _____ rough and thick

8. _____ to feel or show that you are very happy

9. _____ to walk quickly and with firm regular steps like a soldier

10. _____ a group of countries that are all controlled by one ruler or government

## COMPREHENSION CHECK

*Choose the best answer.*

1. Who is **rejoicing**?
   a. "Ow! I hate going to the dentist."
   b. "Yes! I was accepted by my favorite university!"
   c. "I'm sleepy."
   d. "Can I have a piece of cake?"

2. Where can you NOT find **dust**?
   a. on a table that has not been cleaned for a month
   b. on water
   c. on a book that has not been touched for a year
   d. on a dry road

3. Who should study **psychology**?
   a. Gina, who is interested in medicine.
   b. Tobias, who wants to know about animals.
   c. Max, who is good at mathematics.
   d. Jean, who is interested in how the mind works.

4. Which person wants **revenge**?
   a. "I'll make a cake for Sally."
   b. "I want to ask Sally a question."
   c. "Because Sally ate my candy, I'm going to steal her candy!"
   d. "I want to paint a picture of Sally."

5. Which word or phrase CANNOT describe a **valley**?
   a. flat
   b. between mountains
   c. in the ocean
   d. low

6. What would NOT **tremble**?
   a. the voice of a nervous thief
   b. the arms of a confident athlete
   c. the lips of a scared child
   d. the hands of an excited teenager who's driving for the first time

7. Which sentence gives an example of a **colony**?
   a. Anna has three pets: a cat, a dog, and a guinea pig.
   b. India won its independence from Great Britain in 1947.
   c. Six people live in Simon's house.
   d. France is not ruled by another country.

8. Which item is **coarse**?
   a. the skin of a baby
   b. a raindrop
   c. a smooth shell
   d. the cheek of an unshaven man

9. Which sentence gives an example of an **empire**?
   a. Alexander the Great conquered many countries from Egypt to India.
   b. George Washington was president of the United States.
   c. My cousin Joe was the coach for his son's soccer team.
   d. Charlotte owns three coffee shops.

10. Who does NOT **march**?
    a. a tourist
    b. a soldier
    c. a captain
    d. a musician in a marching band

# WORD FAMILIES

Now that you have studied the ten key words and their basic definitions, you are ready to learn words that belong to the same family as some of the key words. A word family includes words that look alike but have different functions (noun, verb, adjective, or adverb). Their meanings are related but different.

**A.** *Look at each model phrase and decide whether the word in* **bold** *is used as a noun, verb, adjective, or adverb.*

|  | NOUN | VERB | ADJECTIVE | ADVERB |
|---|:---:|:---:|:---:|:---:|
| 1. **colony** | | | | |
| • a former **colony** | ✓ | | | |
| • to **colonize** another country | | ✓ | | |
| 2. **dust** | | | | |
| • covered with **dust** | | | | |
| • **dust** the furniture | | | | |
| • a **dusty** attic | | | | |
| 3. **march** | | | | |
| • **march** in a line | | | | |
| • the long **march** | | | | |
| 4. **psychology** | | | | |
| • a **psychology** class | | | | |
| • a **psychological** test | | | | |
| • a professional **psychologist** | | | | |
| 5. **tremble** | | | | |
| • her voice **trembled** | | | | |
| • a **trembling** leaf | | | | |

**B.** *Match the following sentences with the definition of the word in* **bold**.

___b___ 1. Before guests visit her home, Amelia always **dusts** the furniture.

_____ 2. When I saw her **trembling** lips, I knew she was upset.

_____ 3. When France **colonized** Algeria, many French people moved there.

_____ 4. Why did Greg ask our math professor a **psychological** question?

_____ 5. Tom described Gandhi's 1930 **march** against the salt tax.

_____ 6. When Theo opened the **dusty** old book, he coughed.

_____ 7. If you're having problems, you should talk to a **psychologist**.

a. covered or filled with dust

b. to clean the dust from something

c. to control a country or area and send your own people to live there

e. shaking

f. relating to the way people's minds work and the way this affects their behavior

g. someone who is trained in psychology

h. the act of walking with firm, regular steps like a soldier

# ❚ SAME WORD, DIFFERENT MEANING

*Most words have more than one meaning. Study the additional meanings of **coarse**, **colony**, and **march**. Then read each sentence and decide which meaning is used.*

| | | |
|---|---|---|
| a. **coarse** *adj.* | rough and thick |
| b. **coarse** *adj.* | rude and offensive |
| c. **colony** *n.* | a country or area that is ruled by another country |
| d. **colony** *n.* | a group of the same kind of people or animals that live together |
| e. **march** *v.* | the act of walking with firm, regular steps like a soldier |
| f. **march** *n.* | an organized event in which many people walk together to protest about something |

___b___ 1. Jacob's mother covered his ears so that he would not hear the sailors' **coarse** language.

_____ 2. Every summer, Savannah lives in an art **colony**; she lives there with other artists.

_____ 3. Royal guards **march** in a parade.

_____ 4. In 2003, several hundred thousand people participated in a **march** in London to show that they were angry about Great Britain going to war.

_____ 5. The Congo was once a **colony** of Belgium.

_____ 6. Because Marissa's hair felt **coarse**, she used a special shampoo to make it softer and smoother.

# ❚ WORDS IN SENTENCES

*Complete each sentence with one of the words from the box.*

| | | | | |
|---|---|---|---|---|
| coarse | dusts | march | rejoiced | trembling |
| colony | ~~empire~~ | psychologist | revenge | valley |

1. During the Ottoman _____*Empire*_____ , parts of southwest Asia, northeast Africa, and southeast Europe were ruled by Turkish sultans.

2. Felix is going to take part in a(n) _____ to protest the government's new healthcare policy.

3. In a _____ voice, Shingo asked, "I won million dollars?"

4. Jenna _____ the furniture in her living room once a week.

5. Omar's family _____ when they heard that their home had not been destroyed by the earthquake.

6. The princess rejected the dress; the material was too _____.

7. In the long hours of summer sun in Alaska, farmers grow giant vegetables in the Matanuska _____; from their farms, you can see beautiful mountains nearby.

8. Some people commit crimes because they want _____.

9. This week our science class is investigating a large _____ of ants.

10. Dr. Jones, a _____, suggests that people who think positively have happier lives.

## WORDS IN COLLOCATIONS AND EXPRESSIONS

*Following are common collocations (word partners) and expressions with some of the key words. Read the definitions and then complete the conversations with the correct form of the collocations and expressions.*

| | | |
|---|---|---|
| 1. **dust** | | |
| | • **dust (sth) off** | to take the dust off something |
| 2. **empire** | | |
| | • **a business empire** | a group of organizations that are all controlled by one person or company |
| 3. **tremble** | | |
| | • **trembling with fear** | shaking because you are afraid |
| 4. **revenge** | | |
| | • **get revenge on (sb)** | to punish someone for something they did to you |
| | • **in revenge for (sth)** | because you did something bad to me |
| 5. **psychology** | | |
| | • **a psychological problem** | a problem with the mind |

1. DAUGHTER: Look, I found an old picture of you in the attic, Mom. Who is that handsome guy with you?

   MOTHER: I can't see his face. Let's _____*dust*_____ the picture _____*off*_____. Oh, look! It's my brother Martin!

   DAUGHTER: That's Uncle Martin? Wow, he has changed.

2. LUKE: The dog doesn't want to take a bath, Dad! He's scared of it. Look, poor Spot is _____.

   DAD: Sorry, Luke, but the dog doesn't have a choice. Spot smells terrible.

   SPOT: Woof!

3. MARY: Why did you insult me in front of the class?

   ANNE: It was _____ the time that you told a mean joke about me. I was really angry about that!

   MARY: Well now I'm really angry. I'm going to _____ you for this!

4. LOUIS: Doctor, why do I dream about dinosaurs every night?

   DOCTOR: I'm not sure, but it is possible that you have _____.

5. REPORTER: You're one of the most important businessmen in the world. You control _____. What's the secret of your success?

   BUSINESSMAN: I work hard.

## ▌ WORDS IN A READING

*Read this article about Norwegian history. Complete it with words and expressions from the boxes.*

| coarse | marching | ~~psychology~~ | tremble with fear | valleys |
|---|---|---|---|---|

### HOW SKIING CHANGED NORWEGIAN HISTORY

Many countries have national landmarks that represent the nation's skills, power, or greatness. Big Ben in London, New York's Empire State Building, and the Eiffel Tower in Paris are such landmarks. In Oslo, the capital of Norway, the national landmark is a ski jump. This is no accident, as Norwegian history, culture, and ____*psychology*____ are all closely linked to skiing. Rock carvings show that skis
                                    1
have been used in Scandinavia since the Stone Age, 4,000 years ago. However, until the 1850s skiing was a kind of winter time transportation, not a sport.

The use of skis started to change when the Norwegian army created a new kind of soldier in the 17th century. Instead of _____ to war, these soldiers skied to war. Ski soldiers played a
                                2
major role in several wars. They were brave fighters who could make their rivals _____.
                                                                                          3
Skis really evolved, however, in Telemark, a district in southern Norway with many hills and _____. In the 1850s, master craftsmen and skiers in that region began to change the
        4
design of skis. The old _____ skis were dramatically improved. They were made shorter,
                                5
broader, and curved in a new way. This new type of skis became the model for all later developments in skiing, including skiing competitions that took place as early as 1862 in Oslo.

| colony | dust | empire | get revenge on | rejoiced |
|---|---|---|---|---|

Norwegians introduced skis all over the planet (they like to think) when the Norwegian polar explorer Fridtjof Nansen's crossing of Greenland in 1888 caused excitement through Europe and the United States. Several international expeditions had tried to explore the interior of Greenland before him, but failed. While his rivals' hopes had turned to _____, Nansen's expedition was a
                                                                            6
success, mainly because he and his men used skis. Skiing was something completely new to the world. As Norwegians _____ at Nansen's victory, skiing became internationally known for the
                        7
first time—and Norway with it.

Once a(n) _____ of Denmark, Norway was freed from the Danish _____
            8                                                                          9
in 1814, but was immediately thrown into a political union with Sweden. In that union, Sweden was the stronger partner. So, from 1814 to 1888, the people of Norway searched for something purely Norwegian—something that defined them as different from the Swedes, something with which they could identify in order to call for an independent Norway and _____ the Swedes. In 1888,
                                                                    10

they found it in Nansen's victory. Thus skiing provided the inspiration the Norwegians needed to achieve the liberation of their country. Norway became independent in 1905.

*(Based on information in "Skiing and the Creation of a Norwegian Identity." News of Norway, issue 1, 1996.)*

## WORDS IN DISCUSSION

*Apply the key words to your own life. Complete the questionnaire. Then discuss your answers with a classmate. Try to use the key words.*

**EXAMPLE**

Something in my home that is **dusty**: _my German textbook_

**A:** *Why is your German textbook* **dusty***?*

**B:** *I haven't touched it since 1999. Maybe I should* **dust it** *off and start studying again.*

1. A future event that will make me **rejoice**: _____

2. How often I **dust** the furniture in my room: _____

3. What I would say if someone invited me to join a **colony** of people who were going to live on the moon: _____

4. A place where I saw people **marching** in protest: _____

5. Something scary that could make me **tremble**: _____

6. An **empire** that influenced the history of my country: _____

7. The last time I thought, "I will get **revenge**!": _____

8. How much I know about **psychology**: _____

9. The location of a **valley** I have walked in: _____

10. How often I use **coarse** language: _____

## WORDS IN WRITING

*Choose two topics and write a short paragraph on each. Try to use the key words.*

1. If you learned that you would not have to go to school for the rest of your life, would you **rejoice**?

**EXAMPLE**

*Naturally, like most students, I have days when I want to close my books and never open them again. Studying can be exhausting, confusing, and boring. However, learning also can be interesting and exciting. For this reason, I wouldn't* **rejoice** *if I were told I wouldn't have to go to school ever again.*

2. Describe a time when you **trembled** in fear or excitement.

3. Tell a story, real or fictional, about a person who wanted **revenge**.

4. Was your native country ever part of an **empire**? If so, explain why you believe the empire was a positive or negative influence.

5. Imagine what your city will be like 500 years in the future. Which buildings will have turned to **dust**, and which will still exist?

# QUIZ 5

## PART A

*Choose the word that best completes each item and write it in the space provided.*

1. George Washington was _____*elected*_____ president of the United States in 1789.
   - a. ensured
   - b. omitted
   - c. elected
   - d. assumed

2. Garrett felt his legs and hands _____ as he walked on stage; he was very nervous.
   - a. march
   - b. manage
   - c. deceive
   - d. tremble

3. By the 1800s the Russian _____ stretched from Poland to the Pacific Ocean.
   - a. colony
   - b. method
   - c. psychology
   - d. Empire

4. Ian's _____ told him to give the homeless woman some money.
   - a. method
   - b. conscience
   - c. psychology
   - d. task

5. The doctor's manner was very _____ as she delivered the bad news to her patient.
   - a. solemn
   - b. essential
   - c. coarse
   - d. thorough

6. When solving crimes, it often helps for detectives to understand the _____ of criminals; to find a criminal, you often have to think like one.
   - a. method
   - b. conscience
   - c. psychology
   - d. task

7. Mother took lots of water to _____ that we wouldn't go thirsty on the long car ride.
   - a. ensure
   - b. purchase
   - c. omit
   - d. manage

8. Gianna was used to wearing cotton shirts, so the wool sweater felt heavy and _____.
   - a. solemn
   - b. essential
   - c. coarse
   - d. thorough

9. Times of trouble can _____ a community; people more readily help one another.
   - a. ensure
   - b. manage
   - c. unite
   - d. assume

10. The teacher read my paragraph and suggested that I _____ one sentence that gave unnecessary information.
    - a. ensure
    - b. omit
    - c. unite
    - d. display

## PART B

Read each statement and write **T** for true or **F** for false in the space provided.

__F__ 1. If there's a **lack** of skilled workers in your company, business will be good.

_____ 2. Taking an elevator requires a **method**.

_____ 3. If a store **displays** clothes in the front window, it wants you to see them and consider buying them.

_____ 4. Listening skills are **essential** for good communication.

_____ 5. When you **manage** to do something difficult, you should ask for help.

_____ 6. A colony is **independent** from an outside ruler.

_____ 7. Workers who **deceive** their employers will likely lose their jobs.

_____ 8. When you **purchase** clothes, you should wash them and then return them.

_____ 9. If Chloe **assumes** she's right, she can prove this.

_____10. Finding a lost pet is cause to **rejoice**.

## PART C

Complete each item with a word from the box. Use each word once.

| barred | dust | qualify | tasks | valley |
|--------|------|---------|-------|--------|
| ~~deserves~~ | marched | revenge | thorough | volume |

1. Surat _____*deserves*_____ a higher pay because he's a hard worker and he's done a lot for the company.

2. The mechanic did a _____ inspection of the car in order to find the problem.

3. The _____ of sales greatly pleased the store owner.

4. You need at least two years of experience and knowledge of one foreign language to _____ for this job.

5. Everyone cheered as the returning soldiers _____ down Main Street.

6. Flooding is common in this part of the _____ especially in the spring when the rain rolls down from the hills.

7. Because of a serious error made during a patient's care, that doctor will be _____ from practicing medicine ever again.

8. Layla wanted _____ because Ben and Drew had embarrassed her in front of the whole class.

9. My roommate often forgets to do simple _____ like taking out the trash.

10. I sneezed as I began to brush off the _____ from the old photo albums.

**Key Words**

| absence | bend | limb | positive | slight |
|---------|------|------|----------|--------|
| associate | drama | oppose | propose | struggle |

## WORDS IN CONTEXT

*Use the sentences to guess what each key word means. Choose the meaning that is closest to that of the key word in **bold**.*

1. **absence**
   /'æbsəns/
   *-noun*

   • The teachers began to note Gloria's frequent **absences** and questioned her story about being sick each time she missed a class.

   • The manager clearly explained to the new employees that he wouldn't accept **absence** for any reason except an emergency.

   *Absence* means . . .   a. the state of being dishonest   b. the state of being ill   c. the state of not being present

2. **associate**
   /ə'souʃi,eɪt/
   *-verb*

   • I always **associate** watermelon with summer picnics, don't you?

   • Even after many years, people **associated** the actor with his early films, in which he always played the part of a dangerous criminal.

   *Associate* means . . .   a. to connect with   b. to work with   c. to request

3. **bend**
   /bɛnd/
   *-verb*

   • Jacob **bent** deeply as he walked into the room. He's so tall that he's used to not fitting through most doorways.

   • Ow! I can't **bend** my finger. Do you think it's broken?

   *Bend* means . . .   a. to brush lightly   b. to move from a straight position into a curve   c. to be unable to feel or move

4. **drama**
   /'dramə/
   *-noun*

   • My roommate likes action films, but I prefer to watch a good **drama**.

   • The actress is talented, but she's better suited for **drama** than comedy.

   *Drama* means . . .   a. a serious play or story   b. a lively dance   c. a news report

5. **limb**
   /lɪm/
   *-noun*

   • The tree is getting big. We need to cut off that **limb**. It's too close to the window.

   • The children love to play in the oak tree, climbing from **limb** to **limb** and jumping to the ground.

   *Limb* means . . .   a. wood   b. a leaf   c. an arm of a tree

6. **oppose**
   /ə'pouz/
   *-verb*

   • Why must you **oppose** every suggestion I make? Don't you share any of my views?

   • The parents **opposed** the idea of school uniforms, knowing that their children would not want to wear the same thing every day.

   *Oppose* means . . .   a. to fail to understand   b. to disagree with   c. to refuse to listen to

7. **positive**
/ˈpazətɪv/
-adjective

- I'm **positive** that Camargo can do the job well. He's done similar work before.
- Are you certain that Judith isn't coming to the party?— **Positive**.

*Positive* means . . .   a. very sure        b. doubtful        c. interested

8. **propose**
/prəˈpouz/
-verb

- I **proposed** a new format for our weekly reports, and the manager seemed to like it.
- We discussed the problems we've been having with our office computers. Several solutions were **proposed**, but none has been accepted yet.

*Propose* means . . .   a. to consider     b. to improve      c. to suggest

9. **slight**
/slaɪt/
-adjective

- Juan made a **slight** mistake in his speech, but no one noticed except the teacher.
- Bruno had a **slight** bruise on his head from walking into the glass door; it probably caused more embarrassment than pain.

*Slight* means . . .   a. not serious or       b. very unusual     c. surprising
                         important

10. **struggle**
/ˈstrʌgəl/
-verb

- Tyler had to **struggle** for a while after he lost his job. It took about six months before he found another.
- Fatima **struggled** to complete all her work before going on vacation; there was truly a lot to do.

*Struggle* means . . .   a. to deal with      b. to relax        c. to rest
                          a difficult situation

## WORDS AND DEFINITIONS

*Match each key word with its definition.*

1. _____limb_____ a large arm of a tree (a branch)

2. _____ to make a connection in your mind between one thing or person and another

3. _____ a play for the theater, television, radio, etc., usually a serious one

4. _____ to try very hard to deal with a difficult situation

5. _____ not serious or important

6. _____ the state of not being present, of being away from a place

7. _____ to officially suggest that something be done

8. _____ to move a part of your body so that it is no longer straight or so that you are no longer standing upright

9. _____ very sure that something is right or true

10. _____ to disagree strongly with an idea or action

# COMPREHENSION CHECK

*Choose the best answer.*

1. I would **oppose** your plan if
   a. I thought it was very good.
   b. it had everyone's support.
   c. I thought it might bring more harm than help.
   d. it addressed everyone's needs.

2. I **struggled** to open the door because
   a. I had the right key.
   b. the door wasn't locked.
   c. my brother answered when I knocked.
   d. I was holding heavy bags in each hand.

3. What is NOT normally **associated** with winter in Canada?
   a. skiing
   b. sandy beaches
   c. snowstorms
   d. New Year's Eve

4. If I am **positive** about my test answer, I'll
   a. expect the teacher to mark it as correct.
   b. consider changing it.
   c. leave the question blank and move on to the next one.
   d. raise my hand and ask the teacher to explain the question more clearly.

5. Yesterday a friend and I saw a **drama**, and
   a. I enjoyed every painting in the museum.
   b. I will recommend the play to other friends.
   c. I decided to make a copy of the song.
   d. we decided to eat there tonight.

6. When Elias **proposed** a trip to Hawaii,
   a. his wife Sofie happily agreed.
   b. his wife Sofie angrily shouted back at him.
   c. he called his wife Sofie every day while he was gone.
   d. he took a direct flight from Los Angeles to Honolulu.

7. Ayoko has a **slight** accent;
   a. it causes frequent problems with communication.
   b. many people don't even notice it.
   c. she finds it difficult to pronounce many of the sounds in English.
   d. most people know as soon as she speaks that English is a second language for her.

8. All of the following items might hang from a **limb** EXCEPT
   a. a monkey.
   b. a rope to swing on.
   c. fruit.
   d. a picture.

9. You would probably **bend** to do all of the following EXCEPT to
   a. put on sunglasses.
   b. tie your shoe.
   c. pick up a box on the floor.
   d. pet a small dog.

10. You're going on vacation, and before your **absence** from home
    a. you get a good suntan.
    b. you ask your neighbor to collect your mail.
    c. your neighbor comes to visit you.
    d. you work extra hours at the office.

## WORD FAMILIES

Now that you have studied the ten key words and their basic definitions, you are ready to learn words that belong to the same family as some of the key words. A word family includes words that look alike but have different functions (noun, verb, adjective, or adverb). Their meanings are related but different.

**A.** *Look at each model phrase and decide whether the word in* **bold** *is used as a noun, verb, adjective, or adverb.*

|  | NOUN | VERB | ADJECTIVE | ADVERB |
|---|---|---|---|---|
| 1. **absence** | | | | |
| • during my **absence** | ✓ | | | |
| • be **absent** from work | | | ✓ | |
| 2. **bend** | | | | |
| • **bend** your knees | | | | |
| • a **bend** in the river | | | | |
| 3. **drama** | | | | |
| • watch a **drama** | | | | |
| • a **dramatic** ending | | | | |
| 4. **oppose** | | | | |
| • **oppose** an idea | | | | |
| • be completely **opposite** | | | | |
| 5. **slight** | | | | |
| • a **slight** misunderstanding | | | | |
| • move **slightly** closer | | | | |
| 6. **struggle** | | | | |
| • **struggle** alone | | | | |
| • his **struggle** with cancer | | | | |

**B.** *Read the first half of each sentence and match it with the appropriate ending.*

__e__ 1. Frederic and Maria had been arguing. Frederic slammed the door, making a

_____ 2. Are you all right? Your face looks

_____ 3. When you miss a lesson, it's often hard to understand what's going on when your return. Unlike a lot of my classmates, I don't like being

_____ 4. The family had arrived in the country with little money, but they were able to create a successful business and a new life after a

_____ 5. I knew my sister was still angry with me because when I saw her at school she turned and ran in the

_____ 6. We'll see the house after the next

a. **slightly** pale.

b. long **struggle**.

c. **opposite** direction.

d. **bend** in the road.

e. **dramatic** exit.

f. **absent** from school.

# SAME WORD, DIFFERENT MEANING

Most words have more than one meaning. Study the additional meanings of **limb**, **slight**, and **struggle**. Then read each sentence and decide which meaning is used.

| | | |
|---|---|---|
| a. **limb** *n.* | a large arm of a tree (a branch) | |
| b. **limb** *n.* | an arm or leg | |
| c. **slight** *adj.* | not serious or important | |
| d. **slight** *adj.* | thin and delicate | |
| e. **struggle** *n.* | a difficult problem that lasts for a long period of time | |
| f. **struggle** *n.* | a fight between two people for something | |

__c__ 1. Claude had a **slight** fever yesterday. Today he seems to be completely back to normal.

_____ 2. Most female dancers are **slight** in build. It's rare to see a heavy woman dancing on stage.

_____ 3. Working with children for so many years, the nurse had seen everything, from a cut on the finger to broken **limbs**.

_____ 4. Travis went through quite a **struggle** to rebuild his business after the fire.

_____ 5. The storm had knocked down several **limbs** and many smaller branches.

_____ 6. If you are ever robbed on the street, avoid a **struggle**. Nothing you have is so important that you need to fight a dangerous criminal.

# WORDS IN SENTENCES

Complete each sentence with one of the words from the box.

| | | | | |
|---|---|---|---|---|
| absent | bend | limbs | positive | slightly |
| associate | ~~dramatic~~ | opposite | proposed | struggle |

1. The sound of trumpets and the long red carpet made a(n) _____dramatic_____ entrance for the king.

2. I _____ gifts of chocolates and flowers with Valentine's Day.

3. After the long plane ride, Ben stood up to stretch his _____.

4. The fans of the losing team started a fight after the game. Police stopped the _____.

5. Young Micha learned to _____ his knees to keep his balance on the skateboard.

6. I was only _____ embarrassed when my classmate had to remind me who she was. After all, we hadn't seen each other for ten years!

7. The director _____ a new rule for taking sick days. Everyone agreed that it was fair.

8. Let's buy this DVD for Tim's birthday. I'm _____ he'll like it.

9. *Detest* doesn't mean "to love." In fact, it has the _____ meaning.

10. Our teacher, Mrs. Adams, got sick and was _____ for one week. In her place, another teacher covered the next unit in the book.

# WORDS IN COLLOCATIONS AND EXPRESSIONS

*Following are common collocations (word partners) and expressions with some of the key words. Read the definitions and then complete the conversations with the correct form of the collocations and expressions.*

1. **absence**
   - **absence from (sth)**      the state of being away from a place
2. **associate**
   - **associate with (sb/sth)**   to make a connection in your mind between one person or thing and another
3. **bend**
   - **bend down**      to move so that you are no longer standing upright
4. **propose**
   - **propose that**      to officially suggest that something be done
5. **struggle**
   - **struggle to (do sth)**      to try very hard to do something difficult
   - **a power struggle**      a situation in which groups or leaders try to defeat each other and get complete control

1. MOTHER:   After lunch, let's go to Grandma's. She can probably use some help around the house.

   SON:   Is her back hurting again?

   MOTHER:   Yes. She said it hurts even to _____ **bend down** _____ to pick up the cat.

2. LANDLORD:   The elevator should be fixed by the end of this week.

   MS. CASSIDY:   Not earlier? For more than a week already we've all had to _____ climb the stairs. I'm on the fifth floor; I can't imagine how difficult it's been for those on the tenth floor.

3. DIRECTOR:   I _____ Friday be a casual dress day.

   WORKERS:   Great idea!

4. STUDENT:   Why did this particular law take so much time to get passed?

   PROFESSOR:   The question of whether to pass the law caused much argument. Each political party wanted to win on this issue; it became _____.

5. KATE:   There were fireworks at Elisha's wedding?!

   TIA:   Does that seem strange to you?

   KATE:   Well, I think most people in America _____ fireworks _____ the Fourth of July. It's a little odd to have them at a wedding.

6. WORKER 1:   Did I miss anything important at the meeting today?

   WORKER 2:   Not really, but your _____ the meeting was noticed. I think you need to explain what happened to the manager.

# WORDS IN A READING

*Read this article about sumo wrestling. Complete it with words and expressions from the boxes.*

| absence from | ~~associate with~~ | opposite | positive | propose that |
|---|---|---|---|---|

### SUMO IS SPREADING AROUND THE WORLD

Many people naturally _____*associate*_____ sumo wrestling _____*with*_____ Japan, but these
[1]
days the sport is making its way around the world, from Poland to Brazil. What's more, the grand
champion of Japan is actually from Mongolia.

After a twenty-year _____ the United States, the sport recently returned via a Las
[2]
Vegas tournament. New York was next in line to welcome the sport when it became the location of the
first North American tour of international sumo. Wrestlers from _____ ends of the globe
[3]
met one another in the sumo ring; they came from as far away as Norway and Georgia. The event was
held by the Sumo Ultimate Masters Organization (SUMO), which is based in the United States but
hopes to grow on the international level.

Organizers of SUMO are _____ that the sport has a bright future to go along with its
[4]
rich past. In fact, they_____ the old and the new be mixed to attract more spectators.
[5]

| bend | dramatic | limb | slight | struggle |
|---|---|---|---|---|

For example, they plan to keep the traditional prefight greeting (where the two wrestlers must
_____ their knees deeply and sit back on their heels as they face each other) and add
[6]
new practices like use of a theme song. Acrobatics might even be included to increase the
_____ effect.
[7]

Those may all be steps to make the sport more like entertainment, but the fights themselves will
remain real. Though each match lasts less than a minute, there are seventy moves to choose from. The
wrestlers use their knowledge of these moves as _____ comes against limb and one man
[8]
is thrown out of the ring. When a sport involves such a powerful _____, one might
[9]
assume that size is everything. After all, many people associate sumo with heavy men. But according to
Hawaiian-born Kaleo, a former champion in Japan's pro league and now a wrestler in SUMO, technique
matters more than weight. American wrestler Kena Heffernan would agree. Heffernan, a graduate of
Yale University and a math teacher, is catching the attention of many despite his "_____"
[10]
build, which—as the U.S. team coach, Yoshisade Yhoezuka, says—is "only 260 pounds."

Sumo may have started as an ancient religious practice in Japan, but today it has become part of
the modern world of international sports.

*(Based on information in Jeninne Lee-St. John, "Are You Ready for a Sumo Smackdown?" Time Magazine online, October 24, 2005.)*

## WORDS IN DISCUSSION

*Apply the key words to your own life. Read and discuss each question in small groups. Try to use the key words.*

1. What do you **associate with** New Year's Eve?

   **EXAMPLE**

   *New Year's Eve makes me think of family dinners with traditional dishes. I also **associate** fireworks **with** this holiday because every city in my country has them on December 31.*

2. Name a good reason (other than being sick) for a student's **absence from** class.

3. What's your favorite **drama** (either on screen or on stage)?

4. Do you always **bend down** to tie your shoes, or do you ever lift your foot up?

5. Does forgetting someone's name make you **slightly** embarrassed? When was the last time this happened?

6. Name as many words as you can that have the **opposite** meaning of *good*.

7. What changes would you **propose** to your school or workplace?

8. Name a common way a person can break a **limb**.

9. Do you know how to ride a bike? Was it a **struggle** to learn?

10. Are you **positive** that you understand all the words in this chapter?

## WORDS IN WRITING

*Choose two topics and write a short paragraph on each. Try to use the key words.*

1. Describe a decision you **struggled to** make.

   **EXAMPLE**

   *It wasn't easy to leave my country. I thought about it for at least a year. I didn't want to **struggle** all my life, and the job I had didn't pay well. It hasn't been easy here either, but that's okay. I'm **positive** it will get easier.*

2. Have you ever strongly **opposed** the opinions of someone you love? Explain.

3. What was the longest period of time you were **absent** from school? What happened?

4. Describe a time when you were **positive** that you were correct about something only to find out that you were wrong? Did you admit your mistake?

5. Have you ever entered a contest or competition knowing that you had only a **slight** chance of winning? Explain.

**CHAPTER 17**

**Key Words**

| behave | expert | investigate | migrate | roar |
|--------|--------|-------------|---------|------|
| excessive | fierce | joint | outcome | track |

## WORDS IN CONTEXT

*Use the sentences to guess what each key word means. Choose the meaning that is closest to that of the key word in **bold**.*

**1. behave**
/bɪˈheɪv/
-verb

- Scientists watch animals to see how they **behave** in the wild; wild animals live very differently from pet animals.
- Alfonso **behaves** in a different way when he is at school with friends than when he's at home with his parents.

*Behave* means . . .
- (a.) to do things in a particular way
- b. to live naturally
- c. to speak

**2. excessive**
/ɪkˈsɛsɪv/
-adjective

- Oliver has problems at work because of his **excessive** drinking.
- It's a nice restaurant, but the amount of food they serve is really **excessive**. I can't eat all that food.

*Excessive* means . . .
- a. a good amount
- b. not enough
- c. much more than is necessary

**3. expert**
/ˈɛkspɚt/
-noun

- Mandy, who has ten children, is an **expert** at taking care of babies.
- An **expert** on ancient Peruvian art will accompany our group during our visit to Peru.

*Expert* means . . .
- a. a person with special skills or knowledge
- b. an average person
- c. a person who enjoys one activity

**4. fierce**
/fɪrs/
-adjective

- The wrestler got nervous when he saw how **fierce** his opponent looked.
- Josie's umbrella was destroyed by the **fierce** wind.

*Fierce* means . . .
- a. strong and violent
- b. gentle
- c. light

**5. investigate**
/ɪnˈvɛstəˌgeɪt/
-verb

- The police **investigated** the crime, trying to discover who committed the murder.
- Before buying an apartment, the Parks **investigated** the history of the building.

*Investigate* means . . .
- a. to visit
- b. to not pay attention
- c. to study carefully

**6. joint**
/dʒɔɪnt/
-adjective

- I am working on a **joint** project with Patrick; he is researching baby lions and I am researching mother lions.
- Walter, Daphne, and I made a **joint** decision to share the money.

*Joint* means . . .
- a. separate
- b. involving two or more people
- c. individual

7. **migrate**
/ˈmaɪɡreɪt/
-verb

- Every spring, young salmon fish **migrate** from the rivers to the ocean.
- Many birds **migrate** in the fall and spring; for example, yellow warblers spend the winter in Brazil and then **migrate** to southern California by April 1.

*Migrate* means . . .
a. to move with the seasons
b. to fly
c. to stay in the same place

8. **outcome**
/ˈaʊtkʌm/
-noun

- After my aunt Sara voted for a new prime minister, she kept her radio on all evening, waiting to hear the **outcome** of the election.
- We hope that a peaceful agreement will be the **outcome** of the meeting.

*Outcome* means . . .
a. the final result
b. beginning
c. discussion

9. **roar**
/rɔr/
-verb

- When walking alone in the woods, you do not want to hear a hungry bear **roar**.
- During the storm, the ocean **roared** like an angry animal, making us cover our ears with our hands.

*Roar* means . . .
a. to whisper
b. to speak in a normal voice
c. to make a deep, very loud noise

10. **track**
/ˈtræk/
-noun

- When we were children, we walked so many times from the house to the stream that our footprints created a **track** in the field.
- The campers found their way through the forest by following a **track** made by some large animals, probably deer.

*Track* means . . .
a. a natural place
b. a path
c. a home

## ▍WORDS AND DEFINITIONS

*Match each key word with its definition.*

1. _____*fierce*_____ strong and violent

2. _____ much more than is reasonable or necessary

3. _____ to make a deep, very loud noise

4. _____ someone with special skills or knowledge of a subject gained as a result of training or experience

5. _____ the final result

6. _____ involving two or more people, or owned or shared by them

7. _____ to move to another part of the world with the seasons

8. _____ to study carefully in order to find the truth

9. _____ to do or say things in a particular way

10. _____ a narrow path or road with a rough uneven surface, especially one made by people or animals

# COMPREHENSION CHECK

*Choose the best answer.*

1. If Xavier is an **expert** in astronomy, he
   a. knows nothing about planets.
   b. knows a lot about space.
   c. does not know the phases of the moon.
   d. knows the names of a few constellations of stars.

2. Which of the following CANNOT be **fierce**?
   a. a lion
   b. the wind
   c. a warrior
   d. a butterfly

3. Which sentence is about someone **migrating**?
   a. Lucy has always lived in Phoenix, Arizona.
   b. Joe, a farm worker, moves to California every spring to pick fruit.
   c. Brian is moving to Miami next year.
   d. Rebecca wants to visit Maine.

4. Which of the following things does NOT **roar**?
   a. an airplane when it takes off
   b. an angry bear
   c. a lake
   d. the wind on a stormy night

5. How does a baby probably **behave** if he is very hungry?
   a. The baby smiles.
   b. The baby sleeps.
   c. The baby laughs.
   d. The baby cries.

6. Which action is an example of something **excessive**?
   a. Mike ate a sandwich for lunch.
   b. Sasha ordered six pizzas for three people.
   c. Jan bought a simple coat.
   d. Emir gave a balloon to the children.

7. Howard drank too many cups of coffee. What is the **outcome**?
   a. He can't sleep.
   b. He wanted to stay awake.
   c. He needed to write his paper.
   d. He is sleeping well.

8. What word does NOT describe a **track**?
   a. path
   b. rough
   c. tall
   d. narrow

9. If Max is **investigating** a burglary at the Linwood Hotel, what is he doing?
   a. He's enjoying lunch in the hotel restaurant.
   b. He's checking into a room.
   c. He's carefully examining the room where the burglary took place.
   d. He's not interested in the hotel.

10. Which sentence describes a **joint** decision?
    a. Melissa's father tells her to study architecture.
    b. Mellissa decides to study French.
    c. No one knows what Melissa should study.
    d. Melissa and her father decide that she should study law.

## WORD FAMILIES

Now that you have studied the ten key words and their basic definitions, you are ready to learn words that belong to the same family as some of the key words. A word family includes words that look alike but have different functions (noun, verb, adjective, or adverb). Their meanings are related but different.

**A.** *Look at each model phrase and decide whether the word in **bold** is used as a noun, verb, adjective, or adverb.*

| | NOUN | VERB | ADJECTIVE | ADVERB |
|---|---|---|---|---|
| **1. behave** | | | | |
| • **behave** strangely | | ✓ | | |
| • the **behavior** of tigers | ✓ | | | |
| **2. excessive** | | | | |
| • **excessive** force | | | | |
| • **excessively** strict | | | | |
| • an **excess** of information | | | | |
| **3. fierce** | | | | |
| • a **fierce** soccer player | | | | |
| • **fiercely** cold | | | | |
| **4. investigate** | | | | |
| • **investigate** a crime | | | | |
| • a thorough **investigation** | | | | |
| **5. migrate** | | | | |
| • **migrate** every spring | | | | |
| • the spring **migration** | | | | |
| **6. roar** | | | | |
| • The lions **roared**. | | | | |
| • the **roar** of a helicopter | | | | |

**B.** *Read the first half of each sentence and match it with the appropriate ending.*

__d__ 1. When TJ got angry, he yelled

_____ 2. Because Emma cleans for five hours a day, we think she's

_____ 3. Jorge has six pets, so he knows a lot about animal

_____ 4. For my research paper, I'm going to do a(n)

_____ 5. If you want to save money, you should avoid

_____ 6. For many birds, fall is a time for

_____ 7. We knew we were near the waterfall when we heard the

a. **behavior**.

b. **excess** spending.

c. **migration**.

d. **fiercely**.

e. **roar** of falling water.

f. **investigation** of dishonesty in the media.

g. **excessively** neat.

# SAME WORD, DIFFERENT MEANING

*Most words have more than one meaning. Study the additional meanings of **behave**, **joint**, and **track**. Then read each sentence and decide which meaning is used.*

| | | |
|---|---|---|
| a. **behave** *v.* | to do or say things in a particular way |
| b. **behave** *v.* | to be polite and not cause trouble |
| c. **joint** *adj.* | involving two or more people, or owned or shared by them |
| d. **joint** *n.* | a part of the body where two bones connect |
| e. **track** *n.* | a narrow path or road with a rough, uneven surface, especially one made by people or animals |
| f. **track** *v.* | to search for or follow the movements of a person, animal, airplane, or ship |

__c__ 1. Donald and Maria made a **joint** decision to move to Spain.

_____ 2. When you were a child, did your parents tell you to **behave** when you went to a party?

_____ 3. A deer walked along the **track** through the forest.

_____ 4. My grandmother has arthritis—all her **joints**, especially her knees, hurt.

_____ 5. The rescue team **tracked** the lost boys by following their footprints through the forest.

_____ 6. When she is at home, Irene is relaxed, but when she is at the office, she **behaves** differently; she is very professional there.

# WORDS IN SENTENCES

*Complete each sentence with one of the words from the box.*

| | | | | |
|---|---|---|---|---|
| behave | expert | investigation | migrate | roar |
| ~~excessive~~ | fierce | joint | outcome | track |

1. Bo tried to curb his friends' _____excessive_____ enthusiasm.

2. My music professor is a(n) _____ at composing music.

3. Air traffic controllers _____ airplanes in the sky.

4. For her zoology project, Midori will do a(n) _____ into the lives of young gorillas.

5. The _____ of a lion will scare his rival.

6. Because of the _____ wind, it is dangerous to stand close to the edge of the cliff.

7. When Cleopatra, Queen of Egypt, discovered that the _____ of her army's defeat would be the fall of her country to the Roman Empire, she killed herself.

8. Asha is usually a very polite five-year-old girl, but when she visited her cousins, she didn't _____; in fact, she threw mud at them!

9. Every fall, Canadian geese _____ from Canada to Mexico.

10. When asked to show an example of a(n) _____ in the human body, Ally pointed to her hip.

# WORDS IN COLLOCATIONS AND EXPRESSIONS

*Following are common collocations (word partners) and expressions with some of the key words. Read the definitions and then complete the conversations with the correct form of the collocations and expressions.*

1. **behave**
   - **behave yourself**            be polite and don't cause trouble
2. **joint**
   - **a joint effort**            something done together
3. **outcome**
   - **outcome of (sth)**            the final result of something
4. **track**
   - **be on the right/wrong track**    to think in a way that is likely to lead to a correct or incorrect result
   - **railroad tracks**            the two metal lines that a train travels on
   - **race track**            a circular road around which people, cars, horses, etc. race

1. GUEST: Who made this delicious soup?

   MING: My sister and I made it together. It was _____*a joint effort*_____.

2. LITTLE BOY: Mommy, I'm bored!

   MOTHER: Sshhh. You can't talk during the movie, honey. People will get upset.

   LITTLE BOY: But it's so boring!

   MOTHER: Sssshh! _____.

3. DRIVER 1: Do you want to race me to see who's faster?

   DRIVER 2: Okay. Meet me at the _____ in half an hour.

4. TEACHER: In the 1860s, the first transcontinental railroad was built in the U.S. Suddenly _____ connected the East Coast of the United States with California. What was the _____ this project?

   MINGMEI: Many people were able to move to the West Coast, so the cities there grew quickly.

5. SANDRA: In my essay, I'm going to prove that Shakespeare was a bad playwright.

   PROFESSOR: What? I'm sorry, but I think you are _____. Have you read much of Shakespeare's work?

   SANDRA: Only the first three pages of *Hamlet*.

   PROFESSOR: Please read more. When you have a better idea, come talk to me again. Then, when you are _____, you can start writing your essay.

*Read this article about wildlife. Complete it with words and expressions from the boxes.*

| behavior | fierce | ~~investigating~~ | migration | track |
|----------|--------|-------------------|-----------|-------|

### STUDENTS GET POLAR BEAR CYBER VISIT

A couple of polar bears relaxed on the snow-covered ground near Churchill, Manitoba, on Friday. Occasionally, they would get up and walk over to the camera, sending live images of them about 2,000 miles south to Homestead High School.

There, about 150 students were participating in a teleconference with Homestead teacher Doug Waldman and two polar bear experts sitting behind the camera, just feet from the giant bears.

Talking to his class from a video screen, Waldman explained that he and his companions were __investigating__ the polar bears' _____ from inside a "tundra buggy"—a large vehicle specially equipped to _____ the polar bears' _____ into Churchill. This vehicle would also protect them if the polar bears suddenly became _____ and attacked.

| excessively | experts | joint | outcome of | roaring |
|-------------|---------|-------|------------|---------|

Waldman is somewhat of an expert on bears now, but knew little about polar bears before his trip. He spent a week watching the polar bears migrate into Churchill and wanted to share the experience with his students. Computers made the _____ observation possible.

The students asked their teacher and the _____—Steve Amstrup, a polar bear researcher from the Alaska Science Center, and Don Moore of the Wildlife Conservation Society—about the bears, their habitat, and the effects of global warming on the bears.

One of the researcher's key goals was to see how the bears respond to changes in the sea ice. Polar bears need the ice to get to their food: seals and other marine life. And in recent years, ice on the Hudson Bay near Churchill has receded because of global warming. _____ high temperatures have changed the amount of ice on the water and thus the life of the polar bears.

Friday, Waldman said it was thirty-two degrees in Churchill, warm for this time of year. While the polar bears waited for the ice to form, they did not voice their impatience by _____. Instead, they relaxed and occasionally dug around for something—anything—to eat.

What was the _____ this experience for the students in Waldman's advanced ecology class? They learned a lot about global warming and migration from the videoconference. Some students also developed a fondness for the bears.

"It tempted me to ask my mom for a polar bear," one girl said. "I want to pet it."

*(Based on information in Krista J. Stockman, "Homestead Gets Polar Bear Cyber Visit." The Journal Gazette online, November 5, 2005.)*

## WORDS IN DISCUSSION

*Apply the key words to your own life. Complete the questionnaire. Then discuss your answers with a classmate. Try to use the key words.*

**EXAMPLE**

An **expert** whom I would love to meet: _____ *Tiger Woods* _____

**A:** *I'd like to meet Tiger Woods because he could give me **expert** advice about improving my golf skills.*

**B:** *Golf bores me. I'd rather meet a five star-chef who could teach me how to cook.*

1. The **outcome** of my studies if I study hard: _____

2. A **fierce** animal that I do not want to meet: _____

3. Something I am an **expert** at: _____

4. Something in nature or in a city that I have heard **roar**: _____

5. The person who makes me **behave** in a silly way: _____

6. A topic that I would like to **investigate**: _____

7. An animal I have seen **migrating**: _____

8. A course I took for which I had **excessive** homework: _____

9. How I would feel about having a **joint** bank account with my brother/sister: _____

10. How I would feel if I were running on a race **track** in the Olympic Games: _____

## WORDS IN WRITING

*Choose two topics and write a short paragraph on each. Try to use the key words.*

1. Do you believe that there is an **excessive** amount of violence shown on television? Explain why or why not.

**EXAMPLE**

*Car chases, murders, and fights are a normal part of nightly TV. While I understand that many people find this kind of action exciting, I think it's **excessively** violent. I think this **excessive** amount of violence on television is especially dangerous for children.*

2. Do you think that reporters should **investigate** the private lives of politicians? Explain why you think such **investigations** are useful or harmful.

3. Describe a person or an animal who looks **fierce**.

4. Some people **migrate**, moving to a new country to work for a season and then returning home. Other people **immigrate**, moving to a new country forever. Explain which you would prefer to do.

5. What are you an **expert** at? How did you become an **expert** at this?

**Key Words**

| consist | exclude | govern | license | poverty |
|---------|---------|--------|---------|---------|
| define | formula | imitate | nest | tend |

## ▌WORDS IN CONTEXT

*Use the sentences to guess what each key word means. Choose the meaning that is closest to that of the key word in **bold**.*

**1. consist**
/kən'sɪst/
-verb

- Our class **consists** of students from nine different countries. We are a very international group.
- My brother has a large collection of DVDs, but it mainly **consists** of action films, so I don't often ask to borrow any. I prefer romantic comedies.

*Consist means . . .*   a. to gather      b. to organize      c. to be made of

**2. define**
/dɪ'faɪn/
-verb

- I **define** happiness as not wanting more than what you have.
- The teacher asked me to **define** the word for the class, so I tried to think of some similar words to explain its meaning.

*Define means . . .*   a. to explain the meaning  b. to use      c. to remember

**3. exclude**
/ɪk'sklud/
- verb

- I remember how mad I got when my older brothers created a club and **excluded** all girls. The next day my friend and I started a club for girls only.
- Before the 1960s, many blacks were **excluded** from voting in the U.S.

*Exclude means . . .*   a. to invite      b. to not allow      c. to not understand

**4. formula**
/'fɔrmyələ/
-noun

- The audience listened to the entrepreneur and hoped to learn how he made his money. Would he share his **formula**?
- I've always used the same **formula** when learning something new: listen and watch carefully, ask lots of questions, review independently, and practice.

*Formula means . . .*   a. a history      b. a method      c. an attitude

**5. govern**
/'gʌvɚn/
-verb

- Which political party currently **governs** your country?
- Clint Eastwood and Ronald Reagan are examples of actors who later **governed** people from different political offices, from mayor to president.

*Govern means . . .*   a. to control      b. to excite      c. to instruct

**6. imitate**
/'ɪmə,teɪt/
- verb

- The little girl watched her mother drink tea at the breakfast table and **imitated** her. She tried to follow every move, hoping she, too, looked like a lady.
- My husband loves to sing loudly in the shower. He **imitates** popular singers. It's funny to listen to, and he's quite good.

*Imitate means . . .*   a. to look closely      b. to copy      c. to like very much

7. **license**
/ˈlaɪsəns/
-noun

- By law one must have a **license** to own a gun.
- My father helped me learn to drive. We practiced for several months before I took the test and got my driver's **license**.

*License* means . . .  a. an official document  b. an amount of money  c. instruction
that permits something

8. **nest**
/nɛst/
-noun

- The mother bird brought food back to the **nest** for her babies.
- We were excited to find the eagle's **nest**. It was located up high in a tree.

*Nest* means . . .  a. a bird's egg  b. a bird's home  c. the flight of a bird

9. **poverty**
/ˈpavərti/
-noun

- Sadly, people in **poverty** not only live with little money but also must often do without a good education.
- Mick grew up in **poverty** but later became a successful businessman.

*Poverty* means . . .  a. the state of being sick  b. sadness  c. the state of being poor

10. **tend**
/tɛnd/
- verb

- You might want an extra blanket. It **tends** to get cool in our house at night.
- Lara **tends** to laugh when she's nervous, so I understood her need to joke before our big exam.

*Tend* means . . .  a. to usually do  b. to stop from doing  c. to do suddenly

## WORDS AND DEFINITIONS

*Match each key word with its definition.*

1. ____exclude____ to not allow someone to enter a place, or to do something

2. _____ to officially control a country, state, etc. and make all the decisions about things such as taxes and laws

3. _____ a place made or chosen by a bird to lay its eggs in and live in

4. _____ a method that you use to solve a problem or to make sure that something is successful

5. _____ an official document that gives you permission to own or do something

6. _____ to explain the exact meaning of a particular word or idea

7. _____ the situation or experience of being poor

8. _____ to be likely to do a particular thing

9. _____ to be made of or contain a number of different things

10. _____ to copy the way someone else does something

*Choose the best answer.*

1. All of the following things can be **governed** EXCEPT
   a. a country.
   b. a state.
   (c.) a meeting.
   d. a city.

2. All of the following principles could be considered a **formula** for success EXCEPT
   a. Understand what you want and try your best to get it.
   b. Keep good relationships with everyone and ask for help when you need it.
   c. Don't be afraid to take chances and know that sometimes you'll lose.
   d. Give up when a situation gets difficult and don't show interest in new things.

3. Which of the following activities does NOT require a **license**?
   a. cooking food at home
   b. driving a city bus
   c. working as a doctor in a hospital
   d. practicing law as a lawyer

4. A song **consists** of
   a. words and music.
   b. a record, cassette, or CD.
   c. a radio station.
   d. a musical instrument.

5. If a family lives in **poverty**,
   a. they probably eat well at every meal.
   b. they can easily buy two cars.
   c. they might take the children and travel to different countries.
   d. they would likely have trouble paying a doctor's bill.

6. Why might Natalya **imitate** her mother's way of dressing?
   a. Natalya considers her mother's taste in clothes to be poor.
   b. Natalya considers her mother to be very stylish.
   c. Natalya has created her own style.
   d. Natalya wants to go shopping.

7. Linda **tends** to lie, so
   a. don't believe everything she says.
   b. you can trust her.
   c. her information is always correct.
   d. you never have to check her information with others.

8. If you want to know how to **define** a word, you
   a. want to know how to spell it.
   b. want to hear the correct pronunciation.
   c. want to know what it means and how it's used.
   d. are able to use it in a sentence.

9. All of the following statements are true EXCEPT
   a. Many **nests** are in trees.
   b. Some **nests** are underwater.
   c. Birds keep eggs in **nests**.
   d. Some **nests** are not built but found.

10. If an organization chooses to **exclude** a lot of people, then
    a. everyone is welcome.
    b. it's easy to join.
    c. not everyone can become a member.
    d. it considers all people equal.

# WORD FAMILIES

Now that you have studied the ten key words and their basic definitions, you are ready to learn words that belong to the same family as some of the key words. A word family includes words that look alike but have different functions (noun, verb, adjective, or adverb). Their meanings are related but different.

**A.** *Look at each model phrase and decide whether the word in **bold** is used as a noun, verb, adjective, or adverb.*

|  | NOUN | VERB | ADJECTIVE | ADVERB |
|---|:---:|:---:|:---:|:---:|
| **1. define** | | | | |
| • **define** happiness | | ✓ | | |
| • search for a **definition** | ✓ | | | |
| **2. exclude** | | | | |
| • **exclude** certain people | | | | |
| • an **exclusive** hotel | | | | |
| **3. formula** | | | | |
| • a **formula** for happiness | | | | |
| • **formulate** new rules | | | | |
| **4. govern** | | | | |
| • to **govern** a country | | | | |
| • work for the **government** | | | | |
| • elected a new **governor** | | | | |
| **5. imitate** | | | | |
| • **imitate** someone famous | | | | |
| • a careful **imitation** | | | | |

**B.** *Read the first half of each sentence and match it with the appropriate ending.*

__d__ 1. I didn't know the meaning of the word *current,* so I looked it up in the dictionary; I was surprised to find

_____ 2. While I understand and think it's sweet of my little sister to want to be like me, her constant

_____ 3. A new speed limit will be introduced in our state by

_____ 4. The director gave me the job of organizing the move to our new office;

_____ 5. The President, the Senate, the House of Representatives, and the Supreme Court are equally important parts of

_____ 6. They invited us to have dinner with them at

a. lawmakers and supported by the **governor**.

b. I **formulated** a plan and shared it with my co-workers.

c. **imitation** of the way I dress and talk can be annoying.

d. three different **definitions**.

e. the United States **government**.

f. an **exclusive** restaurant in Palm Beach; only people with a lot of money and social status can eat there.

## SAME WORD, DIFFERENT MEANING

Most words have more than one meaning. Study the additional meanings of **exclude**, **govern**, and **tend**. Then read each sentence and decide which meaning is used.

| | | |
|---|---|---|
| a. **exclude** *v.* | to not allow someone to enter a place or to do something |
| b. **exclude** *v.* | to intentionally not include something |
| c. **govern** *v.* | to officially control a country, state, etc. and make all the decisions about things such as taxes and laws |
| d. **govern** *v.* | to control the way a system or situation works |
| e. **tend** *v.* | to be likely to do a particular thing |
| f. **tend** *v.* | to take care of someone or something |

___f___ 1. My aunt asked me to **tend** the store while she ran to the bank.

_____ 2. The children were thoughtful enough not to **exclude** the new student from their games on the playground at lunchtime.

_____ 3. It must be difficult to be a king or a queen; many rules **govern** your life, from how to dress to whom you must marry.

_____ 4. People of the Jewish and Islamic religions **exclude** pork from their diet.

_____ 5. I don't like to read books by that author. His stories **tend** to be a little too unrealistic.

_____ 6. The mayor **governed** the city for seven years.

## WORDS IN SENTENCES

Complete each sentence with one of the words from the box.

| | | | | |
|---|---|---|---|---|
| consisted | exclusive | government | license | poverty |
| definition | ~~formulated~~ | imitation | nest | tend |

1. The children carefully _____formulated_____ the rules for their game.

2. An army general, a mayor, and a mail carrier all work for the _____.

3. Experience has taught me the true _____ of "friend": someone who knows both good things and bad things about you and accepts you as you are.

4. That's a very _____ hotel. Not many can afford to stay there.

5. The teacher's _____ of a game show host made us laugh. Every time we answered a question correctly, he told us what we had won.

6. I wear socks to bed because my feet _____ to get cold.

7. The main streets of the city were alive with business and entertainment, but farther out from the center were families living in _____, and the dirty sidewalks and small homes there made a sad contrast.

8. What are you doing behind the wheel of a car?! Do you even have a driver's _____?

9. We found a robin's egg on the ground. It must have fallen from the _____ we saw in the tree above us.

10. I laughed when I saw Gretchen's costume for the party: it _____ of a metal ring above her head and a shower curtain hanging down from it.

## WORDS IN COLLOCATIONS AND EXPRESSIONS

*Following are common collocations (word partners) and expressions with some of the key words. Read the definitions and then complete the conversations with the correct form of the collocations and expressions.*

| | | |
|---|---|---|
| 1. **consist** | | |
| | • **consist of (sth)** | to be made of or contain a number of different things |
| 2. **exclude** | | |
| | • **exclude (sth) from (sth)** | to not allow someone to enter a place or to do something; to intentionally not include something |
| 3. **formula** | | |
| | • **magic formula for (sth)** | an especially successful method or set of principles that you use to solve a problem or to make sure that something is successful |
| 4. **license** | | |
| | • **apply for a license** | to officially request a document giving permission to do something |
| 5. **nest** | | |
| | • **leave the nest** | to leave you parents' home when you become an adult |
| 6. **tend** | | |
| | • **tend to (do sth)** | to be likely to do a particular thing |

1. FATHER: Did you feed the dog yet?

   SON: Yes.

   FATHER: Did you remember to take out the trash?

   SON: Yes, Dad.

   FATHER: And is your homework done?

   SON: Yes!

   FATHER: Don't get upset. I'm just checking. You \_\_\_\_\_*tend to*\_\_\_\_\_ forget these things.

2. PHYLLIS: Are you and your husband going to go ahead with your plans to open a restaurant?

   GRACE: Yes. In fact, we're going to _____ this month.

3.   SON:      Mom, when Traci comes for dinner, remember not to serve things like cheese, sour cream, or ice cream.

   MOTHER:   Why does she _____ so much _____ her diet?

   SON:      Traci has an allergy to milk.

4.   LIBRARIAN:   How can I help you?

   STUDENT:   This is my first time in a library here in the United States. Can you explain the different parts of the library system? What does it _____?

5.   NANCY:    I hate being in a new school. No one there wants to be friends with me.

   FATHER:   Well, there's no _____ making friends. These kinds of relationships just happen naturally. Give it some time.

6. CHARLOTTE:   Going to college will be so exciting!

   MOTHER:   I'm excited for you, too, honey. But I'll admit I'm also sad that my only child is ready to _____.

## ▌WORDS IN A READING

*Read this article about people who live long and healthy lives. Complete it with words and expressions from the boxes.*

| consists of | excluding...from | license | ~~magic formula for~~ |
|---|---|---|---|

### LIVING LONG, LIVING WELL

Is there a(n) _magic formula for_ a long, healthy life? Ask the experts, people who can share from
<sub>1</sub>

experience, like the super seniors in Loma Linda, California; Okinawa, Japan; or Sardinia, Italy.

We can all learn a lot from people like Marge Jetton, who, upon turning 100, renewed her

California driver's _____ for another five years. Her lifestyle _____ good
$_2$                                                          $_3$

habits that many other centenarians* share: she centers her life around family and friends; she stays

physically and socially active (she walks and lifts weights!); she doesn't smoke; and she eats fruits,

vegetables, and whole grains. But when asked what has really kept her alive and healthy for more than

a century, Marge will tell you it's her faith. As a Seventh Day Adventist,** her strong religious beliefs

guide her every day, from _____ "unclean" meats _____ her diet to doing
$_4$

community work in her town of Loma Linda.

---

*A centenarian *is a person 100 or older.*
**A Seventh Day Adventist *belongs to the Adventist Church—a Christian sect that preaches and practices a message of health.*

| definition | imitate | poverty |
|---|---|---|
| governed | left the nest | tend to |

What else do some super seniors have in common? Interestingly enough, Marge shares a similar childhood with Okinawan-born Ushi Okushima. Both women, now over 100, knew _____ 5 in their early years. In fact, Ushi's diet, which also doesn't include much meat, isn't _____ 6 by religion but is the result of growing up poor. To this day Ushi, like many other older Okinawans, doesn't _____ 7 eat a lot in one sitting. This habit follows the teaching of Confucius: *Hara hachi bu*–"eat until your stomach is eighty percent full."

Marge and Ushi share one more thing: a sense of purpose. Marge does her community work as part of her religion. Similarly, Ushi believes in *ikigai*– "that which makes life worth living," and her *ikigai* is her circle of friends.

Giovanni Sannai of Sardinia, Italy, questions why he's lived past 100, but like Ushi and Marge, he finds purpose and activity close to the home where he and his wife have lived all their lives. Their children _____ 8 long ago, but they all live nearby and are often invited to share a meal with their parents. And Giovanni stays active, taking pleasure in a morning of hard work: milking cows, chopping wood, and tending sheep.

In summary, each one of these three super seniors has his or her own _____ 9 of a healthy lifestyle. It's up to us to choose which one to _____ 10 . Or perhaps you just want to be like Lydia Newton, 112, who believes the best part of the day is when she takes a nap.

(Based on information in Dan Buettner, "The Secrets of Living Longer." National Geographic, November 2005.)

## ▌ WORDS IN DISCUSSION

*Apply the key words to your own life. Read and discuss each question in small groups. Try to use the key words.*

1. What do you **tend to** do when you get nervous?

   **EXAMPLE**

   *When I'm nervous, I **tend to** sneeze. I don't know why this happens.*

2. Do you have a driver's **license**? If you do, when did you get it? If you don't, will you apply for one?

3. Which political party **governs** your country at the present?

4. Name an animal children like to **imitate**.

5. Do you **exclude** anything from your diet?

6. Is **poverty** easily seen in your country? Is it located in big cities or other places?

7. Name a good age for a child to **leave the nest** in your opinion.

8. Is there a **magic formula for** learning a language?

9. Look at your class. Who does it **consist of**? Where is everyone from?

10. What's your **definition** of a good friend?

## WORDS IN WRITING

*Choose two topics and write a short paragraph on each. Try to use the key words.*

1. Do you have a **formula** for a healthy life?

> **EXAMPLE**
>
> *I think I'm quite healthy. I try to eat well, get enough sleep, and exercise. However, my **formula** doesn't necessarily work for everybody. Each person should find his or her own **formula**, use it, and be happy.*

2. Do you know of any **exclusive** places like a hotel or restaurant? Have you ever visited such a place?

3. What does your diet usually **consist of**?

4. Identify the major people or parts of your country's **government**.

5. Have you ever tried to **imitate** another person's style of speaking, dressing, or other behavior? Explain.

# QUIZ 6

## PART A

*Choose the word that best completes each item and write it in the space provided.*

1. Jacques Cousteau was a(n) _____*expert*_____ on the undersea world.
   - a. outcome
   - b. expert
   - c. track
   - d. limb

2. Abby's father couldn't come to her wedding. His _____ saddened her, but she managed to smile brightly.
   - a. struggle
   - b. poverty
   - c. absence
   - d. drama

3. Avery can't seem to stop herself from buying things that she doesn't need and can't really afford; her spending is _____.
   - a. slight
   - b. excessive
   - c. positive
   - d. fierce

4. The police are _____ the cause of the fire; they believe it wasn't an accident.
   - a. investigating
   - b. associating
   - c. defining
   - d. excluding

5. Most early American universities _____ women. That's why women's colleges like Smith and Mount Holyoke opened.
   - a. opposed
   - b. excluded
   - c. struggled
   - d. governed

6. Many people _____ good food and opera with Italy.
   - a. propose
   - b. associate
   - c. define
   - d. exclude

7. Throughout history many warriors have used face paint to look more _____ going into battle.
   - a. slight
   - b. excessive
   - c. positive
   - d. fierce

8. My cat is _____ strangely; usually it acts this way when it's sick, so I'm a bit worried.
   - a. governing
   - b. proposing
   - c. behaving
   - d. struggling

9. The wind was strong, and I _____ to close the door.
   - a. struggled
   - b. roared
   - c. migrated
   - d. tended

10. My father _____ that from now on we have our family dinner at a restaurant on New Year's Eve to save my mother from having to cook.
    - a. governed
    - b. roared
    - c. defined
    - d. proposed

## PART B

*Read each statement and write **T** for true or **F** for false in the space provided.*

___T___ 1. Lions and tigers **roar.**

_____ 2. You can watch a **drama** at the circus.

_____ 3. A person who lives in **poverty** has little money even for basic things.

_____ 4. All scientific research begins with an **outcome.**

_____ 5. Dictionaries **define** words.

_____ 6. Most soups **consist** of broth, or liquid flavored from meat or vegetables.

_____ 7. If I **oppose** your suggestion, I wholly agree with your idea.

_____ 8. Children might try to **imitate** their parents' manners if they admire them and want to be like them.

_____ 9. You need a **license** in order to travel to foreign countries.

_____ 10. If you have a **slight** fever, you should call a doctor immediately.

## PART C

*Complete each item with a word from the box. Use each word once.*

| bend | governed | limb | nest | tends |
|------|----------|------|------|-------|
| formula | joint | ~~migrate~~ | positive | track |

1. When gray whales _____migrate_____, they cover well over 12,000 miles in a single year.

2. The monkey made us laugh when it hung upside down from the tree's longest _____.

3. Bryce and Isidore have _____ ownership of the business.

4. All of Mrs. Wasserman's sons had grown so tall that they had to _____ deeply to hug their mother.

5. U.S. President William Henry Harrison _____ the country for only thirty days in the year of 1841. He was the first President to die in office.

6. The bird busily worked on its _____, adding grass and leaves.

7. The hikers followed the _____ up the mountain.

8. Tiffany is reading a book on how to have a happy career. I told her that no book will give a magic _____ for any kind of happiness; good things come naturally.

9. I'm _____ that I won't need my bike this weekend, so you can borrow it.

10. Alana _____ to bite her nails when she's nervous. It's a bad habit.

## WORDS IN CONTEXT

*Use the sentences to guess what each key word means. Choose the meaning that is closest to that of the key word in **bold**.*

1. **administration**
   /əd,mɪnəˈstreɪʃən/
   *-noun*

   - The new director has a lot of experience in **administration**, so I think he'll be a good manager.
   - A good boss needs **administration** skills in order to manage and organize an office.

   *Administration means . . .*
   a. conversation
   b. organizing and managing
   c. team work

2. **claim**
   /kleɪm/
   *-verb*

   - Walter **claims** to be the best skier in Vermont, but I have no idea if that's true.
   - If both Giorgia and Elena **claim** to be the most beautiful woman in Italy, one of them must be wrong.

   *Claim means . . .*
   a. to say that something is true when it might not be
   b. to discuss
   c. to have no opinion

3. **credit**
   /ˈkrɛdɪt/
   *-noun*

   - Since Emma didn't have any money, she bought her new TV on **credit**, planning to pay the money to the bank later.
   - Would you rather pay cash for something or use a **credit** card?

   *Credit means . . .*
   a. cash
   b. a check
   c. an arrangement to pay later

4. **earnest**
   /ˈɚnɪst/
   *-adjective*

   - In the job interview, Silvester gave **earnest** answers to all the questions, deeply believing in what he said, and telling the complete truth.
   - When Tom spoke about the joys of repairing old cars, we thought he was joking, but he was giving an **earnest** answer.

   *Earnest means . . .*
   a. funny
   b. half true
   c. serious and sincere

5. **heap**
   /hip/
   *-noun*

   - On Wednesday mornings, there are **heaps** of garbage bags on my street before the trash collectors arrive.
   - There is a **heap** of dirty laundry on Maureen's bedroom floor.

   *Heap means . . .*
   a. a large, messy pile of things
   b. a neat pile of things
   c. one or two things

**6. key**
/ki/
*-adjective*

- Our history professor asked us to explain the **key** ideas of the article.
- Exercise is a **key** part of good health.

*Key* means . . .   a. unimportant   b. very important   c. slightly important

**7. option**
/ˈapʃn/
*-noun*

- If you want to go to Faneuil Hall, you have two **options**: you can take the subway or you can take the bus.
- When she finishes college, she'll have the **option** of going to graduate school. If she doesn't want to do that, she can look for a job.

*Option* means . . .   a. something you must do   b. an idea   c. a choice

**8. restrict**
/rɪˈstrɪkt/
*-verb*

- The zoo keepers are careful to **restrict** the lions to their own area.
- Should parents **restrict** the number of video games their children play?

*Restrict* means . . .   a. to limit   b. to be free   c. to enjoy

**9. sacrifice**
/ˈsækrəˌfaɪs/
*-noun*

- It was a **sacrifice** for Peter to give up his freedom to take care of his sick child.
- Quitting smoking was a **sacrifice** that Claire made for her baby's health.

*Sacrifice* means . . .   a. refusing to give up anything   b. giving up something you value   c. giving up something you don't value

**10. strike**
/straɪk/
*-verb*

- A baseball player **strikes** the ball with a bat.
- Whenever Josh gets angry, he **strikes** his hand against a wall.

*Strike* means . . .   a. to hit   b. to play   c. to throw

## ▌WORDS AND DEFINITIONS

*Match each key word with its definition.*

1. _____*option*_____ a choice you can make in a particular situation

2. _____ a large, messy pile of things

3. _____ giving up something that you value to get something that is more important

4. _____ to control something or keep it within limits

5. _____ the activities that are involved in organizing and managing a company or institution; the people who manage a company, etc.

6. _____ to hit someone or something

7. _____ serious and sincere

8. _____ very important and necessary for success or to understand something

9. _____ an arrangement with a bank, store, etc. that allows you to buy something and pay for it later

10. _____ to say that something is true even though it might not be

# COMPREHENSION CHECK

*Choose the best answer.*

1. Which person is **claiming** something?
   a. "Is the party on Friday?"
   b. "This is the best restaurant in the world."
   c. "You can have this seat."
   d. "I don't know what's true."

2. What will an **earnest** person do if you ask him a question?
   a. lie
   b. give a silly answer
   c. give a serious answer
   d. tell you the question is stupid

3. Which is NOT an example of something **striking** something else?
   a. A car hits another car.
   b. The heavy rain pounds against the window.
   c. A student slams her hand against the desk when she is angry.
   d. A child plays with another child in the park.

4. If a **heap** of book bags is in the corner of a drama class, how many bags are probably there?
   a. none
   b. one
   c. two
   d. many

5. Who is making a **sacrifice**?
   a. Nielson, who eats the last piece of cake
   b. Marie, who skips the dance so that she can take care of her sick mother
   c. Carrie, who steals her sister's sweater
   d. Liam, who buys himself a new sports car

6. What is not a **key** reason why people wear clothing?
   a. warmth
   b. privacy
   c. costume parties
   d. fashion

7. In which situation does a person have an **option**?
   a. Ian can go to the movies, or he can hang out with his friends.
   b. Heather has to do her homework tonight.
   c. Emeril must cook dinner.
   d. Marla can't leave her office until she finishes the project.

8. Which job is part of hotel **administration**?
   a. deciding the cost of each room
   b. relaxing in the hotel pool
   c. cooking meals for the guests
   d. vacuuming the guests' rooms

9. If you buy a piano on **credit**, you
   a. pay cash for the piano.
   b. get the piano for nothing.
   c. will pay for the piano later.
   d. steal the piano.

10. In which situation is someone **restricting** someone else?
   a. Lucy's boss allows her to arrive at work whenever she wants.
   b. The children give their grandmother a present.
   c. Brian tells his daughter that they can go anywhere on vacation.
   d. The police officer locks Bob in a jail cell.

## ▌WORD FAMILIES

Now that you have studied the ten key words and their basic definitions, you are ready to learn words that belong to the same family as some of the key words. A word family includes words that look alike but have different functions (noun, verb, adjective, or adverb). Their meanings are related but different.

**A.** *Look at each model phrase and decide whether the word in* **bold** *is used as a noun, verb, adjective, or adverb.*

| | NOUN | VERB | ADJECTIVE | ADVERB |
|---|:---:|:---:|:---:|:---:|
| **1. claim** | | | | |
| • **claim** to know | | ✓ | | |
| • believe the man's **claim** | ✓ | | | |
| **2. heap** | | | | |
| • a **heap** of books | | | | |
| • **heap** the bags into the truck | | | | |
| **3. key** | | | | |
| • a **key** idea | | | | |
| • the **key** to happiness | | | | |
| **4. option** | | | | |
| • consider the **options** | | | | |
| • an **optional** task | | | | |
| **5. restrict** | | | | |
| • **restrict** smoking | | | | |
| • several **restrictions** | | | | |
| • **restricted** entry | | | | |
| **6. sacrifice** | | | | |
| • a great **sacrifice** | | | | |
| • **sacrifice** a lot | | | | |

**B.** *Match the following sentences with the definition of the word in* **bold**.

___c___ 1. Julia **sacrificed** her dinner to feed her hungry friend.

_____ 2. Reading is the **key** to increasing your vocabulary.

_____ 3. We should investigate Larry's **claim** to see if what he's saying is true.

_____ 4. In this area there is **restricted** parking; only doctors can park here.

_____ 5. Clara **heaped** her books on the desk.

_____ 6. The class tonight is **optional**, so you don't have to come unless you feel like it.

_____ 7. After Todd had a heart attack, the doctor placed many **restrictions** on his diet.

a. a rule or set of laws that limits what you can do or what is allowed to happen

b. to put a lot of things on top of each other in a messy way

c. to willingly give up something that you value to get something that is more important

d. a statement that something is true even though it might not be

e. something you do not need to do or have but can choose if you want it

f. controlled or limited

g. a very important part of a plan or action

# SAME WORD, DIFFERENT MEANING

*Most words have more than one meaning. Study the additional meanings of* **claim**, **credit**, *and* **strike**. *Then read each sentence and decide which meaning is used.*

| | | |
|---|---|---|
| a. | **claim** *v.* | to say that something is true even though it might not be |
| b. | **claim** *v.* | to ask for or take something that belongs to you |
| c. | **credit** *n.* | an arrangement with a bank, store, etc. that allows you to buy something and pay for it later |
| d. | **credit** *n.* | praise given to someone for doing something |
| e. | **strike** *v.* | to hit someone or something |
| f. | **strike** *n.* | a time when a group of workers stop working because of a disagreement about pay, working conditions, etc. |

__*b*__ 1. When you arrive at an airport, is it easy to **claim** your luggage?

_____ 2. The vase fell and **struck** the ground.

_____ 3. I give Mrs. Smith **credit** for teaching me how to play the flute.

_____ 4. Even though he only started studying fifteen minutes ago, Warren **claims** that he has finished his homework.

_____ 5. Because the university does not give them health care benefits, the cafeteria workers are going on **strike** today.

_____ 6. Because I don't have much money now, I'm going to buy the sofa on **credit**.

# WORDS IN SENTENCES

*Complete each sentence with one of the words from the box.*

| | | | | |
|---|---|---|---|---|
| administration | credit | heap | options | sacrificed |
| claims | earnest | ~~key~~ | restricted | strike |

1. One _____*key*_____ to success is hard work.

2. Because the truck drivers are unhappy about their pay, they are planning not to work next week; they are organizing a(n) _____.

3. At the beach, the children _____ a lot of sand in a pile to make a sandcastle.

4. Thank you for saying that I'm a good driver! I have to give Jim _____ for that—he taught me how to drive.

5. The town's water supply comes from the lake, so swimming there is _____.

6. Steve _____ that he makes the world's best chili; let's taste it and find out if he's right!

7. It's a good idea to have experience in _____ before starting a business.

8. A(n) _____ person will tell you what she is really thinking.

9. Professor Silver _____ her lunch break so that she could explain the equation to the confused student.

10. In the afternoon, you have three _____: you can swim in the ocean, take a hike in the rainforest, or go shopping on the island.

## WORDS IN COLLOCATIONS AND EXPRESSIONS

*Following are common collocations (word partners) and expressions with some of the key words. Read the definitions and then complete the conversations with the correct form of the collocations and expressions.*

1. **credit**
   - **give (sb) credit for (sth)**   to say that someone is the reason that something good happened

2. **heap**
   - **be heaped with (sth)**   to have a lot of things on top of something

3. **key**
   - **key points**   most important ideas

4. **restrict**
   - **a restricted area**   an area where only a particular group of people is allowed in because it is secret or dangerous

5. **strike**
   - **strike (sb) as (sth)**   to seem to someone to have a particular quality
   - **strike without warning**   for something bad to happen suddenly and unexpectedly

1. STUDENT:   For my astronomy project, I'm going to discover a new galaxy.

   PROFESSOR:   I'm sorry, but your plans _____ *strike* _____ me
   _____ *as* _____ being unrealistic. I'm going to have to ask you to think of a new idea.

2. ELLEN:   How do you know that I'm not on a diet anymore?

   RAMI:   Your plate is _____ food!

3. REPORTER:   Is it true that a UFO once landed in this desert, and that you have bodies of aliens hidden in that building?

   GUARD:   I'm sorry, but you can't ask any questions, and you have to leave.
   This is _____.

4. JOSÉ:   You speak Spanish beautifully.

   ELENA:   Thanks. I have to _____ my Spanish teacher, Señor Sanchez, _____ my fluency. He really helped me with my speaking.

5.  MAYOR:        What am I going to talk about in my speech tonight?

    ASSISTANT:    You're going to talk about how the city will be prepared if an earthquake
                  _____. Here are the notes that you wrote this morning
                  about your three _____.

    MAYOR:        Thank you.

## WORDS IN A READING

*Read this article about earth science. Complete it with words and expressions from the boxes.*

| administrations | earnest | heaped with | options | restricted | struck |
|---|---|---|---|---|---|

### HOW HURRICANES CHANGED HISTORY

News reports about hurricanes often explain how fierce storms damage towns and cause headaches for government __administrations__. The next time you see such a report, remember that
1

these seasonal storms are nothing new.

More than 400 years ago the _____ explorer Tristan de Luna had some ambitious
2

plans—he aimed to establish the first permanent Spanish settlement in a land called Florida. In June 1559, in Vera Cruz, Mexico, de Luna and 1,500 colonists boarded a dozen ships _____
3

food and supplies. They expected to reach their destination in two weeks. But it was a stormy summer on the Gulf of Mexico, and for two months storms _____ the ships' progress, blowing
4

them back and forth across the water.

In mid-August, the colonists finally landed in Florida. Most of their food was gone, and many of their horses had been killed in the long, stormy crossing. Still, de Luna tried to remain optimistic. But only a few weeks later, a hurricane _____ without warning and smashed into de Luna's
5

settlement, killing hundreds and destroying nine ships. In 1561, they had no more _____.
6

Spain evacuated de Luna's surviving colonists.

| claims | give...credit | key | struck |
|---|---|---|---|

De Luna's ill-fated colony was among the earliest recorded examples of how hurricanes have
played a _____ role in history, but the powerful summer storms have been influencing
7

history for perhaps millions of years.

No humans were around to make permanent records of prehistoric hurricanes. But Kerry Emanuel, professor of meteorology at the Massachusetts Institute of Technology, _____
8

conditions may have existed about sixty-five million years ago that could have created prehistoric hypercanes far more powerful than modern storms.

Scientists have long thought that the dinosaurs may have died after an asteroid

_____ Earth and caused dramatic climate changes. Emanuel and other researchers
⁹

think the asteroid could have heated the ancient oceans to as much as fifty degrees Celsius (about 120

degrees Fahrenheit). Hurricanes draw their energy from warm ocean water, and this superheated

water could have fueled enormous storms, causing deadly changes on our planet that would have

killed the dinosaurs.

More recently, the ancient Maya Indians, the dominant power in Central America from about A.D.

250 to 900, were quite familiar with the storms that regularly blew off the Atlantic. We probably can

_____ the Maya Indians _____ for inventing the word "hurricane." They called their
¹⁰

god of storms Hurukan, and it is likely that our term for the storms evolved from this name.

*(Based on Willie Drye, "Hurricanes of History—From Dinosaur Times to Today." National Geographic Channel, January 28, 2005.)*

## ▌WORDS IN DISCUSSION

*Apply the key words to your own life. Read and discuss each question in small groups. Try to use the key words.*

### EXAMPLE
I would **sacrifice** a romantic date if: *my friend needed help studying for a test*

*A: Are you crazy? I wouldn't **sacrifice** a romantic date for any reason.*

*B: But what if your friend was in danger of failing the test?*

*A: I'd feel sorry for my friend, but I'd go on my date!*

1. Something parents should **restrict** in their children's meals: _____

2. How many **options** I like to see on a restaurant menu: _____

3. How often I throw my clothing into a **heap** on the floor: _____

4. An **earnest** person I know: _____

5. A person I know who made a lot of **sacrifices**: _____

6. If my father **claimed** to be an excellent driver, I would say: _____

7. How many times I have **struck** a wall with my hand when I was angry:

   _____

8. Something that is **key** to my happiness: _____

9. How talented I am at **administration**: _____

10. The person whom I **credit** for teaching me how to do my favorite thing:

    _____

# ▌WORDS IN WRITING

*Choose two topics and write a short paragraph on each. Try to use the key words.*

1. Who do you know who is really **earnest**? Describe him or her.

   **EXAMPLE**

   > *My cousin Charlie is the most **earnest** person I know. Even though he's only nineteen, he is really serious about life. When I talk to him, I know that he's speaking from his heart.*

2. Describe a person you admire who has **sacrificed** a lot in his or her life.

3. Do you feel that your culture places too many **restrictions** on teenagers, too few, or the correct amount? Explain.

4. Would you go on **strike** if you were unhappy with your job? Explain why or why not.

5. Describe a person to whom you **give credit** for teaching you an important lesson.

## WORDS IN CONTEXT

*Use the sentences to guess what each key word means. Choose the meaning that is closest to that of the key word in **bold**.*

1. **aid**
   /eɪd/
   *-noun*

   - The families who had lost their homes were thankful for the **aid** they received. After the hurricane, many were in need of shelter and basic clothing.
   - People in poverty often receive government **aid**, especially to buy food.

   *Aid means . . .*　a. a form of help　b. sympathy　c. work

2. **basis**
   /ˈbeɪsɪs/
   *-noun*

   - I chose my college on the **basis** of cost; money was a limiting factor.
   - I was told that some companies hire new employees on the **basis** of age and sex; they try to avoid choosing young women who might get married and have children.

   *Basis means . . .*　a. a question　b. a reason　c. an attitude

3. **caution**
   /ˈkɔʃən/
   *-noun*

   - **Caution** is needed when you handle tools; serious accidents can easily happen.
   - Using a little **caution** to avoid danger is a good idea for a tourist.

   *Caution means . . .*　a. acting carefully　b. planning　c. taking risks

4. **conscious**
   /ˈkanʃəs/
   *-adjective*

   - What makes Oksana so special is that she's not even **conscious** of her own beauty.
   - As I became **conscious** of all the heads turned towards me and the silence in the room, I got nervous and couldn't think clearly enough to give an answer.

   *Conscious means . . .*　a. confident　b. pleased　c. aware

5. **culture**
   /ˈkʌltʃɚ/
   *-noun*

   - I studied the Japanese language for four years, but I still know very little about Japanese **culture**. That's why I want to study in Tokyo for a semester.
   - Surprisingly, there are similarities between Russian and Brazilian **cultures**. They share beliefs about the importance of family, friends, and good times.

   *Culture means . . .*　a. a group of people　b. the beliefs and behavior of a people　c. a country's geography

6. **deed**
   /did/
   *-noun*

   - My grandfather believes that there are no evil people, only evil **deeds**. He says that even good people do bad things sometimes.
   - The mother complimented her son after watching him help an elderly lady carry grocery bags. "That was a good **deed** you did," the mother said, smiling.

   *Deed means . . .*　a. a statement　b. a suggestion　c. an action

7. **distinguish**
/dɪˈstɪŋgwɪʃ/
-verb

- Brenda and Bianca are twins, and they usually laugh when people cannot **distinguish** between them.
- My little sister is learning to write. She's doing well, but it's hard to **distinguish** between her *p*'s and *q*'s and her *m*'s and *n*'s.

*Distinguish* means . . .
    a. to describe    b. to see a difference    c. to treat equally

8. **idle**
/ˈaɪdl/
-adjective

- The factories have been **idle** for a week. The workers are on strike.
- I couldn't understand why Tony would let a fine sports car sit **idle** in his garage. I'd love to have a car like his; I'd drive it around every day.

*Idle* means . . .
    a. not working or being used    b. working    c. active

9. **profit**
/ˈprɑfɪt/
-noun

- The **profit** from the singer's album was huge. Now she's a millionaire.
- Jerry didn't expect any share of the **profit** when he helped his parents sell their house. He did it because he cared for them.

*Profit* means . . .
    a. a large house    b. money received    c. excitement

10. **worth**
/wɚθ/
-adjective

- My parents bought this house thirty years ago for $70,000. Today it's **worth** $400,000.
- I looked at my cards, and I was happy. My queen was **worth** ten points, and my ace would get me eleven. That's twenty-one.

*Worth* means . . .
    a. appearing important    b. having a certain value    c. needing a certain amount

## ▌WORDS AND DEFINITIONS

*Match each key word with its definition.*

1. _____caution_____ the quality of doing something carefully, not taking risks, and avoiding danger

2. _____ noticing or realizing something, aware

3. _____ money, food, or services that an organization or government gives to help people

4. _____ to recognize or understand the difference between two similar things or people

5. _____ to have a particular value, especially in money

6. _____ a particular fact or reason

7. _____ the art, beliefs, behavior, ideas, etc. of a particular society or group of people

8. _____ money that you gain from selling things or doing business

9. _____ not working or being used

10. _____ an action

# COMPREHENSION CHECK

*Choose the best answer.*

1. Which action is the best example of a kind **deed**?
    a. telling a lie
    b. washing clothes
    c. playing a computer game
    d. making dinner for your sick neighbor

2. All these things are part of a country's **culture** EXCEPT
    a. paintings.
    b. the weather.
    c. the way of making introductions.
    d. holiday celebrations.

3. If I treat other people kindly or unkindly on the **basis** of their skin color,
    a. I consider their personalities to be most important.
    b. I take time to get to know them before forming an opinion.
    c. I'm prejudiced.
    d. I'm respectful towards everyone.

4. I want to know the current **worth** of my car, so I'll
    a. take it for a ride to see how well it drives.
    b. give it a new paint job before I sell it.
    c. ask the mechanic if he can fix it.
    d. do some research to see what people are paying for similar cars.

5. If a person is NOT **conscious** of his mistake,
    a. he'll apologize for it sincerely.
    b. he'll learn to do better next time.
    c. he isn't able to correct it.
    d. he'll probably feel embarrassed.

6. If an employee's work brings a large **profit** to the company,
    a. the boss gets angry.
    b. the employee will usually quit.
    c. the employee may get a raise.
    d. the company must be sold.

7. Which of the following things is **idle**?
    a. a radio turned up high
    b. an exercise bike with a heavy layer of dust on it
    c. an ugly vase
    d. a dirty floor

8. We can **distinguish** alligators from crocodiles because
    a. alligators have a U-shaped nose, and crocodiles have V-shaped nose.
    b. crocodiles can be aggressive, and so can alligators.
    c. alligators can reach fifteen feet in length, and some crocodiles can be a little larger.
    d. both have sharp teeth.

9. All the following people accept some form of **aid** EXCEPT
    a. a student who receives money to help pay for college.
    b. a family that lost their home in a fire and sleeps in a shelter.
    c. a homeless woman who gets a free lunch from a church.
    d. an artist who sells his paintings at an outdoor market.

10. You need to use **caution** when you are walking on snow and ice because it's
    a. fun; you can build a snowman.
    b. slippery; you can fall.
    c. beautiful.
    d. cold.

# WORD FAMILIES

Now that you have studied the ten key words and their basic definitions, you are ready to learn words that belong to the same family as some of the key words. A word family includes words that look alike but have different functions (noun, verb, adjective, or adverb). Their meanings are related but different.

**A.** Look at each model phrase and decide whether the word in bold is used as a noun, verb, adjective, or adverb.

| | NOUN | VERB | ADJECTIVE | ADVERB |
|---|---|---|---|---|
| 1. **aid** | | | | |
| • give **aid** | ✓ | | | |
| • **aid** others | | ✓ | | |
| 2. **caution** | | | | |
| • act with **caution** | | | | |
| • **caution** kids against smoking | | | | |
| • **cautious** drivers | | | | |
| 3. **culture** | | | | |
| • British **culture** | | | | |
| • **cultural** differences | | | | |
| 4. **conscious** | | | | |
| • a **conscious** action | | | | |
| • **consciously** move away | | | | |
| 5. **profit** | | | | |
| • look for a **profit** | | | | |
| • **profit** from an experience | | | | |

**B.** Read each sentence and match the word in **bold** with the correct definition.

_e_ 1. Computers can greatly **aid** one's studies. School children often use the Internet to do homework.

____ 2. The tour guide **cautioned** us against buying artwork on the street instead of at a store.

____ 3. My parents wanted us to attend some **cultural** events while we were in Sydney, so we went to a folk concert and a food festival.

____ 4. I'm always **cautious** when strangers speak to me.

____ 5. Everyone should have the opportunity to **profit** from a good education.

____ 6. I didn't **consciously** move closer to the table of food. I guess I was so hungry that my stomach had a mind of its own.

a. related to the art, beliefs, behavior, etc. of a particular society

b. to warn someone that something might be dangerous or difficult

c. to get and advantage from something (money or something else of use)

d. doing something with full awareness of your actions

e. to help or give support to someone

f. careful to avoid danger

## SAME WORD, DIFFERENT MEANING

Most words have more than one meaning. Study the additional meanings of **basis**, **distinguish**, and **idle**. Then read each sentence and decide which meaning is used.

| | | |
|---|---|---|
| a. **basis** *n.* | a particular fact or reason | |
| b. **basis** *n.* | the information or ideas from which something develops | |
| c. **distinguish** *v.* | to recognize or understand the difference between two similar things or people | |
| d. **distinguish** *v.* | to be the thing that makes someone or something different from other people or things | |
| e. **idle** *adj.* | not working or being used | |
| f. **idle** *adj.* | lazy | |

___e__ 1. The machine wasn't **idle** for long; it automatically shuts off if it's not used for more than five minutes.

_____ 2. What's the **basis** for your plan to start a new career? Can you explain how you came to this decision?

_____ 3. I can't **distinguish** between Portuguese and Spanish because I haven't studied either one.

_____ 4. I hate to be **idle**; I like to be busy and make each day have meaning.

_____ 5. In gym class the teacher made me the captain of a team. Since we were going to play volleyball, I chose my teammates on the **basis** of their height; I wanted tall people.

_____ 6. The speed of the skater clearly **distinguished** him from the rest of the athletes.

## WORDS IN SENTENCES

Complete each sentence with one of the words from the box.

| | | | | |
|---|---|---|---|---|
| aid | cautious | ~~cultural~~ | distinguished | profited |
| basis | consciously | deed | idle | worth |

1. Until we had a foreign student live in our home last year, I didn't think there were so many _____cultural_____ differences between Americans and Japanese.

2. My summer job was very special. I _____ from the experience.

3. I _____ tried to speak more slowly so that Yuri would understand me. His English isn't very good.

4. The accident involved a bus and two cars. The medical staff ran to _____ the injured passengers.

5. Extreme kindness and a lifetime of service _____ Mother Theresa from ordinary people.

6. My mother never let me remain _____ during summer vacation. She got me to read, help her around the house, and go for long walks.

7. I once burned myself while drinking hot tea too quickly. I'm now more _____.

8. You helped me when everyone else turned away. Your good _____ will never be forgotten. Thank you.

9. The clock in our family room once belonged to my great-grandfather. It must be _____ a small fortune.

10. My parents' small lessons about honesty and responsibility in childhood became the _____ for many of my choices and actions later in life.

## ❚ WORDS IN COLLOCATIONS AND EXPRESSIONS

*Following are common collocations (word partners) and expressions with some of the key words. Read the definitions and then complete the conversations with the correct form of the collocations and expressions.*

| | |
|---|---|
| 1. **basis** | |
| • **on the basis of (sth)** | because of a particular fact or reason |
| 2. **conscious** | |
| • **be conscious of (the fact that)** | noticing or realizing something (or some fact) |
| 3. **distinguish** | |
| • **distinguish between** | to recognize or understand the difference between two similar things, people, etc. |
| • **distinguish (sth or sb) from (sth or sb)** | to be the thing that makes someone or something different from other people or things |
| 4. **profit** | |
| • **profit from (sth)** | to get an advantage from something (money or something else of use) |
| 5. **worth** | |
| • **be worth it** | to be helpful, valuable, or good for you |

1. ROOMMATE 1: I'm so tired. It would be nice to come home before 9 P.M. for once.

   ROOMMATE 2: You work so hard at your job. Do you think it's _____ *worth it* _____?

2. GARY: You actually thought Marty was Lorraine's boyfriend?

   JIM: I wasn't _____ Marty was Lorraine's brother. I noticed that they looked alike, but I never thought to ask if they were related.

3. SPECTATOR 1: So these are the best high school wrestlers in the state?

   SPECTATOR 2: Yeah. Athletes were invited to this final competition _____ their individual performances during the regular season.

4.    GRANDSON:    Grandma, can we eat any mushroom we find in the woods?

     GRANDMOTHER:    Size and color can _____ one kind of mushroom _____ another. It's important to recognize which ones you can eat and which ones you can't.

5.    ERIN:    Irene's had a lot of interviews, but she's still without a job.

     DAVE:    Well, at least she knows how to _____ a job interview. Even if she doesn't get a job, she uses the experience to practice interview skills and become familiar with a company in the field.

6.    CHRISSY:    I find it difficult to _____ your voice and your brother's when I call your house.

     JASON:    Really? I always thought Rob's voice was a bit deeper.

## WORDS IN A READING

*Read this article about student travel. Complete it with words and expressions from the boxes.*

| basis | culture | deeds | ~~idle~~ | worth it |
|-------|---------|-------|----------|----------|

### TRAVELING ABROAD WITH A PURPOSE

Many American students are not sitting on a beach, remaining _____idle_____ during their
                                               1

summer vacation. Instead, they are traveling to other countries to combine sightseeing with community

service. Of course, foreign travel is not new among students. But in the past, young adults would go to

western Europe for a vacation as tourists; now they fly to places such as Ghana, Thailand, and Guatemala

to do construction work, help in children's homes, and perform other good _____ during
                                                                                  2

their summer break.

Another change in the student travel business is the age of the students going overseas. High school

students are signing up for work-travel programs in large numbers. What's the _____ for a
                                                                               3

teenager's decision to join one of these overseas programs? The reasons include the chance to see the

world, experience another _____, and learn a foreign language. Parents support the trips,
                                                      4

explaining that education must go beyond the classroom. Matthew Greene, an independent educational

consultant, adds that the programs offer a chance for self-development. The students themselves agree that

the expense is _____. Byron Langford, sixteen, who will take a trip to teach English in
                       5

China, argues, "I think it will teach me lessons about how other people live."

| aid | conscious of the fact that | profit from |
|---|---|---|
| cautious | distinguish ... from | |

Such lessons come at a price. A two-week program in China runs at $2,279 plus airfare. But companies are _____ and do not accept just any student who can afford to pay. Emily
<sub>6</sub>
Braucher of the company Where There Be Dragons explains, "Our programs are challenging emotionally and physically." Some students with only personal goals in mind look to _____ the
<sub>7</sub>
experience, hoping that the international travel and community service will make their college application stronger. Braucher does not think such teens are the right people for the programs.

The high school students who travel to give unpaid _____ in foreign countries are
<sub>8</sub>
_____ their work is a plus on college applications, but this is not the main reason they
<sub>9</sub>
do it. That's good since Matthew Greene says that such community service will _____
<sub>10</sub>
one application _____ another only if everything else is equal. Even then, a good student can have a powerful learning experience through a summer job at a coffee shop. After all, when it comes to getting into college, a strong performance in school is still the most important.

*(Based on information in Margaret Farley Steele, "What I Did on My Summer Vacation." The New York Times online, June 12, 2005.)*

## WORDS IN DISCUSSION

*Apply the key words to your own life. Read and discuss each question in small groups. Try to use the key words.*

1. Name a situation in which you need **caution**.

   **EXAMPLE**

   > *I'm a **cautious** person. I don't take risks very often. I think **caution** is especially important when you're driving.*

2. How often do you sit **idle**? Are you someone who needs to stay busy all the time?

3. What kinds of businesses bring a large **profit** to people?

4. How can you **aid** a classmate?

5. Look at the watch that someone near you is wearing. How much do you think it's **worth**?

6. When's the last time you performed a good **deed**? What did you do?

7. Name something that you do **consciously** as one of your study habits.

8. Name at least two cities in your country that a foreigner should visit in order to understand the **culture** better. Why do those cities have **cultural** importance?

9. Can you easily **distinguish between** good movies and bad ones? On what **basis** can you call a movie good?

10. How carefully do you listen when someone **cautions** you against doing something risky?

## ■ WORDS IN WRITING

*Choose two topics and write a short paragraph on each. Try to use the key words.*

1. Have you ever lost a night's sleep for a good reason? Why was it **worth it**?

   **EXAMPLE**

   > *I've lost sleep for different reasons. I sometimes don't sleep much because I want to talk to my friends on the phone or write e-mail. I think it's **worth it** every time because friendships make us healthy and happy.*

2. Explain a **cultural** difference that you have noticed or seen.

3. On what **basis** do you choose your friends?

4. Describe a **deed** you've done in the past that you are now sorry about.

5. Besides money, how can you **profit from** a job?

## ▌WORDS IN CONTEXT

*Use the sentences to guess what each key word means. Choose the meaning that is closest to that of the key word in **bold**.*

1. **agriculture**
   /ˈægrɪˌkʌltʃɚ/
   -noun

   • Mitch is studying **agriculture** because he intends to become a farmer.
   • Knowledge of **agriculture** helps you grow excellent vegetables.

   *Agriculture means . . .*    a. ocean science    b. the science of medicine    ⓒ the science of farming

2. **fate**
   /feɪt/
   -noun

   • At their wedding, Fatma and Omar said that **fate** brought them together.
   • Do you believe in **fate**, or do you believe that nothing in our lives was planned before we were born?

   *Fate means . . .*    a. science    b. a power that controls peoples' lives    c. a dream

3. **mend**
   /mɛnd/
   -verb

   • When I had a hole in the pocket of my jacket, my sister **mended** it for me.
   • A tree fell on the fence during the storm, but the fence was not destroyed; Tom was able to **mend** the broken fence.

   *Mend means . . .*    a. to throw away    b. to start over    c. to repair

4. **occur**
   /əˈkɚ/
   -verb

   • Earthquakes often **occur** in and around San Francisco.
   • Power failures sometimes **occur** when there are big storms. The last time we had a big storm, we were without electricity for two days.

   *Occur means . . .*    a. to happen    b. to surprise    b. to see

5. **quantity**
   /ˈkwantəti/
   -noun

   • A single office can consume a large **quantity** of paper, but thankfully most businesses today recycle.
   • With six kids and two adults in the family, I have to buy huge **quantities** of groceries every week.

   *Quantity means . . .*    a. quality    b. amount    c. location

6. **region**
   /ˈridʒən/
   -noun

   • Many people believe that the Lake District is the most beautiful **region** of England.
   • Lapland is the northernmost **region** of Finland.

   *Region means . . .*    a. total area    b. town    c. part of a state or country

**7.** **relate**
/rɪˈleɪt/
-verb

- In this paper, we will **relate** exercise and diet to health.
- The musician **related** his love of classical guitar to the music his grandfather had played to him when he was a child.

*Relate* means . . .

a. to describe a difference
b. to ask a question
c. to show a connection

**8.** **rid**
/rɪd/
-verb

- Putting screens in the windows will **rid** the restaurant of its mosquito problem.
- That law enforcement program was very successful: it **rid** the country of dangerous criminals.

*Rid* means . . .

a. to remove something or someone
b. to keep
c. to fill

**9.** **stem**
/stem/
-noun

- Be careful when you touch the **stem** of a rose; the thorns on the **stem** could hurt you!
- When you put a flower in a vase, the long green **stem** goes in the water.

*Stem* means . . .

a. a plant
b. the colorful part of a flower
c. the long thin part of a plant

**10.** **urge**
/ɚdʒ/
-verb

- Jan **urged** his grandfather to go to the hospital when the old man had chest pains.
- Annie shops every day in expensive stores and is in serious debt, so her friends have **urged** her to destroy her credit card.

*Urge* means . . .

a. to suggest
b. to strongly advise
c. to have no opinion

## ▌WORDS AND DEFINITIONS

*Match each key word with its definition.*

1. _____occur_____ to happen, especially without being planned first

2. _____ to remove something or someone bad or harmful from a place or organization

3. _____ to repair

4. _____ a fairly large area of a state, country, etc.

5. _____ to strongly advise someone to do something

6. _____ the science or practice of farming

7. _____ to show or prove a connection between two or more things

8. _____ an amount of something that can be counted or measured

9. _____ a power that is believed to control what happens in people's lives

10. _____ the long thin part of a plant from which leaves or flowers grow

# COMPREHENSION CHECK

*Choose the best answer.*

1. If I **relate** my idea to your idea, our ideas are
   a. completely different.
   b. opposite.
   c. equal.
   d. connected.

2. Which speaker is **urging** someone to do something?
   a. "You can go to the basketball game if you want to."
   b. "I don't know what you should do."
   c. "You really should go to the game!"
   d. "It might be fun for you to go to the basketball game."

3. Which sentence describes a **quantity**?
   a. The blouses are made of silk.
   b. The apples are red.
   c. The stone is smooth.
   d. There are six dolls.

4. Which one has a **stem**?
   a. a rose
   b. a mountain
   c. a tree
   d. a rock

5. If Chen plans to **rid** his city of litter, he'll
   a. throw trash out his car window.
   b. leave soda cans on the grass in the park.
   c. pick up any bottles or trash that he finds on the ground.
   d. throw cigarettes butts into the street.

6. If Giselle believes in **fate**, what does she think about life?
   a. Something controls everything that happens to her.
   b. She can control every part of her life.
   c. There's no greater power that has a plan for her.
   d. Everything in her life happens by accident.

7. Which item CANNOT be **mended**?
   a. a sock that has a hole in the toe
   b. a broken fence
   c. torn blue jeans
   d. a glass that broke into a hundred pieces

8. Which **region** of the United States is the coldest?
   a. the Northeast
   b. the Midwest
   c. the South
   d. the far North (Alaska)

9. Why would Dan study **agriculture**?
   a. He wants to live in a big city.
   b. He's interested in mathematics.
   c. He wants to be a farmer.
   d. He loves learning new languages.

10. When is lightning most likely to **occur**?
    a. on a sunny afternoon
    b. during a thunderstorm
    c. in the winter
    d. in perfect weather

## WORD FAMILIES

Now that you have studied the ten key words and their basic definitions, you are ready to learn words that belong to the same family as some of the key words. A word family includes words that look alike but have different functions (noun, verb, adjective, or adverb). Their meanings are related but different.

**A.** *Look at each model phrase and decide whether the word in **bold** is used as a noun, verb, adjective, or adverb.*

|  | NOUN | VERB | ADJECTIVE | ADVERB |
|---|---|---|---|---|
| 1. **agriculture** | | | | |
| • to study **agriculture** | ✓ | | | |
| • an **agricultural** project | | | ✓ | |
| 2. **region** | | | | |
| • an unexplored **region** | | | | |
| • **regional** differences | | | | |
| 3. **relate** | | | | |
| • **relate** one idea to another | | | | |
| • **related** topics | | | | |
| • a clear **relation** | | | | |
| • a difficult **relationship** | | | | |
| 4. **occur** | | | | |
| • find out what **occurred** | | | | |
| • a strange **occurrence** | | | | |
| 5. **urge** | | | | |
| • **urge** people to vote | | | | |
| • **urgent** business | | | | |

**B.** *Match the following sentences with the definition of the word in **bold**.*

_f_ 1. The senators met to discuss ways to improve **regional** business.

____ 2. Is there any **relation** between Hank's drinking and his car accident?

____ 3. To find more information about planting seeds, search the **agricultural** library.

____ 4. The hospital has an **urgent** need for blood donations.

____ 5. Jim Yong and Hyung Min look like brothers! Are they **related**?

____ 6. Although there are many bears in Alaska, a bear attack is an uncommon **occurrence** there.

____ 7. Emily and her mom have a close **relationship**.

a. a connection between two things

b. very important and needing to be dealt with immediately

c. something that happens or exists

d. the way in which two people, groups, or things behave toward each other

e. related to the science of farming

f. relating to a particular region

g. connected by family, ideas, or subjects

# SAME WORD, DIFFERENT MEANING

Most words have more than one meaning. Study the additional meanings of **relate**, **stem**, and **urge**. Then read each sentence and decide which meaning is used.

| | | |
|---|---|---|
| a. **relate** *v.* | to show or prove a connection between two or more things |
| b. **relate** *v.* | to tell someone about something that has happened |
| c. **stem** *n.* | the long, thin part of a plant from which leaves or flowers grow |
| d. **stem** *v.* | to stop something from growing |
| e. **urge** *v.* | to strongly advise someone to do something |
| f. **urge** *n.* | a strong wish or need |

__*b*__ 1. We listened carefully as Barbara **related** the news.

_____ 2. Professors often **urge** their students to come to class on time.

_____ 3. More police will work on the border to **stem** illegal immigration.

_____ 4. Zack had the **urge** to laugh when he saw his boss's strange haircut.

_____ 5. In his article, the doctor **related** the amount of sleep a person gets to his or her ability to concentrate.

_____ 6. Madison cut the **stem** of the flower before she put it in a vase.

# WORDS IN SENTENCES

Complete each sentence with one of the words from the box.

| | | | | |
|---|---|---|---|---|
| agriculture | mend | quantity | relation | ~~stem~~ |
| fate | occurrence | regional | rid | urgent |

1. Speed bumps are used in the high school parking lot to _____*stem*_____ speeding.

2. Maura used a needle and thread to _____ the tear in her shirt.

3. If you believe in _____, you think that life has a plan for you.

4. Robbery is a rare _____ in a safe neighborhood.

5. In the beautiful Tatra mountains of southern Poland, you can eat delicious _____ dishes such as *pierogi* and *bigos*.

6. Gardeners want to _____ their gardens of weeds.

7. Is there any _____ between the cake I made and Jim's stomachache?

8. Farmers in the American Midwest are experts at _____.

9. Allegra received a(n) _____ voice mail message that told her to call work immediately.

10. Our shoe store will order a large _____ of shoes from Milan, Italy.

# WORDS IN COLLOCATIONS AND EXPRESSIONS

*Following are common collocations (word partners) and expressions with some of the key words. Read the definitions and then complete the conversations with the correct form of the collocations and expressions.*

| | | |
|---|---|---|
| 1. **occur** | | |
| | • **occur to (sb) to** | to suddenly come into your mind |
| 2. **relate** | | |
| | • **relate to (sb/sth)** | to understand how someone feels |
| | • **be in a relationship** | to be romantically involved with someone |
| | • **an important relationship** | an important connection between people, things, or ideas |
| 3. **rid** | | |
| | • **get rid of (sth)** | to throw away or make something stop |
| 4. **stem** | | |
| | • **stem from (sth)** | develop from something |

1.    ERIKA:    Not only is my bike ugly, its brakes don't work.

     VANESSA:    And it was made in 1983! Don't you think it's time to buy a new bike?

     ERIKA:    Yeah, I think it's time to _____ *get rid of* _____ it. Let's go bike shopping.

2.    CAMPER 1:    We're lost!

     CAMPER 2:    Relax. We're not lost! Look down the mountain to the right. Do you see the village?

     CAMPER 1:    You're smart. It never _____ me _____ look that way.

3.    JOE:    I'm tired of being single. You're lucky to be _____ .

     PIERRE:    Having a girlfriend isn't always easy. We fight a lot.

     JOE:    Why?

     PIERRE:    Our problems _____ my lack of money. She expects me to take her to fancy restaurants, but I'm broke.

4.    STUDENT:    Why are the oceans getting higher?

     EXPERT:    There's _____ between the rise in ocean levels and the fact that the Earth is slowly getting warmer. This is called global warming. When the temperatures rise, more ice melts at the North and South Poles, creating more water in the ocean.

5.    RYAN:    I'm really sorry I fell asleep in your class. I'm exhausted because I'm working at two jobs to help pay for college.

     PROFESSOR:    I can _____ that. I also had a part-time job when I was a university student. But please drink some coffee before our next class. If you're not awake, you can't learn.

# WORDS IN A READING

*Read this article about wildlife. Complete it with words and expressions from the boxes.*

| agriculture | occur | quantity | relationship | ~~regions~~ | stem from |
|---|---|---|---|---|---|

## DIVERSITY PROTECTS THE HEALTH OF THE WORLD

In Oaxaca, Mexico, people from many _____regions_____ of the world are meeting to discuss the
**1**
global importance of biodiversity. Biodiversity is having many different kinds of plants and animals in
the world. Sponsored by the international science organization Diversitas, the meeting brings together
experts from the natural and social sciences who can share a large _____ of information.
**2**

A key idea at the conference will be the _____ between humans and the environment
**3**
in terms of public health. Diversitas organizer Peter Daszak calls biodiversity a kind of global health
insurance. "If you really look at some of the big diseases that are affecting humans—diseases like
SARS,[*] avian influenza—there is something common to all of them," he says. He explains that these
diseases _____ changes to the environment, such as building roads into forests or
**4**
changing methods of _____. He wants people to think about the causes that make these
**5**
diseases _____.
**6**

| Fate | get rid of | mend | urges |
|---|---|---|---|

Researchers believe that the bird flu virus first passed to humans in the crowded poultry markets
of Vietnam and is being spread by migratory birds.

Peter Daszak says SARS, the highly infectious respiratory illness that emerged in 2002, also began
with the sale of wildlife—in this case bats and civet cats in Chinese markets. Because the animals were
kept so closely together, a SARS-like virus in bats was able to move to the civets and from them to
people. Daszak _____ people to use this information to stop SARS from appearing again.
**7**

How can we _____ the health of our planet? One way is for public health officials to
**8**
pay closer attention to human–wildlife interaction. Wildlife, even animals that people may want to
_____, can play a positive role in the environment. For example, bats are important to
**9**
agriculture because they eat insects.

Diversitas organizer Peter Daszak thinks that the Mexico meeting will raise awareness about the
complex relationship between humans and wildlife. _____ isn't behind such diseases as
**10**
SARS; it's the way humans hunt and trade wildlife. If we look at the way we interact with wildlife
around the world and act on the knowledge, we can prevent diseases like SARS from appearing and
protect both humans and wildlife.

*(Based on Rosanne Skirble, "Experts Say Biodiversity Is a Form of Global Health Insurance." Voice of America, November 4, 2005.)*
[*]*SARS (Severe Acute Respiratory Syndrome) is a viral illness. Symptoms include high fever, headache, body ache, and eventually pneumonia.*

## WORDS IN DISCUSSION

*Apply the key words to your own life. Read and discuss each question in small groups. Try to use the key words.*

#### EXAMPLE

Something I would like to see **occur**: _____ *a solar eclipse* _____

**A:** *I saw a solar eclipse* **occur** *when I was a kid. The moon covered the sun and it became dark in the middle of the day.*

**B:** *It sounds very interesting . . . Do you know when the next eclipse will* **occur**?

1. Something that often **occurs** in my neighborhood: _____

2. Someone I am **related** to whom I don't know well: _____

3. How deeply I believe in **fate**: _____%

4. Something or someone I want to get **rid** of: _____

5. How much I know about **agriculture**: _____

6. Someone who **urged** me to improve my English: _____

7. How I helped a friend **mend** his/her broken heart: _____

8. A **region** of the world that interests me: _____

9. A place where I hope the police will **stem** the growing crime: _____

10. The **quantity** of water that I have drunk today: _____

## WORDS IN WRITING

*Choose two topics and write a short paragraph on each. Try to use the key words.*

1. When you go to a restaurant, do you care more about the **quantity** or the quality of the food?

#### EXAMPLE

*I prefer to go to a restaurant where the food is excellent than to a restaurant where huge portions of food are served. However, my brother disagrees. One time he went to a gourmet restaurant where the portions were very small. He paid a fortune for the meal but was still hungry when he left the restaurant. Since then, when he goes out to eat, he wants quality and* **quantity**.

2. Do you believe in **fate**? Explain why or why not.

3. Describe a **region** of your country that interests you.

4. Describe something that was difficult for you to **get rid of**.

5. What famous person would you like to be **related** to? Explain.

# QUIZ 7

## PART A

*Choose the word that best completes each item and write it in the space provided.*

1. When restaurant servers ask "For here or to go?" they are giving you the _____*option*_____ of eating in the restaurant or taking your food with you.
   - a. aid
   - b. credit
   - c. option
   - d. basis

2. I had to cut the long _____ of the flowers a bit before I put them in the vase.
   - a. stems
   - b. fates
   - c. deeds
   - d. regions

3. My mother _____ me to spend more time with my grandparents. She reminded me how much my visits mean to them.
   - a. claimed
   - b. urged
   - c. restricted
   - d. related

4. Drive with _____ on wet or icy roads.
   - a. fate
   - b. caution
   - c. deed
   - d. aid

5. Gracie will receive financial _____ from her university. Like many others, her family cannot pay for her college education without some kind of help.
   - a. credit
   - b. caution
   - c. profit
   - d. aid

6. My sister sometimes says things that don't _____ to the conversation at our dinner table, but that's because she's too little to understand all the topics.
   - a. claim
   - b. relate
   - c. urge
   - d. distinguish

7. This restaurant _____ to have the best barbecued ribs in the state of Texas.
   - a. claims
   - b. relates
   - c. restricts
   - d. distinguishes

8. Marissa believes that _____ put her and Cooper on the same plane from London to New York; they talked the entire flight and left as good friends.
   - a. fate
   - b. credit
   - c. deed
   - d. culture

9. Because business wasn't as good this year, the president needed to _____ company spending.
   - a. claim
   - b. urge
   - c. restrict
   - d. distinguish

10. To really understand a people's _____ you need to spend time among them.
    - a. credit
    - b. basis
    - c. culture
    - d. deed

## PART B

*Read each statement and write **T** for true or **F** for false in the space provided.*

__T__ 1. When you purchase something on **credit**, you don't have to pay immediately.

_____ 2. It's a good practice to **rid** your closet of clothes you particularly like.

_____ 3. Loving parents make **sacrifices** for their children's health and happiness.

_____ 4. Forest fires can easily **occur** during hot, dry weather.

_____ 5. Sometimes the exercise equipment at a gym can be **idle**.

_____ 6. An **earnest** conversation is full of laughter.

_____ 7. Needle and thread can help you **mend** torn clothing.

_____ 8. If you want to work in **administration**, it helps to have leadership and organization skills.

_____ 9. **Agriculture** is very important to the economy of big cities like New York.

_____ 10. The Northeast is the closest **region** of the United States to Mexico.

## PART C

*Complete each item with a word from the box. Use each word once.*

| basis | deeds | heap | profit | struck |
|-------|-------|------|--------|--------|
| conscious | distinguish | key | quantity | ~~worth~~ |

1. Some baseball cards, especially the older ones, are _____worth_____ hundreds of dollars.

2. My uncle says it's best to buy cars on the _____ of how they perform rather than how they look.

3. Cord doesn't always read his mail right away, so there's usually a _____ of letters, bills, and magazines on his kitchen table.

4. A person's _____ say more about their personality than any spoken or written recommendation.

5. The smaller boxer _____ the other man in the stomach with a strong fist.

6. Without my glasses, I couldn't _____ the house numbers. 3's and 8's looked very similar. So did 4's and 9's.

7. Molly is very _____ of her new haircut since she has never worn her hair this short before.

8. Salespeople are interested in _____.

9. My piano teacher believes that practice is _____ to becoming a good musician.

10. Compared to Ellie, Trevor eats a large _____ of food at every meal.

## WORDS IN CONTEXT

*Use the sentences to guess what each key word means. Choose the meaning that is closest to that of the key word in **bold**.*

**1. burst**
/bɚst/
-verb

- The girl was having fun chewing her bubble gum. She kept blowing bubbles bigger and bigger until they **burst**.
- Leaving balloons in a hot car isn't a good idea; they are likely to **burst**.

*Burst* means . . .    a.  to become larger    (b.)  to break open suddenly    c.  to be stolen

**2. commerce**
/'kɑmɚs/
-noun

- It's amazing to think of how much **commerce** takes place over the Internet. Everyone in my family does some shopping online.
- A century ago, this area near the river was a place of **commerce** because many goods were transported by water.

*Commerce* means . . .    a.  buying and selling    b.  communication    c.  gift giving

**3. creep**
/krip/
-verb

- The mother tried her best to **creep** into the room without a sound, but the baby woke up the minute she turned to leave.
- The thief **crept** through the open window and began to look for things to steal.

*Creep* means . . .    a.  to disappear    b.  to run quickly    c.  to move carefully and quietly

**4. descend**
/dɪ'sɛnd/
-verb

- The eagle **descended** toward the water and caught a fish.
- The sky was turning dark and the mountain air was growing cool; it was time to **descend**. It had been a great day of hiking.

*Descend* means . . .    a.  to go down    b.  to fly    c.  to rush

**5. harbor**
/'harbɚ/
-noun

- People on land stood and watched as our ship pulled into the **harbor**.
- The fireworks over the **harbor** were beautiful. From our boat, we watched the colors light up the sky and reflect off the water.

*Harbor* means . . .    a.  a resort    b.  an island    c.  a protected body of water

**6. major**
/'meɪdʒɚ/
-adjective

- Automobile, truck, and bus traffic is a **major** problem in most large cities. Other forms of transportation must be found.
- This collection of paintings brought the artist **major** success. He became famous around the world.

*Major* means . . .    a.  large or important    b.  lasting for a long time    c.  unique

**7. odd**
/ad/
*-adjective*

- Kim thought it was **odd** that so few people were on the train. Usually it was crowded with people headed to school and work. What had happened?
- Aidan had an **odd** look on his face when I told him that Shannon was coming to the party with Patrick. I wonder what he was thinking.

*Odd* means . . .    a. sad          b. strange          c. peaceful

**8. prompt**
/prɑmpt/
*-verb*

- The news about my friend's illness **prompted** me to get in touch with her.
- The baby-sitter knew from experience that she'd need to **prompt** the children to do their homework.

*Prompt* means . . .    a. to surprise          b. to remember          c. to make someone do something

**9. roast**
/roʊst/
*-verb*

- Let's **roast** the chicken. Roasted chicken is healthier than fried chicken.
- I love the smell and sound when we **roast** chestnuts over a fire at Christmastime.

*Roast* means . . .    a. to cut up          b. to cook in an oven or over a fire          c. to sweeten with sugar

**10. suspect**
/ˈsʌspɛkt/
*-noun*

- There are two **suspects** for the crime. The police hope to prove that one of them is the real bank robber.
- At the police station, I was asked to look at several **suspects** and identify the criminal.

*Suspect* means . . .    a. a person who may be guilty          b. a gang          c. a person who suffers from a crime

## WORDS AND DEFINITIONS

*Match each key word with its definition.*

1. _____prompt_____ to make someone do something or to help him/her remember to do it

2. _____ to cook something in an oven or over a fire

3. _____ different from what is expected; strange

4. _____ to break open or apart suddenly

5. _____ the buying and selling of goods and services

6. _____ to move very carefully and quietly so that no one will notice you

7. _____ someone who may be guilty of a crime

8. _____ a calm area of water next to the land where ships can safely rest

9. _____ to go down or move from a higher level to a lower one

10. _____ very large or important

# COMPREHENSION CHECK

*Choose the best answer.*

1. If tourism is a **major** industry in Hawaii,
   a. it receives few visitors throughout the year.
   b. many people visit Hawaii throughout the year.
   c. other industries like the forest industry are much more important.
   d. there's little need for large hotels.

2. Mihae and Bill live near a **harbor**;
   a. they keep their fishing boat there.
   b. it's quite noisy with all the passing cars.
   c. the green trees and comfortable benches make it a nice place to relax.
   d. when they hike to the top, they have a wonderful view.

3. The boy is **creeping** into the room. He
   a. is running after his dog.
   b. wants to make enough noise to wake up his father.
   c. always jumps around like this when he's excited.
   d. plans to come from behind and yell "Boo!" at his father.

4. The police already have a **suspect**;
   a. the person saw the whole crime and can describe it in detail.
   b. he's a good detective. I'm glad they chose him.
   c. they're planning to arrest the person and question him.
   d. I'm glad the judge sent the guilty person to jail.

5. The hot air balloon gently **descended**;
   a. I watched it rise until the clouds blocked my view.
   b. I ran to meet my friends and ask them how their ride was.
   c. the wind continued to carry it to the east.
   d. we all watched as the air filled the balloon and made it larger.

6. My cousin developed a lung disease; this **prompted** me to
   a. move to a city with high air pollution.
   b. become a coal miner.
   c. give up smoking and start exercising more regularly.
   d. continue smoking.

7. They **roasted** the lambs;
   a. the noisy animals were kept outside next to the cows.
   b. more and more families were interested in caring for lambs as pets.
   c. nothing is more delicious than fried meat.
   d. everyone at the festival enjoyed a lamb dinner that evening.

8. Historically, the town square was a place where much **commerce** took place;
   a. today cars race through instead of horses.
   b. people sold many different things, from food to animals.
   c. today weddings, festivals, and parades continue to be held there.
   d. thankfully, crime is much lower today and the square is a safe place.

9. Which one CANNOT **burst**?
   a. a tall tree
   b. a big balloon
   c. an old water pipe
   d. a heavy trash bag

10. We all thought Helena's sudden marriage was **odd**;
    a. I'd like a big wedding just like hers.
    b. her family spent a lot of money on the wedding.
    c. she met him only last month and didn't even like him much at first.
    d. she and her husband did a fine job arranging it all so quickly.

## WORD FAMILIES

Now that you have studied the ten key words and their basic definitions, you are ready to learn words that belong to the same family as some of the key words. A word family includes words that look alike but have different functions (noun, verb, adjective, or adverb). Their meanings are related but different.

**A.** *Look at each model phrase and decide whether the word in **bold** is used as a noun, verb, adjective, or adverb*

| | NOUN | VERB | ADJECTIVE | ADVERB |
|---|---|---|---|---|
| **1. major** | | | | |
| • **major** city | | | ✓ | |
| • choose your **major** | ✓ | | | |
| • the **majority** of students | ✓ | | | |
| **2. prompt** | | | | |
| • **prompt** me to answer | | | | |
| • a **prompt** response | | | | |
| • arrive **promptly** | | | | |
| **3. roast** | | | | |
| • **roast** a turkey | | | | |
| • **roasted** peanuts | | | | |
| **4. suspect** | | | | |
| • be a **suspect** | | | | |
| • **suspect** your co-worker | | | | |

**B.** *Read the first half of each sentence and match it with the appropriate ending.*

_b_ 1. Last week a family in our building was robbed. I was shocked to learn that the police

___ 2. The director asked me if I would accept the new position, and he expected

___ 3. For the big family dinner, my grandmother served

___ 4. I like taking oral tests, but written exams are preferred by

___ 5. Christina loves the world of politics. That's why she chose political science as her

___ 6. I don't understand why I received the package so late. I like my mail to be

a. **roasted** chicken.

b. **suspected** my neighbor of the crime.

c. delivered **promptly**.

d. a **prompt** answer.

e. the **majority** of students in my class.

f. college **major**.

# SAME WORD, DIFFERENT MEANING

Most words have more than one meaning. Study the additional meanings of **creep**, **odd**, and **suspect**. Then read each sentence and decide which meaning is used.

| | | |
|---|---|---|
| a. **creep** *v.* | to move very carefully and quietly so that no one will notice you |
| b. **creep** *v.* | to move very slowly |
| c. **odd** *adj.* | different from what is expected; strange |
| d. **odd** *adj.* | used to describe numbers not divisible by two |
| e. **suspect** *v.* | to think that someone may be guilty |
| f. **suspect** *v.* | to think that something is likely, especially something bad |

_c_ 1. My aunt, who lives alone with eight cats, is considered **odd** by some people.

____ 2. The spider **crept** up the wall, and the cat watched it curiously for quite some time.

____ 3. In Russia, gifts of flowers are given in **odd** numbers, so bouquets sold on the street often have three or five flowers.

____ 4. Although Rene never complained, I **suspect** it was very difficult trying to work, study, and take care of her ill father.

____ 5. It was 3 A.M. I didn't want to wake my parents, so I **crept** up the stairs.

____ 6. The detective **suspected** that the husband had something to do with the murder of his wife, but he had no proof.

# WORDS IN SENTENCES

Complete each sentence with one of the words from the box.

| | | | | |
|---|---|---|---|---|
| burst | creep | harbor | odd | roasted |
| commerce | ~~descended~~ | major | promptly | suspected |

1. The firefighter _____descended_____ the ladder. He took each step down very carefully because he held a small child in his arms.

2. My two friends and I wanted to ride the roller coaster, but only two people could sit together. One person would have to ride alone. That's the problem with _____ numbers.

3. Yukihisa attends Middlebury College, and his _____ is economics.

4. The minutes seemed to _____ by as I waited for my cousins' train to arrive. It was late, and I was impatient to see my relatives.

5. We took a walk near the water and looked at all the boats in the _____.

6. My mother taught us to _____ take off dirty shoes when we entered the house.

7. The clown's big red nose looked like a tomato that was ready to _____.

8. My father _____ that I had skipped school when I arrived home without any books. Later, I admitted that he was right.

9. The world of _____ excites my uncle. He's been in the business of buying and selling foreign cars for many years now.

10. It's hot in the car. Now I know what a(n) _____ duck feels like!

## ▌ WORDS IN COLLOCATIONS AND EXPRESSIONS

*Following are common collocations (word partners) and expressions with some of the key words. Read the definitions and then complete the conversations with the correct form of the collocations and expressions.*

| | |
|---|---|
| 1. **burst** | |
| • **bursting with (sth)** | to be very full of something |
| 2. **creep** | |
| • **creep in** | to gradually begin to appear |
| 3. **descend** | |
| • **descend upon/on (sth)** | to arrive at a place or a home in large numbers |
| 4. **major** | |
| • **majority of** | most of the people or things in a particular group |
| 5. **prompt** | |
| • **(sb) needs prompting** | someone needs to be reminded to do something |
| 6. **suspect** | |
| • **suspect that** | to think that something is likely, especially something bad |

1.   REESE: You look like you're _____*bursting with*_____ joy.

CHANG-LIN: I am! I haven't seen my brother for ten years. He's arriving tomorrow for a one-month visit.

2.   CHARLENE: I introduced Greg to my roommate Carrie yesterday. They have a lot in common, so I hope they'll get along.

MARCUS: I think there's a good chance of that. I saw them together at lunch today. By the way Greg was looking at Carrie, I _____ he is quite fond of her.

3.   VICTOR: You're from a small town, aren't you?

CLAUDE: Yeah. I go home once a year to visit. Last year I was a little sad to see that modern businesses had started to _____. I wish they had stayed out and left the quiet way of life untouched.

4.    NADINE:    While I'm here in Paris, I'd like to see Notre-Dame and Sacré-Coeur.

    GABRIELLE:    It's good that you came now and not on Easter weekend, when hundreds of tourists _____ the city and make a special point of visiting Notre-Dame and Sacré-Coeur.

5. MRS. REILLY:    Please make sure Danny brushes his teeth before bedtime. He definitely _____.

    BABY-SITTER:    All right. I'll remind him.

6.    CLARK:    Wow! You have a lot of books. I didn't know you read that much.

    ROGER:    Well, the _____ them are for school. I don't have much time to read for pleasure.

## ▌WORDS IN A READING

*Read this article about New Zealand. Complete it with words and expressions from the boxes.*

| crept in | descending upon | promptly | ~~roast~~ | suspect that |
| --- | --- | --- | --- | --- |

### NEW ZEALAND: ON AND OFF CAMERA

My visit to the South Island of New Zealand shows the country for what it is: a mix of the old and the new. The farm at Houston's Lakeview Homestay is very traditional, with many sheep to tend—and ____roast____ for a delicious meal.
           1

In contrast, the farmer's home is quite modern. It's built along a hilltop, and its floor-to-ceiling windows give amazing views of Pukaki Lake and Mount Cook. I can't help but think that the beauty is perfect, and I _____ if New Zealand were closer to the Northern Hemisphere, 100 million
        2
people would live here instead of just 4 million.

However, because of the popular film trilogy *The Lord of the Rings*, tourists have been _____ New Zealand to see the land they know from cinema as Middle-Earth. Even in the
   3
emptier land of the South Island, tourism has _____. When I incorrectly note how the
        4
area seems untouched by all the excitement caused by the trilogy, the farmer's wife _____
                                                     5
points out a nearby film location. "You can even take a tour, if you like."

| bursting with | commerce | harbor | major | odd |
| --- | --- | --- | --- | --- |

Not knowing the popular trilogy, tourists would still find reason to visit the South Island. Queenstown, a(n) _____ recreational center, offers activities like skiing, jet boating, and
        6
fly-fishing. What else could you ask for?

Well, if it's more film sites you want, then it's to the North Island you go—or "up North," as the South Islanders say. Rotorua, in particular, is a hot spot, and there's a reason why the city is being called "Roto-vegas." It's nearly _____ motels and tourist shops. But as I mentioned, New Zealand is the mix of old and new. Look past all the _____ that tourism has brought, and Rotorua is a center of Maori culture. The Maoris are a Polynesian people, and it was the Polynesians who first discovered the beauty of New Zealand thousands of years before *The Lord of the Rings*.

The North Island is also home to the nation's capital, Auckland, which has yet another mix, one of the familiar and the strange. Not far from the _____, Victoria Park shows me orderly gardens like those in England, yet the trees and plants are not anything like the ones I'd see in London. And as I dine in a steakhouse near the water, I think I'm having a common experience—until I'm served a thick cut of ostrich. It's this mix of ancient and modern as well as the usual and the _____ that makes this country the interesting place it is. New Zealand has magic on and off screen.

(Based on information in Steve Hendrix, "New Zealand Has True Ring of Enchantment." The Seattle Times online, December 31, 2004.)

## ▌WORDS IN DISCUSSION

*Apply the key words to your own life. Read and discuss each question in small groups. Try to use the key words.*

1. Tell about something you do that others might find **odd**.

   **EXAMPLE**

   *I like to eat cold pizza for breakfast. Some might think this is **odd**, but it tastes very good. I don't think I'm the only one who does this.*

2. When you chew gum, do you blow bubbles and let them **burst**? Does this habit bother you when others do it?

3. Have you ever been afraid to **descend** from a great height? Explain.

4. If someone were to **creep** into your room at night do you think you would hear the person? Or are you a heavy sleeper?

5. Describe a popular place of **commerce** in your hometown or country.

6. What foods do you like to eat **roasted**?

7. Name something you do **promptly** after arriving at school or work. How about when you come home?

8. Does your hometown have a **harbor**? Name a well-known **harbor** in your country.

9. Whether you are in college or not, name two different **majors** that you find interesting.

10. Think of detective stories you know. What kinds of questions would the police ask the **suspects** of a bank robbery?

*Choose two topics and write a short paragraph on each. Try to use the key words.*

1. When is it important to act **promptly**?

   **EXAMPLE**

   > *You should act quickly in an emergency. In other situations it's usually better to think first and then take action, even if it takes longer. Sometimes when I try to answer **promptly** in class, I rush to say anything. Then my **prompt** answer becomes silly.*

2. Describe a **major** source of joy in your life.

3. Is there something you sometimes **need prompting** to do? Who or what prompts you?

4. Why might you **suspect that** someone is lying to you? Can you easily tell the difference between a lie and the truth?

5. How do the **majority of** people in your age group spend their free time? Are you part of the **majority**, or do you spend your free time differently than most?

# CHAPTER 23

**Key Words**

| achieve | corporation | nuisance | represent | sweat |
|---------|-------------|----------|-----------|-------|
| constant | latter | pale | sting | wreck |

## WORDS IN CONTEXT

*Use the sentences to guess what each key word means. Choose the meaning that is closest to that of the key word in **bold**.*

1. **achieve**
   /ə'tʃiv/
   -verb

   • Our students can **achieve** great results in science only if they have excellent science teachers.

   • Marco feels proud because he **achieved** each one of his goals this year.

   *Achieve* means . . .   a. to succeed   b. to have good luck   c. to fail

2. **constant**
   /'kɑnstənt/
   -adjective

   • My three-year-old daughter needs your **constant** attention; if you look away for even one minute, she might run into the street.

   • A person who enjoys a comfortable routine will not enjoy a job that requires **constant** change.

   *Constant* means . . .   a. happening all the time   b. happening once in a while   c. changing often

3. **corporation**
   /ˌkɔrpə'reɪʃən/
   -noun

   • After getting his business degree, Matteo got an executive position in an important **corporation**.

   • Would you like to buy stock that would let you own a tiny part of a large **corporation**?

   *Corporation* means . . .   a. a small family business   b. a school   c. a large business organization

4. **latter**
   /'lætɚ/
   -noun

   • Both green and blue are nice colors, but I prefer the **latter**.

   • Ella could choose a vacation in Switzerland or a vacation in Senegal; because she likes hot countries, she picked the **latter**.

   *Latter* means . . .   a. the first one   b. the second one   c. the most important one

5. **nuisance**
   /'nusəns/
   -noun

   • Faith was jumping in the living room while her father was trying to read the newspaper. He said, "Don't be a **nuisance**."

   • There aren't enough public toilets in this city. It's a real **nuisance**!

   *Nuisance* means . . .   a. someone or something that interests you   b. someone or something that helps you   c. someone or something that annoys you

6. **pale**
/peɪl/
-adjective

- Jill's face looks so **pale**—I hope she isn't sick!
- Which color do you prefer, **pale** blue or dark blue?

*Pale* means . . .    a. light in color    b. dark in color    c. white

7. **represent**
/ˌrɛprɪˈzɛnt/
-verb

- On the map, the squares **represent** subway stops.
- Very often, modern art **represents** ideas.

*Represent* means . . .   a. to paint    b. to direct    c. to be a sign for something else

8. **sting**
/stɪŋ/
-verb

- If a bee **stings** your hand, you might yell in pain.
- The smoke might make your eyes **sting**.

*Sting* means . . .    a. to give you no pain    b. to feel    c. to give you a sharp pain

9. **sweat**
/swɛt/
-verb

- If you walk for three miles in the hot sun, take some water with you because you're going to **sweat** a lot and get very thirsty.
- Jared was so nervous during his final exam that he **sweat** a lot.

*Sweat* means . . .    a. to have liquid come out through your skin    b. to feel sleepy    c. to cough

10. **wreck**
/rɛk/
-verb

- If Harry doesn't quit smoking three packs of cigarettes every day, he is going to **wreck** his health.
- The children built a house of cards, but the dog **wrecked** it.

*Wreck* means . . .    a. to destroy    b. to damage slightly    c. to be in fine condition

## ▌WORDS AND DEFINITIONS

*Match each key word with its definition.*

1. ____constant____ happening regularly or all the time

2. _____ a large business organization

3. _____ the second of two people or things that are mentioned

4. _____ someone or something that annoys you or causes problems

5. _____ to have liquid coming out through your skin when you are hot or nervous

6. _____ to completely destroy something

7. _____ to cause or feel a sharp pain

8. _____ to succeed in getting a good result or in doing something you want

9. _____ light in color

10. _____ to be a sign for something else

## COMPREHENSION CHECK

*Choose the best answer.*

1. What does ☺ **represent**?
   a. anger
   b. confusion
   (c.) happiness
   d. fear

2. Which action does NOT **sting**?
   a. A bee bites your arm.
   b. Someone you care about insults you.
   c. You clean a cut on your hand with antiseptic.
   d. A feather touches your face.

3. Which person is probably NOT **sweating**?
   a. Claire, who is sitting in a hot sauna.
   b. Nick, who is climbing Mt. Everest.
   c. Isabella, who is reading a magazine.
   d. Andrew, who must give a presentation in front of 100 people, but he isn't well prepared.

4. Which is a **nuisance**?
   a. a gift
   b. loud music coming from the apartment above yours
   c. a delicious meal
   d. friendship

5. If Hugo **wrecks** his car in an accident, what does he need to do?
   a. repair the car
   b. buy a new car
   c. paint the car
   d. Nothing—the car is okay.

6. Sasha **achieved** all her goals. What kind of person is she?
   a. successful
   b. unhappy
   c. unsuccessful
   d. unfortunate

7. Which is a **pale** color?
   a. light pink
   b. black
   c. brown
   d. red

8. We have two plans, A and B; which is the **latter**?
   a. A
   b. B
   c. neither
   d. both

9. If Kelly wants to work for a **corporation**, she wants to work
   a. alone.
   b. for a small family business.
   c. in another country.
   d. for a large company.

10. Which sentence describes someone or something that is **constant**?
    a. Della's emotions change several times an hour.
    b. The museum's security guard checked the statue twice during the night.
    c. Fernando smiles all day long.
    d. My grandmother sometimes works in her garden.

## WORD FAMILIES

Now that you have studied the ten key words and their basic definitions, you are ready to learn words that belong to the same family as some of the key words. A word family includes words that look alike but have different functions (noun, verb, adjective, or adverb). Their meanings are related but different.

**A.** *Look at each model phrase and decide whether the word in **bold** is used as a noun, verb, adjective, or adverb.*

| | NOUN | VERB | ADJECTIVE | ADVERB |
|---|:---:|:---:|:---:|:---:|
| **1. achieve** | | | | |
| • **achieve** a lot | | ✓ | | |
| • a great **achievement** | ✓ | | | |
| **2. constant** | | | | |
| • **constant** stress | | | | |
| • **constantly** making excuses | | | | |
| **3. corporation** | | | | |
| • an important **corporation** | | | | |
| • the **corporate** headquarters | | | | |
| **4. latter** | | | | |
| • the **latter** | | | | |
| • the **latter** option | | | | |
| **5. represent** | | | | |
| • **represent** an idea | | | | |
| • a clear **representation** | | | | |
| **6. sweat** | | | | |
| • **sweat** in the gym | | | | |
| • covered in **sweat** | | | | |

**B.** *Read the first half of each sentence and match it with the appropriate ending.*

___f___ 1. You told me about two plans. Can you describe

_____ 2. A manager in a large company is

_____ 3. Graduating from college is

_____ 4. After running for five miles in the desert, Todd stopped to wipe

_____ 5. Why are you

_____ 6. The art professor explained how the color red was

a. a **corporate** executive.

b. a major **achievement**.

c. **constantly** talking on the phone?

d. a **representation** of passion in the painting.

e. the **sweat** off his face.

f. the **latter** plan in greater detail?

## SAME WORD, DIFFERENT MEANING

Most words have more than one meaning. Study the additional meanings of **constant**, **represent**, and **wreck**. Then read each sentence and decide which meaning is used.

| | | |
|---|---|---|
| a. | **constant** *adj.* | happening regularly or all the time |
| b. | **constant** *adj.* | staying at the same level for a long period of time |
| c. | **represent** *v.* | to be a sign for something else |
| d. | **represent** *v.* | to do things or speak officially for someone else |
| e. | **wreck** *v.* | to completely destroy something |
| f. | **wreck** *n.* | something that is so damaged it cannot be repaired |

__d__ 1. Mr. Edwards **represents** the people of his state in the United States Senate.

_____ 2. After the terrible accident, Bart's car was a **wreck**.

_____ 3. Heather's **constant** questions are beginning to annoy me!

_____ 4. Michelangelo wanted his art to **represent** ideal beauty.

_____ 5. When James jumped on his sister's paper doll, she yelled, "You **wrecked** my doll!"

_____ 6. Marie likes to drive at a **constant** speed.

## WORDS IN SENTENCES

Complete each sentence with one of the words from the box.

| | | | | |
|---|---|---|---|---|
| achievements | Corporation | nuisance | ~~represents~~ | sweat |
| constant | latter | pale | stung | wreck |

1. Yuko _____represents_____ the freshman class on the student council.

2. Elizabeth wants to get a suntan because her skin is so _____.

3. Joe says that a secret of barbecuing is keeping the grill at a(n) _____ temperature.

4. Bill Gates is the president of Microsoft _____.

5. Some people use anti-perspirant so that they won't _____.

6. I wish Chris would stop calling me. He's such a(n) _____.

7. Let's make a list of the _____ we hope to accomplish in our lifetime.

8. Divers have just discovered a ship that sank forty years ago; the _____ is 1500 feet under the ocean.

9. Ow! A bee _____ me.

10. The boss described the two projects; Cassandra volunteered to work on the _____ project.

# WORDS IN COLLOCATIONS AND EXPRESSIONS

*Following are common collocations (word partners) and expressions with some of the key words. Read the definitions and then complete the conversations with the correct form of the collocations and expressions.*

| | | |
|---|---|---|
| 1. | **constant** | |
| | • **remain constant** | to stay at the same level |
| 2. | **nuisance** | |
| | • **make a nuisance of (yourself)** | to be annoying to someone else |
| 3. | **pale** | |
| | • **pale in comparison with** | to seem less important, good, etc. when compared with something else |
| 4. | **sting** | |
| | • **feel the sting (of sth)** | to feel the bad effect of a bad situation |
| 5. | **sweat** | |
| | • **no sweat** | used to say that you can do something easily |
| 6. | **wreck** | |
| | • **I'm a wreck** | used to say that you are very nervous, tired, or sick |

1. ROBERT: Why won't Virginia talk to me anymore?

   JEN: Remember how you told her that she was a bad actress? She really
   _____*felt the sting*_____ of your criticism.

   ROBERT: Oops. I'd better apologize.

2. CARRIE: Can you fix my sink?

   PLUMBER: _____. It's an easy job. I can fix it in fifteen minutes.

3. BERNARDO: You look really pale. Are you sick?

   JOEY: Yes, because I'm scared. I don't know if I can get married
   today. _____!

   BERNARDO: Relax. You and Sara really love each other. I'm sure your love will
   _____ in the future. Now take a deep breath. You'll be
   fine.

4. MICHELANGELO: My painting's in the Sistine Chapel are beautiful, aren't they?

   LEONARDO: Yes, but I have to be honest with you. I think your paintings
   _____ my *Mona Lisa*.

5. MARCIA: How was class?

   FRED: Fine, except Dan had to _____ himself, as usual. He
   was asking a lot of questions that had nothing to do with what the professor
   was talking about. Everyone was irritated with him for wasting our time.

## WORDS IN A READING

*Read this article about the music business. Complete it with words and expressions from the boxes.*

| achieve | feel the sting | ~~remained constant~~ | sweating | wrecked |
|---------|----------------|-----------------------|----------|---------|

### iPODS NOT HELPING MUSIC SALES

The popularity of Apple's portable digital music player, iPod, is not causing more downloads. Digital music sales in the United States have not improved in the past five months; they have _remained constant_₁ . The iPod, with more than 28.2 million sold, isn't going to _____₂ what the music industry hoped: that people would pay for a large quantity of downloads.

Music industry executives are starting to _____₃ and they are _____₄. In the spring, many believed that digital sales would give new life to the $34 billion recorded music market. Now that it is clear that digital sales are not rising, their hopes are _____₅. Digital sales are unlikely to offset falling CD sales, which are causing global revenue to drop for a sixth straight year.

| Corporation | latter | nuisance | pale in comparison | represents |
|-------------|--------|----------|--------------------|-----------| 

The download numbers suggest that the iPod's success, which has increased Apple _____₆'s share price dramatically since 2001, isn't translating into new music sales the way the evolution from vinyl albums to cassettes and then CDs did. New music sales from iPods _____₇ with those that came after the invention of CDs. For many users, the portable devices are just another way of stocking and listening to music, not a reason to buy new music.

Apple's iTunes Music Store has a catalog of 2 million titles on sale for 99 cents apiece. Many people, however, don't want to pay anything for downloads. Given the choice between paying for a download and transferring music from their CDs or their friends' CDs to their iPod, they prefer the _____₈ option. In the United States, yearly downloads per iPod fell from twenty-five to fifteen in the last year.

Although this change worries some, others in the music industry think that it is a _____₉ but not a major problem. Music sales often change sharply by geography and season, so it may be a mistake to think that this short period of time in the United States _____₁₀ the future of downloads worldwide. Even if the download market in the United States does not improve, companies may find digital opportunities elsewhere in the world, from song downloads to ring tones for mobile phones.

*(Based on information in Charles Goldsmith, "Music Sales Fail to Match iPod's." The Seattle Post-Intelligencer, November 3, 2005.)*

## WORDS IN DISCUSSION

*Apply the key words to your own life. Read and discuss each question in small groups. Try to use the key words.*

**EXAMPLE**

Something that I will **achieve** this year: <u>*I'll graduate from high school*</u>

**A:** *Will graduating from high school be the greatest **achievement** of your life?*

**B:** *So far, yes, but I hope to **achieve** a lot more in the future.*

1. How much I think about starting my own **corporation**: _____

2. One kind of exercise that really makes me **sweat**: _____

3. Something that was a **nuisance** to me today: _____

4. One group of people whom I could **represent**: _____

5. My favorite **pale** color: _____

6. Something I **wrecked**: _____

7. Something or someone I pay **constant** attention to: _____

8. How many times I have been **stung** by a bee: _____

9. I can travel to Las Vegas or Miami. My opinion of the **latter** city: _____

10. Something that I hope to **achieve** in my lifetime: _____

## WORDS IN WRITING

*Choose two topics and write a short paragraph on each. Try to use the key words.*

1. If you could have dinner tonight with any person you love or with any famous person, would you pick the first choice or the **latter**?

   **EXAMPLE**

   *I love many people and would enjoy having dinner with any of them. However, the **latter** choice, having dinner with a famous person, is more interesting. I'm not sure if I'd rather meet the president of my country or my favorite writer.*

2. Describe a great **achievement** of someone close to you.

3. Imagine that you find out that your fifteen-year-old sister is planning to go on a date with a nineteen-year-old boy. Would you try to **wreck** her plans? Explain why or why not.

4. What do the colors and shapes in the flag of your country **represent**?

5. Which **corporation** would you like to work for? Explain why.

## WORDS IN CONTEXT

*Use the sentences to guess what each key word means. Choose the meaning that is closest to that of the key word in **bold**.*

1. **bear**
   /bɛr/
   -verb

   • We received a lower grade because our group project was late. However, my part was done on time, so I won't **bear** any blame.
   • Every tax payer **bears** some of the expense of keeping people in prison.

   *Bear* means . . .    a. to refuse to help    (b.) to be responsible    c. to want to forget

2. **delicate**
   /ˈdɛlɪkɪt/
   -adjective

   • The glass decorations were very **delicate**. I packed them in a box with care.
   • The new father nervously held his daughter; he was afraid that the **delicate** little baby would fall apart in his arms.

   *Delicate* means . . .    a. pretty    b. noisy    c. easy to harm or damage

3. **individual**
   /ˌɪndəˈvɪdʒuəl/
   -adjective

   • Each **individual** tile on the wall was hand painted. The entire room was a work of art.
   • Jane got out an old photo of her high school class and looked at it for a long time. She wanted to recall each **individual** face.

   *Individual* means . . . a. considered separately    b. limited    c. part of a group

4. **legal**
   /ˈligəl/
   -adjective

   • Casino games are **legal** activities.
   • Is it **legal** to make copies of CDs?

   *Legal* means . . .    a. entertaining    b. secretive    c. allowed by law

5. **offend**
   /əˈfɛnd/
   -verb

   • Denise **offended** Lance by not saying hello. She didn't even look at him.
   • Mrs. Ross was **offended** by the strong language we used while watching the football game.

   *Offend* means . . .    a. to make someone upset    b. to joke about someone    c. to confuse someone

6. **previous**
   /ˈpriviəs/
   -adjective

   • In her **previous** job, Li had to travel a lot. Now she's always in her office.
   • I joined my roommate to watch his favorite TV program, but it was hard to understand because I didn't know what had happened on the **previous** show.

   *Previous* means . . .    a. today's    b. regular    c. before now

7. **prohibit**
/proʊˈhɪbɪt/
-verb

- Most movie theaters **prohibit** children from seeing adult films.
- Roller skating, rollerblading, and skateboarding are **prohibited** in this park.

*Prohibit* means . . .    a. to invite          b. to not allow          c. to make happen

8. **pronounce**
/prəˈnaʊns/
-verb

- I find it difficult to **pronounce** words with "th" like *Thursday* and *math*.
- Although some languages share letters, they're often **pronounced** differently. The letters *r*, *j*, and *h* are good examples.

*Pronounce* means . . .    a. to say          b. to read          c. to understand

9. **reasonable**
/ˈriznəbəl/
-adjective

- I need a day off to help my mother move to a new apartment. I'm a good employee and my boss is a **reasonable** man, so he agreed to let me go.
- The father thought his son's request for $15 a week was **reasonable**. The boy needed money for lunch, and there would be a little extra for going out with friends.

*Reasonable* means . . .    a. very generous          b. fair and sensible          c. likable

10. **seize**
/siz/
-verb

- The police **seized** the robber as he was coming out of the store.
- When I saw my favorite TV star eating dinner at the next table, I **seized** the chance to meet him. I told him my name and asked for an autograph.

*Seize* means . . .    a. to wait for          b. to let go          c. to take hold of someone or something quickly

## ▌WORDS AND DEFINITIONS

*Match each key word with its definition.*

1. ____individual____ considered separately from other people or things in the same group

2. _____ to be responsible for something

3. _____ to make someone angry or upset

4. _____ to make the sound of a letter or word in the correct way

5. _____ to not allow an activity officially or by law

6. _____ happening or existing before a particular event, time, or thing

7. _____ can be easily harmed or damaged

8. _____ fair and sensible

9. _____ allowed, ordered, or approved by law

10. _____ to take hold of someone or something quickly and forcefully

# COMPREHENSION CHECK

*Choose the best answer.*

1. If Juanita complains that people often have trouble **pronouncing** her name, it means that they
   a. don't know whether it's a boy or girl's name until they meet her.
   b. don't spell it correctly.
   c. cannot remember what her name is.
   d. don't say it correctly.

2. The **legal** voting age is eighteen. In other words, you can
   a. vote until the age of eighteen.
   b. vote only if you're older than eighteen.
   c. vote if you're eighteen or older.
   d. vote only for a period of eighteen years.

3. Isis looked in each **individual** box for her parents' wedding album;
   a. she didn't take much time to search.
   b. she was very thorough in her search.
   c. she carefully searched only one box.
   d. there were too many boxes to search.

4. The mother **seized** her little boy's arm
   a. just as he was about to step out onto the busy street.
   b. and they began to play.
   c. as they strolled through the park.
   d. because he said it was itchy.

5. Rogerio doesn't want to **bear** any blame for the failed marriage;
   a. Olivia tried hard to make things right again, but he said it was over.
   b. he believes it was Olivia who ruined their relationship.
   c. both he and Olivia made their share of mistakes.
   d. Rogerio is having a hard time learning to forgive himself.

6. Smoking is **prohibited** here;
   a. feel free to enjoy a cigarette.
   b. they complain about the smoke, but no one will stop you.
   c. you'll have to pay a fine if you light a cigarette.
   d. they expect smokers to use an ashtray.

7. The chair is old and in **delicate** condition;
   a. it can probably hold the weight of two people.
   b. I'm certain it will last another fifty years.
   c. it's comfortable as well as strong. Go ahead and sit down. Relax.
   d. I don't suggest standing on it to hang the curtains.

8. Abigail's behavior **offended** other guests at the party;
   a. everyone laughed and thought she had a good sense of humor.
   b. some felt so upset that they left early.
   c. she is really quite a boring person.
   d. she really has wonderful conversational skills.

9. Which of your roommate's suggestions is the most **reasonable**?
   a. I can't pay for the food, but I can help make the list of what to buy.
   b. It would be nice if you did all the shopping.
   c. Let's not keep any food in the house. We can go to restaurants.
   d. Why don't we take turns going to the grocery store?

10. Jamie and Sheree exchanged business cards at a **previous** meeting;
   a. they've had each other's contact information for some time.
   b. they plan to share contact information at their next meeting.
   c. they'll have their first business meeting soon.
   d. they haven't met in person yet.

## WORD FAMILIES

Now that you have studied the ten key words and their basic definitions, you are ready to learn words that belong to the same family as some of the key words. A word family includes words that look alike but have different functions (noun, verb, adjective, or adverb). Their meanings are related but different.

**A.** *Look at each model phrase and decide whether the word in* **bold** *is used as a noun, verb, adjective, or adverb.*

| | NOUN | VERB | ADJECTIVE | ADVERB |
|---|:---:|:---:|:---:|:---:|
| 1. **individual** | | | | |
| • each **individual** worker | | | ✓ | |
| • a responsible **individual** | ✓ | | | |
| 2. **legal** | | | | |
| • **legal** action | | | | |
| • **illegal** activity | | | | |
| 3. **offend** | | | | |
| • **offend** another person | | | | |
| • **offensive** language | | | | |
| 4. **previous** | | | | |
| • a **previous** relationship | | | | |
| • met **previously** | | | | |
| 5. **pronounce** | | | | |
| • **pronounce** his name | | | | |
| • learn the correct **pronunciation** | | | | |
| 6. **reasonable** | | | | |
| • a **reasonable** suggestion | | | | |
| • to **reason** that it was all right | | | | |

**B.** *Read each sentence and match the word in* **bold** *with the correct definition.*

__d__ 1. The first day of Italian class was easy for me because I had studied the language **previously**.

_____ 2. Freedom is a basic right of every **individual**.

_____ 3. I know it's best to ask before taking something, but I **reasoned** that my brother didn't need his CD player since he was at work.

_____ 4. Some of the jokes in the movie were **offensive** to me. I can't watch it again or else I'll just get angry and upset.

_____ 5. What's the correct **pronunciation** of your last name?

_____ 6. Hunting in this state is **illegal** if you don't have a license.

a. one person, considered separately from the rest of the society he or she lives in

b. very rude and likely to upset people

c. to make a particular decision after thinking about the facts

d. before now, or before a particular time

e. the way in which a particular word is said

f. not allowed by the law

## SAME WORD, DIFFERENT MEANING

Most words have more than one meaning. Study the additional meanings of **bear**, **delicate**, and **reasonable**.
Then read each sentence and decide which meaning is used.

| | |
|---|---|
| a. **bear** *v.* | to be responsible for something |
| b. **bear** *v.* | to deal with something painful or unpleasant |
| c. **delicate** *adj.* | can be easily harmed or damaged |
| d. **delicate** *adj.* | needing to be done very carefully to avoid causing problems |
| e. **reasonable** *adj.* | fair and sensible |
| f. **reasonable** *adj.* | a reasonable amount, number, or price is not too much or too big |

___f___ 1. The teacher gave us a **reasonable** amount of time to write our essay, so I'm not sure why Bo
said he had to rush in order to finish.

_____ 2. The **delicate** pin was made of pearl and ivory. Mia handled it gently for fear of breaking it.

_____ 3. I'm sorry for what I did, and I can't **bear** the thought of your hating me. Forgive me.

_____ 4. You're not being **reasonable**. How can I let you have the car for the whole weekend when
other people in this family also have places to go?

_____ 5. If you caused the accident, you'll have to **bear** the cost of all the repairs.

_____ 6. The boss felt uncomfortable talking to Marlene about her poor performance lately. He knew
she was having personal problems at home, so it was a **delicate** matter.

## WORDS IN SENTENCES

Complete each item below with a word from the box.

| | | | | |
|---|---|---|---|---|
| **bear** | ~~illegal~~ | **offensive** | **prohibited** | **reasoned** |
| **delicate** | **individual** | **Previously** | **pronunciation** | **seized** |

1. Isn't it ____illegal____ to make a left turn on red? I don't think any state has a law that allows
that.

2. When the plane is taking off and landing, the use of cell phones is _____.

3. _____ such rules about clothing didn't exist, so students wore whatever they wanted.
Now they cannot wear jeans, sweatshirts, T-shirts, or sneakers.

4. I like to hear what people really think about my music. I don't find any comment _____.

5. When I was a little child, my _____ of the letter *s* wasn't very good.

6. The excited shoppers _____ clothes off the hangers and shoes off the shelves.
Everything was on sale and everyone wanted to take something home.

7. The care of his two aging parents was a lot for Daniel to _____.

8. We _____ that it would be better to take our vacation in the fall because plane tickets are cheaper and fewer people are traveling then.

9. In Korea, people eat meat and vegetables from common dishes, but they have _____ bowls of rice and soup.

10. Kenichi's troubled childhood is a _____ topic. He doesn't like to talk much about it, so be careful asking questions.

## ▌ WORDS IN COLLOCATIONS AND EXPRESSIONS

*Following are common collocations (word partners) and expressions with some of the key words. Read the definitions and then complete the conversations with the correct form of the collocations and expressions.*

| 1. **bear** | |
|---|---|
| • **bear (sth) in mind** | to consider a fact when you are deciding or judging something |
| • **can't bear (sb/sth)** | to dislike someone or something a lot and get upset or annoyed about it |
| 2. **legal** | |
| • **take legal action** | to go to court |
| 3. **prohibit** | |
| • **prohibit (sb) from (doing sth)** | to officially or by law not allow an activity |
| 4. **reason** | |
| • **reason that** | to form a particular judgment after thinking about the facts |
| • **reason with (sb)** | to talk to someone in order to persuade him/her to be more sensible |

1.  REGGIE: Hey, Aunt Lily! I didn't know you had an exercise bike.

    LILY: Feel free to use it while you're here. Just _____ *bear in mind* _____ that it's quite old, so sometimes the wheels are hard to turn.

2.  JUSTIN: Did you try to talk to Mitch? He was really upset when he left the party last night.

    RAYMOND: I called him this morning, but I couldn't _____ him. He was too angry to listen to anyone.

3.  NED: Our landlord has failed to repair many things in our building.

    DENZEL: It's true, and the problems are only getting worse. It may be necessary to _____ against him.

4.  DOG OWNER 1: More and more beaches are starting to _____ people _____ taking their dogs for walks near the water.

    DOG OWNER 2: Frankly, I understand why some people are against having pets on beaches.

5. **GRANDMA:** I've enjoyed your visit so much. I _____ the thought of you leaving!

   **SHEILA:** Grandma, I'm not leaving for another week. And I promise to visit again during the fall break.

6. **EVAN:** Are you getting a new computer to replace the one you have? I thought you bought that computer just last year.

   **SETH:** We did, and it's still good. But Bri and I _____ two computers are necessary at home. We both need a computer for our work, and sharing has become difficult.

## ▌WORDS IN A READING

*Read this article about having an accent in the American workplace. Complete it with words and expressions from the boxes.*

| individual | ~~previously~~ | prohibits . . . from | reasonable | seizing |
|---|---|---|---|---|

### WORKING WITHOUT AN ACCENT

In half a year's time, thirty-nine-year-old Mercedes Woodward experienced some changes at work. The sales executive now holds a higher position that requires three secretaries. More important, her salary is three times more than it was ___*previously*___ . What brought about these changes for
\[1\]
Woodward? Accent reduction classes.

More and more immigrants are trying to find better career opportunities by "Americanizing" the way they speak. Private companies, in turn, are _____ the chance to make a profit. A
\[2\]
single accent reduction lesson can cost about $100. Is that a _____ price? For Woodward
\[3\]
it was. The Guatemalan-born woman argues that her accent stopped her from moving ahead in her career. So she took the advice of a supervisor and enrolled in an accent reduction course. Woodward believes that six months of doing drills and exercises played a part in her promotion.

Neill D. Hicks, who operates classes at Los Angeles Mission College in Sylmar, confirms Woodward's opinion: "Unless you speak English well, you can never be the boss." Even lower positions in an American workplace might not be open to those who speak with accents. Although the law _____
\[4\]
employers _____ judging a(n) _____ on the basis of his or her accent, an employer
\[5\]
can choose not to work with that person if the accent puts the safety of others at risk or if the job requires oral communication and the accent does not allow communication to take place.

Putting this law into practice is a(n) _____ matter, however. Some immigrants have
been _____ by their employer's behavior, feeling that their accent was the cause for being
mistreated in the workplace. The number of times that employees _____ in response to
such unfair treatment was twice as high in 2004 (eighty-five cases) as in 1996 (forty-two cases).

_____ that 10 percent of the population is foreign-born and such cases are often not
reported at all.

So, understandably, companies like Chicago-based Executive Language Training will continue to
make money, teaching the British to _____ their r's after vowels and Spanish speakers to
stop rolling theirs.

Of course, some feel that Americanizing their speech is equal to a loss of identity. But Joel Goldes,
a dialect coach for hopeful actors in Hollywood, sees it differently. "I don't like to think I am taking
away an accent. I am teaching them another."

*(Based on information in Rachel Uranga, "Their Accent Is on Success." LA Daily News, November 5, 2005.)*

## ▌WORDS IN DISCUSSION

*Apply the key words to your own life. Read and discuss each question in small groups. Try to use the key words.*

1. Give an example of a difficult name to **pronounce** in English.

   **EXAMPLE**

   *It's hard for me to **pronounce** words with the letter "L." So names such as Lily, Lee, Laura, and William are difficult.*

2. Name one way a guest could **offend** his or her host in your culture.

3. What is a **reasonable** time for a teenager to come home on a school night?

4. Do you own anything that is **delicate**? What is it made of?

5. Why might an employee **take legal action** against his or her employer?

6. What is something that you **can't bear** to do?

7. What is something that the law **prohibits** children from doing? Do you agree with the law, or do you think the **legal** age for this activity should change?

8. Name an **individual** whom you admire.

9. Do you remember what you studied in your **previous** lesson?

10. When was the last time a strong fear **seized** you?

## ▌WORDS IN WRITING

*Choose two topics and write a short paragraph on each. Try to use the key words.*

1. Have you ever **reasoned that** it was all right to lie?

   **EXAMPLE**

   *Sometimes I **reason that** it's better to keep quiet than say something. Many say that this is a form of lying. But if I choose not to tell someone something, it's because I've **reasoned that** knowing the information would hurt them.*

2. If you hear a joke that's **offensive**, how do you react?

3. How important do you think **pronunciation** is when learning to speak a foreign language? How do you feel about your own **pronunciation** in English?

4. Do you find it easy or hard to **bear** the blame for mistakes you make? Explain.

5. Describe a time when it was difficult to **reason with** a friend.

# QUIZ 8

## PART A

Choose the word that best completes each item and write it in the space provided.

1. The passenger next to me on the bus was using her cell phone, and her _____*constant*_____ talking made it hard for me to read.
   - a. constant
   - b. delicate
   - c. previous
   - d. reasonable

2. The prince and princess _____ the stairs to the ballroom slowly and gracefully.
   - a. seized
   - b. crept
   - c. wrecked
   - d. descended

3. Students are _____ from leaving the school until their last class has ended.
   - a. seized
   - b. crept
   - c. prompted
   - d. prohibited

4. I had to review the _____ chapter because it had been a while since I had looked at the book. Only then did I go on to the next chapter.
   - a. odd
   - b. legal
   - c. previous
   - d. delicate

5. The police are investigating the crime, but they don't have a _____ yet.
   - a. harbor
   - b. nuisance
   - c. suspect
   - d. corporation

6. Sebastian and Nicole don't know if they will have a boy or a girl, so they decided to paint the baby's room in _____ green. The soft color is good for any baby.
   - a. odd
   - b. pale
   - c. previous
   - d. reasonable

7. Mother's tea cups are very _____, so we wash them by hand and not in the dishwasher.
   - a. odd
   - b. legal
   - c. previous
   - d. delicate

8. The _____ has grown even larger in the past few years. Two new offices have opened in the U.S., and another will soon open in London.
   - a. harbor
   - b. nuisance
   - c. commerce
   - d. corporation

9. Losing things such as a good dictionary and my favorite sunglasses has _____ me to be more organized and careful with my belongings.
   - a. prompted
   - b. stung
   - c. prohibited
   - d. seized

10. The child knocked the tall cake onto the floor and _____ it.
    - a. roasted
    - b. crept
    - c. wrecked
    - d. descended

## PART B

Read each statement and write **T** for true or **F** for false *in the space provided.*

_F_ 1. You find planes and helicopters in a **harbor**.

_____ 2. There is generally more **commerce** in cities than in the countryside.

_____ 3. If Donny **creeps** into the room, he doesn't want someone to see or hear him.

_____ 4. Smooth silk **stings** your skin.

_____ 5. A responsible person will **bear** blame for mistakes he or she makes.

_____ 6. A balloon will **burst** if you try to put too much air in it.

_____ 7. A fly sitting on the TV screen during your favorite show is a **nuisance**.

_____ 8. It's important to **offend** people in positions of authority such as police officers and teachers.

_____ 9. 4:30 A.M. is a **reasonable** time to have an English lesson at school.

_____ 10. Frankfurt, Munich, and Berlin are **major** cities in Germany.

## PART C

Complete each item with a word from the box. Use each word once.

| achieved | latter | odd | ~~represented~~ | seized |
|----------|--------|-----|-------------|--------|
| individual | legal | pronounced | roasted | sweat |

1. When I first looked at my test, I thought I did well, but then the teacher explained that the check marks ____represented____ incorrect answers not correct ones.

2. Don't you find it _____ that Lisha never talks about her family?

3. It was necessary for Leon to wear a suit to the wedding, but he knew he would _____ in the July heat.

4. On our first night of camping we _____ hot dogs over an open fire.

5. Adik and Aaron interviewed with the same company, but only the _____ got a job offer. Adik has no hard feelings.

6. In most places around the world it's not _____ to sell tobacco to children.

7. Dasha noticed that her English teachers _____ the word *either* two different ways. She reasoned that both ways must be correct.

8. Bailey has _____ a lot through hard work. He has a successful career.

9. The airport official _____ the woman who was trying to get on the plane without a ticket.

10. The appetizer wasn't served on _____ plates, so we helped ourselves from the same dish. I think my brother took more than anyone.

## ▌WORDS IN CONTEXT

*Use the sentences to guess what each key word means. Choose the meaning that is closest to that of the key word in **bold**.*

**1. branch**
/bræntʃ/
-noun

- In the spring, new leaves grow on a tree's **branches**.
- A red bird in my garden likes to sit on a **branch** of the oak tree.

*Branch* means . . .    a. leaf        b. tree roots        c. an arm of a tree

**2. coward**
/ˈkaʊɚd/
-noun

- When the *Titanic* was sinking, Richard jumped into a lifeboat without his wife and child. Everyone said that he was a **coward**.
- Yolanda is a **coward**: she runs away from every difficult situation.

*Coward* means . . .    a. someone who has no fear        b. someone who is not brave        c. a courageous person

**3. district**
/ˈdɪstrɪkt/
-noun

- There are many important buildings in the financial **district** in New York City.
- Ana Paola lives in Brazil in the Federal **District**.

*District* means . . .    a. the entire country        b. a particular area of a city or country        c. a shopping mall

**4. guarantee**
/ˌgærənˈti/
-verb

- Flowers Express **guarantees** that your roses will be delivered in twenty-four hours.
- A salesperson often **guarantees** that you will be satisfied with what you buy.

*Guarantee* means . . .    a. to be polite        b. to suggest something    c. to promise something

**5. justice**
/ˈdʒʌstɪs/
-noun

- If there were more **justice** in the world, no person would be judged by the color of his or her skin.
- There is a problem with **justice** if poor people have to pay higher taxes than rich people.

*Justice* means . . .    a. unfairness        b. inequality        c. fairness

**6. kneel**
/nil/
-verb

- Some people **kneel** when they pray.
- In a knighthood ceremony, the person who is becoming a knight **kneels** in front of the queen.

*Kneel* means . . .    a. to rest your body on your knees        b. to sit        c. to jump up and down

7. **merchant**
/ˈmɚtʃənt/
-noun

• Marat is a powerful rug **merchant**; he buys rugs in Turkey and sells them in a large store in London.
• Over 1,000 **merchants** have shops in the South China Mall in Dongguan, China, making it one of the largest malls in the world.

*Merchant* means . . .   a. someone who sells   b. someone who shops   c. someone who buys and sells goods

8. **punctual**
/ˈpʌŋktʃuəl/
-adjective

• You must be **punctual** for the test; if you are late, you will not be allowed to take it.
• Are trains **punctual** in your native country, or are they late?

*Punctual* means . . .   a. early   b. on time   c. late

9. **temper**
/ˈtɛmpɚ/
-noun

• Be careful when you talk to Bill; he has a terrible **temper** and might yell at you.
• Risako cannot control her **temper** and starts many fights.

*Temper* means . . .   a. a tendency to talk a lot   b. a tendency to sudden anger   c. a tendency to be depressed

10. **vain**
/veɪn/
-adjective

• That actor is so **vain**, he demanded that his picture be in the center of every advertisement for the play.
• Gloria is a **vain** girl who always looks at herself in the mirror and thinks that every boy must be in love with her.

*Vain* means . . .   a. talented   b. modest and humble   c. too proud of your appearance

## WORDS AND DEFINITIONS

*Match each key word with its definition.*

1. _____*district*_____ a particular area of a city or country

2. _____ too proud of your appearance or your abilities

3. _____ to be in or move into a position where your body is resting on your knees

4. _____ part of a tree that has leaves, fruit, or smaller branches growing from it

5. _____ someone who buys and sells large quantities of goods

6. _____ someone who is not brave at all

7. _____ arriving or happening at exactly the time that has been arranged

8. _____ to promise that something will happen or be done

9. _____ fairness in the way people are treated

10. _____ a tendency to become suddenly angry

# COMPREHENSION CHECK

*Choose the best answer.*

1. Which is the **branch** of an apple tree?
   a. the part of the tree where apples grow
   b. the biggest part of the tree
   c. the part of the tree that grows underground
   d. an apple

2. Which part of your body do you put your weight on when you **kneel**?
   a. your head
   b. your stomach
   c. your feet
   d. your knees

3. Which person is **punctual**?
   a. Ben, who is ten minutes late.
   b. Ala, who is on time.
   c. Oliver, who kept us waiting for an hour.
   d. Wendy, who never showed up.

4. What would a **vain** person say?
   a. "I am an average person."
   b. "Everyone on our team helped us win."
   c. "Claude is a better singer than I am."
   d. "I am incredibly handsome, aren't I?"

5. Which is NOT a common **district** in a big city?
   a. the theater district
   b. the financial district
   c. the mathematics district
   d. the fashion district

6. Who has a bad **temper**?
   a. Hank, who gets angry if he cannot find a seat on the subway.
   b. Nora, who is patient with the children.
   c. Lucy, who rarely yells.
   d. AJ, who laughs when he slips in the snow.

7. Which speaker is **guaranteeing** something?
   a. "This computer might break. Sorry."
   b. "I don't know if we can deliver the package on time."
   c. "If your new TV has any problems, we will fix it for free."
   d. "I can't promise you anything."

8. Which is an example of **justice**?
   a. The innocent man goes to jail.
   b. The judge rules that the murderer is guilty.
   c. The rich children get newer books than the poor children.
   d. The guilty man does not have to go to jail.

9. Who is a **coward**?
   a. Henri, who ran into the burning building to save the old woman.
   b. Kyle, who parachuted into the Amazon jungle.
   c. Tim, who ran away from the wrestling match when he saw his big opponent.
   d. Mikel, who jumped into ocean to save the drowning dog.

10. What does a **merchant** do at work?
    a. exercise
    b. read literature
    c. eat
    d. buy and sell goods

# WORD FAMILIES

Now that you have studied the ten key words and their basic definitions, you are ready to learn words that belong to the same family as some of the key words. A word family includes words that look alike but have different functions (noun, verb, adjective, or adverb). Their meanings are related but different.

**A.** *Look at each model phrase and decide whether the word in **bold** is used as a noun, verb, adjective, or adverb.*

|  | NOUN | VERB | ADJECTIVE | ADVERB |
|---|:---:|:---:|:---:|:---:|
| **1. coward** | | | | |
| • a terrible **coward** | ✓ | | | |
| • an act of **cowardice** | ✓ | | | |
| • a **cowardly** act | | | | ✓ |
| **2. guarantee** | | | | |
| • **guarantee** it will happen | | | | |
| • give a **guarantee** | | | | |
| **3. justice** | | | | |
| • work toward **justice** | | | | |
| • a **just** decision | | | | |
| **4. punctual** | | | | |
| • always be **punctual** | | | | |
| • with amazing **punctuality** | | | | |
| **5. vain** | | | | |
| • a **vain** child | | | | |
| • tremendous **vanity** | | | | |

**B.** *Read the first half of each sentence and match it with the appropriate ending.*

___b___ 1. Superman was never

_____ 2. Oliver is worried about the future. He wants

_____ 3. A person who treats others fairly is

_____ 4. You're always at work on time. Thank you for your

_____ 5. I'd thought Alice and Caroline were modest, so I was surprised by their

_____ 6. Tellie's father said that he was ashamed of her

a. **punctuality**.

b. a **cowardly** person.

c. **just**.

d. **vanity**.

e. a **guarantee** that he will have a job.

f. **cowardice**.

# SAME WORD, DIFFERENT MEANING

Most words have more than one meaning. Study the additional meanings of **branch**, **justice**, and **temper**. Then read each sentence and decide which meaning is used.

| a. **branch** *n.* | part of a tree that has leaves, fruit, or smaller branches growing from it |
|---|---|
| b. **branch** *v.* | to divide into two or more smaller, narrower, or less important parts |
| c. **justice** *n.* | fairness in the way people are treated |
| d. **justice** *n.* | the system by which people are judged in courts of law and criminals are punished |
| e. **temper** *n.* | a tendency to become suddenly angry |
| f. **temper** *v.* | to make something less difficult or severe |

__*b*__ 1. In my town, the Blue River **branches** into two narrower rivers.

_____ 2. Legal cases in the criminal **justice** system are supposed to be fair for everyone.

_____ 3. Mr. Ricardson is not a popular teacher because he has a terrible **temper**.

_____ 4. I had better grades than Quinn, but the university rejected me and accepted him; where is the **justice**?

_____ 5. On a windy night, a **branch** tapped against the window of the children's room.

_____ 6. The doctor **tempered** the bad news by explaining that the hopes of recovery were excellent.

# WORDS IN SENTENCES

Complete each sentence with one of the words from the box.

| branches | district | Justice | ~~merchants~~ | tempered |
|---|---|---|---|---|
| coward | guarantee | knelt | punctuality | vain |

1. Thirty ___*merchants*___ have stores in the shopping mall.

2. _____ is important for this class; you should never be late.

3. Elizabeth _____ on the ground as she planted the flowers in her garden.

4. When State Street _____ into two roads, take the left road.

5. When Derik was too scared to ride on the motorcycle, his brother said, "You're a _____."

6. The United States Department of _____ is the government agency that enforces the law.

7. Many powerful businesses are located in the financial _____.

8. When Amelia put a giant picture of herself on her desk, her co-workers said, "She is so _____."

9. This shampoo comes with a _____; if you are not satisfied, you can return the shampoo and get your money back.

10. Zarina _____ her criticism by speaking in a soft voice.

## ▌WORDS IN COLLOCATIONS AND EXPRESSIONS

*Following are common collocations (word partners) and expressions with some of the key words. Read the definitions and then complete the conversations with the correct form of the collocations and expressions.*

| | |
|---|---|
| 1. **branch** | |
| • **branch office** | a local office of a larger business |
| 2. **guarantee** | |
| • **there's no guarantee that** | it is not sure to happen |
| 3. **justice** | |
| • **do (sb/sth) justice** | to treat or represent someone or something in a way that is fair and shows the best qualities of the person or thing |
| 4. **temper** | |
| • **have a temper tantrum** | to have a sudden fit of uncontrolled anger and emotion |
| • **lose/keep your temper** | to suddenly become angry/to stay calm |
| 5. **vain** | |
| • **in vain** | without success |

1. PROFESSOR: Your research paper is really weak. You have to start again.

   JEFFREY: You can't be serious! I worked on that paper for two months!

   PROFESSOR: Calm down. There is no reason to ____lose your temper____.

   JEFFREY: You're right. I'm sorry, Professor.

2. POLITICIAN 1: Did you see the newspaper article about me in the *Times* today? It didn't _____ me _____! I'm much more important than that article said.

   POLITICIAN 2: Sorry, but I disagree. I read the article, and I thought it was fair. Don't be vain, Tom. You're not that important.

3. INSTRUCTOR: After you jump out of the plane, pull on the string and your parachute will open.

   STUDENT: Can you promise me that?

   INSTRUCTOR: Well, _____ that your parachute will open, but why worry about that? Jump!

   STUDENT: No way!

4.    THEO:    How is business?

      ERIC:    Great. The company is so successful that we're going to open a
               _____ in San Francisco. How is your business?

      THEO:    Not good. I have financial problems. I asked the bank for a loan, but it was
               _____. The bank wouldn't give me a penny.

5. YOUNG CHILD:    Buy me the toy robot!!!

      MOTHER:    Shhh! I told you I won't buy it. Please be quiet.

YOUNG CHILD :    No!!! I WANT THE ROBOT!!

 STORE OWNER:    Excuse me, but your son is disturbing the other customers.
               He can't _____ here. Please take him outside.

## ▌WORDS IN A READING

*Read this article about ancient trails in Peru. Complete it with words and expressions from the boxes.*

| district | do justice to | kneel | lose your temper | vain |
|----------|---------------|-------|------------------|------|

### EXPLORING ANCIENT INCA TRAILS

Are you bored by the idea of spending your next vacation in the shopping ____district____ of a
                                                                              1
modern city? Do you believe it is _____ to spend your vacation in a beauty spa? Do you
                                            2
think you will _____ if you go on another boring family vacation? If so, perhaps you
                      3
should consider a more adventurous trip walking the ancient Inca trails in South America.

Each day up to 2,000 tourists flood the ancient Inca mountaintop city of Machu Picchu in southern
Peru. They come to admire temples built from perfectly cut blocks of granite. Here tourists explore and
take photographs. There are even some people who _____ to pray there.
                                                              4

Most of the tourists travel by train from nearby Cuzco. Others ride the bus. A few hundred more
daring people feel that taking public transportation does not _____ the famous Inca Trail
                                                                       5
to Machu Picchu. They arrive on foot after a four-day journey along that amazing road. If you are truly
adventurous, you too might want to attempt the trip.

| branched | cowardly | guarantee | merchants |
|----------|----------|-----------|-----------|

The World Conservation Union is heading a project to restore and bring new life to sections of the Inca
High Road or Gran Ruta Inca. The High Road followed the spine of the Andes and served as the main road
in a network of ancient trails. Inca rulers used this network of roads to keep their empire running smoothly.
Many roads _____ off the High Road. One followed the coastline. Several roads connected
                      6
the coastal route to the Andes. Other roads trailed from the Andes into the jungle toward the Amazon.

The Gran Ruta Inca has been covered or destroyed where it passes through major cities and towns. But in rural villages, it is in better condition. These rural communities are occupied mainly by indigenous people living in extreme poverty. While there is no _____ that the local
7
people will be helped by the Gran Ruta Inca project, it seems very likely that they will gain a lot.

Adventurer Karin Muller encourages the tourists who hike the Inca Trail to Machu Picchu or other trails linked to the Gran Ruta Inca to find the courage to participate in the Inca culture. Most travelers would love to get involved in the culture, but are a bit _____ because they fear rejection. In
8
truth, the local people are very friendly. Tourists can try to start conversations with _____
9
in local shops or with people on the road. By involving themselves in the culture, tourists will have a much richer experience.

*(Based on information in John Roach, "Restoration Afoot for Ancient Inca Trails." National Geographic News, August 17, 2004.)*

## ▌WORDS IN DISCUSSION

*Apply the key words to your own life. Read and discuss each question in small groups. Try to use the key words.*

### EXAMPLE

How important I think it is to be **punctual**: *not very important*

***A:*** *Why don't you think it's important to be **punctual**?*

***B:*** *None of my friends are on time, so I don't see why I should be.*

***A:*** *Don't you need to be **punctual** if you're going to a meeting or a class?*

1. How often I am **punctual**: _____
2. I think a **coward** is a person who always: _____
3. A famous person who is **vain**: _____
4. The last place where I **kneeled**: _____
5. What I would do if a tree **branch** fell in front of my car, during a storm:
   _____
6. The number of times I have lost my **temper** and shouted at someone this year:
   _____
7. The **district** of my city in which I would like to work: _____
8. A place where **merchants** sell souvenirs to tourists in my country:
   _____
9. How interested I am in the criminal **justice** system: _____
10. Something I will try to do even if there is no **guarantee** of success:
    _____

*Choose two topics and write a short paragraph on each. Try to use the key words.*

1. What makes you **lose your temper**?

   **EXAMPLE**

   *I am usually a calm person, and I tend not to get angry easily. However, if someone wakes me up very early in the morning, I **lose my temper** and exclaim, "Go away!" I have had this bad habit for as long as I can remember. When I was a small child, I would have a terrible **temper tantrum** if I was awoken early.*

2. Describe a person whom you think is a **coward**.

3. Imagine that a visitor is coming to your home city for a day. Describe the **districts** that he or she should visit.

4. Do you believe that being **vain** can help you succeed in life? Explain why or why not.

5. For what events do you feel that it is important to be **punctual**? Explain.

## WORDS IN CONTEXT

*Use the sentences to guess what each key word means. Choose the meaning that is closest to that of the key word in **bold**.*

1. **accord**
/əˈkɔrd/
-noun

   • Sadly, the city council members couldn't reach an **accord** on how to solve the problem of homeless animals. Several plans were suggested, but none were accepted by all.

   • When Morocco asked to join the European Union, members of the EU were in **accord**: Morocco wasn't a European country, so their answer was no.

   *Accord* means . . .    a. anger    (b.) agreement    c. confusion

2. **desert**
/ˈdɛzərt/
-noun

   • The Sahara **desert** is one of the hottest regions in the world: temperatures there can rise over 136°F (57°C).

   • In the **desert**, few plants grow well besides the cactus, which can hold up to 760 liters of water.

   *Desert* means . . .    a. hot, dry land    b. a rainy area of land    c. high hills

3. **efficient**
/ɪˈfɪʃənt/
-adjective

   • The housekeeper was very **efficient**. All the rooms were tidy and clean by lunchtime.

   • Most airports I've been to have an **efficient** way to check bags and tickets to get passengers to their planes on time.

   *Efficient* means . . .    a. moving slowly    b. careful    c. working well and quickly

4. **gap**
/gæp/
-noun

   • The rabbit found a **gap** in the fence and easily got through to the vegetable garden.

   • When Nicky lost a baby tooth, he had a **gap** between his two front teeth.

   *Gap* means . . .    a. a piece of wire    b. a piece of food    c. an empty space

5. **income**
/ˈɪnkʌm/
-noun

   • Adam makes only $2,000 a month. It's hard to support himself and his son on that **income**.

   • Each year you must report your family's **income** to the government.

   *Income* means . . .    a. money earned    b. job    c. number of members in a group

6. **injure**
/'ɪndʒɚ/
-verb

- Ghalib is lucky that he didn't **injure** himself seriously when he fell down.
- The dog's leg was obviously broken. Was it an accident or did a cruel person **injure** the poor animal?

*Injure* means . . .     a. to kill           b. to hurt          c. to throw

7. **resign**
/rɪ'zaɪn/
-verb

- After Barbara had her second child, she decided to **resign** and stay at home.
- Wallace **resigned** when he got a better job offer at another company.

*Resign* means . . .     a. to start a career      b. to quit your job      c. to move to a new home

8. **scarce**
/skɛrs/
-adjective

- With no rivers or streams nearby, water was **scarce**, and the hikers had to use what they had very carefully.
- Information about that historical event was **scarce**. I had to look in many places just to learn a few facts.

*Scarce* means . . .     a. everywhere        b. not easy to find      c. plentiful

9. **stock**
/stɑk/
-noun

- Do we have this bag in red? I think so. Let me check my **stock**.
- My grandmother always has a **stock** of canned food for emergencies.

*Stock* means . . .     a. a supply          b. a sale           c. a display

10. **survey**
/'sɚveɪ/
-noun

- Researchers did a **survey** to find out what students eat and if they eat well.
- Customers were asked to do a **survey** in order to improve service.

*Survey* means . . .     a. a report          b. a lesson         c. a set of questions

## ❙ WORDS AND DEFINITIONS

*Match each key word with its definition.*

1. ____*income*____ money that you earn from working or making investments

2. _____ a large area of land where it is always hot and dry

3. _____ an empty space between two things or two parts of something

4. _____ to officially leave your job or position because you want to

5. _____ not easy to find because not enough is available

6. _____ a set of questions that you ask a large number of people in order to find out about their opinions and behavior

7. _____ a formal agreement between groups or countries

8. _____ to hurt a person or animal

9. _____ a supply of something that is kept to be sold or used later

10. _____ working well, quickly, and without wasting time, energy, or effort

# COMPREHENSION CHECK

*Choose the best answer.*

1. An **efficient** restaurant staff will
   a. confuse your order with the order of another table.
   b. take a long time to give you your bill.
   c. seat you at a table that hasn't been cleared.
   (d.) serve a good meal in a short amount of time.

2. Amal's new job as a salesperson gives him a higher **income**. Now he
   a. must be careful about his spending.
   b. can get the car he's wanted to buy for a long time.
   c. will need to drive farther to reach his office.
   d. won't be able to spend as much time with his family.

3. If you asked people to complete a **survey** about hobbies, you would
   a. recommend your own hobby.
   b. warn them that not exercising is bad for one's health.
   c. create a set of questions to find out how they spend their free time.
   d. ask people to teach you new skills like dancing and playing tennis.

4. Food might be **scarce** because
   a. wartime can slow down the delivery of food and make it very expensive.
   b. the supermarkets offer a wonderful selection of fruits and cheeses.
   c. a chef might choose to make a dish without meat.
   d. some people don't eat fish.

5. The following are all ways you can **injure** yourself EXCEPT
   a. running on an icy sidewalk.
   b. cutting onions quickly with a sharp knife.
   c. wiping the kitchen table with a wet sponge.
   d. picking up a very heavy bag and carrying it up the stairs.

6. The school keeps a **stock** of office supplies;
   a. teachers have to buy their own markers and erasers.
   b. teachers always have use of pens, paper, and staples.
   c. teachers have asked the school to buy paper more than once.
   d. the school is unable to provide paper at this time.

7. What would NOT be a reason for Divya to **resign**?
   a. She loves her job and respects her co-workers.
   b. She gets paid very little, and the company will not pay her more.
   c. She received a great job offer in another city.
   d. She needs to be at home to take care of her mother, who is very sick.

8. There was a large **gap** between the bookcase and the wall, so
   a. the cat couldn't hide behind the bookcase.
   b. the cat got stuck while running behind the bookcase.
   c. I couldn't really see if the cat was hiding there.
   d. the cat used the space to hide in.

9. What are you NOT likely to find in a **desert**?
   a. a cactus
   b. a camel
   c. a lake
   d. sand

10. If a group of business people are in **accord**, they
    a. are likely to argue.
    b. still need to address the most important problem.
    c. can move forward with their business plans.
    d. will need time to research other solutions.

# WORD FAMILIES

Now that you have studied the ten key words and their basic definitions, you are ready to learn words that belong to the same family as some of the key words. A word family includes words that look alike but have different functions (noun, verb, adjective, or adverb). Their meanings are related but different.

**A.** Look at each model phrase and decide whether the word in **bold** is used as a noun, verb, adjective, or adverb.

| | NOUN | VERB | ADJECTIVE | ADVERB |
|---|:---:|:---:|:---:|:---:|
| **1. desert** | | | | |
| • live in the **desert** | ✓ | | | |
| • **desert** a place | | ✓ | | |
| **2. efficient** | | | | |
| • an **efficient** system | | | | |
| • to work **efficiently** | | | | |
| **3. injure** | | | | |
| • **injure** yourself | | | | |
| • a back **injury** | | | | |
| **4. resign** | | | | |
| • **resign** from your job | | | | |
| • a letter of **resignation** | | | | |
| **5. stock** | | | | |
| • a **stock** of food | | | | |
| • **stock** weapons | | | | |
| **6. survey** | | | | |
| • fill out a **survey** | | | | |
| • **survey** the students | | | | |

**B.** Read each sentence and match the word in **bold** with the correct definition.

___b___ 1. Messages are not delivered **efficiently** in our office. They often come late.

_____ 2. The enemy was close; people **deserted** the village for the mountains.

_____ 3. I'm unhappy in my present job. As soon as I get another job offer, I'll hand in my **resignation**.

_____ 4. I like to be prepared, so I **stock** light bulbs and batteries in my closet.

_____ 5. Eli is suffering from serious **injuries** he received in the car accident.

_____ 6. I **surveyed** my classmates as part of my research on how teenagers spend money. Their answers will help me write my paper.

a. physical harm or damage that is caused by an accident or attack

b. done in a manner in which time, energy, and effort are not wasted and the result is good

c. to leave a place so that it is completely empty

d. to ask a large number of people a set of questions to find out their opinions or behavior

e. to have a supply of something available to be sold or used

f. the act of leaving your job; a written statement to say you are doing this

# SAME WORD, DIFFERENT MEANING

*Most words have more than one meaning. Study the additional meanings of **desert**, **gap**, and **injure**. Then read each sentence and decide which meaning is used.*

| a. **desert** *v.* | to leave a place so that it is completely empty |
| b. **desert** *v.* | to leave someone alone without any help |
| c. **gap** *n.* | an empty space between two things or parts |
| d. **gap** *n.* | a difference between two situations, groups, amounts, etc. |
| e. **injure** *v.* | to hurt a person or animal |
| f. **injure** *v.* | to harm or damage something such as someone's position, feelings, or chances of doing something |

__a__ 1. The approaching storm forced the townspeople to **desert** their homes and businesses.

_____ 2. My necklace broke and fell through a narrow **gap** between two boards of the old walkway.

_____ 3. Bend your knees when you lift heavy boxes or you'll **injure** your back.

_____ 4. Only two years separate my older sister and me, but the age **gap** between my brother and me is much larger. He's almost ten years younger than I am.

_____ 5. The man **deserted** his family, and they were left with no income.

_____ 6. My failure to win **injured** my pride, but the whole experience also taught me an important lesson in modesty.

# WORDS IN SENTENCES

*Complete each sentence with a word from the box.*

| accord | efficiently | income | resignation | stock |
| ~~deserted~~ | gap | injury | scarce | surveyed |

1. The house looked empty and was in need of care. How long ago had the family ___deserted___ it?

2. Water is very _____ in the desert.

3. Marbella _____ her co-workers and learned that everyone had smoked at one point but gave it up to become healthier.

4. The team of mechanics worked on the race car so _____ that in seconds the car was ready to go again.

5. Darius, a firefighter, recently suffered a back _____. He won't be able to work for at least a month.

6. Many expected Russell's _____ after he won the lottery, but he surprised everyone by stating that he wanted to keep working.

7. The _____ between the two nations' plans was large. They had completely different views on the economy and military weapons.

8. Our family has a limited _____, so we are careful about how much we spend on groceries and entertainment each month.

9. The countries took a long time to reach a(n) _____, but they finally agreed where to draw the border.

10. My sister refuses to _____ her refrigerator with lots of food. She likes to buy only what she needs for a day or two.

## WORDS IN COLLOCATIONS AND EXPRESSIONS

*Following are common collocations (word partners) and expressions with some of the key words. Read the definitions and then complete the conversations with the correct form of the collocations and expressions.*

| | |
|---|---|
| 1. **accord** | |
| • **be in accord with (sb/sth)** | to be in agreement with someone or something |
| 2. **gap** | |
| • **gap between** | an empty space or a difference between two things |
| 3. **income** | |
| • **income tax** | tax paid on the money you earn |
| 4. **resign** | |
| • **resign yourself to (doing sth)** | to accept something that is unpleasant but cannot be changed |
| 5. **stock** | |
| • **in/out of stock** | available/unavailable to be sold |
| • **take stock of (sth)** | to think carefully about a situation in order to decide what to do next |

1.    JAMIE:    Wasn't Svetlana a director back in Ukraine?

    OLIVIA:    Yes, and she has a lot of experience in the field, but she'll have to
    _____*resign*_____ herself _____*to*_____ working in a
    low-paying job until her English improves.

2.    CAREY:    Did you know that Somwang used to work in a bank?

    SAM:    Yeah. He told me that after losing his job there, he needed to
    _____ his life. He realized he wanted to be a chef.

3.  PRESIDENT:    If everyone in the club is _____ my recommendation to
    meet twice a month, then let's choose two dates for next month.

    MEMBER:    I say we always meet on the first and third Monday of the month.

    PRESIDENT:    That's a good idea. Everyone agreed?

4. MRS. LEWIS: How long has Mr. Griffin been retired?

   MRS. GRIFFIN: Just one year. The _____ our ages is quite large. I plan to work for another fourteen years before I retire.

5. JOURNALIST: There's talk that the government may have to raise the _____ to support the war.

   POLITICIAN: It's difficult to say how much longer the war will last. So far we've been able to meet our military goals without asking for additional money.

6. KEISHA: I thought you went to the mall to buy winter boots.

   SAMANTHA: I did, but winter boots are no longer _____. All the stores are selling spring shoes. Can you imagine? It's still January!

## WORDS IN A READING

*Read this article about a problem Irish parents face. Complete it with words and expressions from the boxes.*

| deserted | efficiently | injure | ~~surveyed~~ |
|----------|-------------|--------|----------|

### GOVERNMENT HELP FOR PARENTS

A recent study shows the unhappiness of many stay-at-home and working parents in Ireland. Of the 1,081 people ___surveyed___ by the Irish Examiner/Lansdowne Market Research, eighty-four percent stated that government has not dealt _____ with the issue of quality childcare. The information suggests that politicians will _____ their chances of getting elected in the future if they do not address the issue of childcare now.

Women who have returned to work after having a child feel as if the state has _____ them. They are encouraged to return to their jobs, but then no help is given for childcare. Presently, many parents turn to relatives for free help. When both parents work, one out of three households ask the grandparents to look after children of preschool age. However, changing economics often require families to move to new places like Dublin, taking them away from relatives' support. Of course, using a childcare center is another possibility for working parents, but the cost is high. Only one in ten believes that childcare costs are reasonable.

| gap between | income tax | scarce |
|-------------|------------|--------|
| in accord | resigned themselves to | take stock of |

When asked who should receive government assistance, all Irish parents are _____: working parents *and* stay-at-home parents need financial help. Most working parents—eighty-four percent—support the idea of a state payment to parents remaining at home. According to the survey, almost half of all parents want the _____ raised by one percent to help pay for childcare in general.

The whole situation has caused a number of problems, but solutions are _____. The
7
survey showed that full-time parenting is considered to be the best form of childcare, but not all families
can afford it. Moreover, many parents have already _____ limiting their family size: in
8
homes where both the mother and father work, parents say that having another child would mean that
one parent would have to quit working. This is especially true if the family already has two children.

In short, it is time for the Irish government to _____ the situation. Families are asking
9
for help, and the _____ the people's needs and the state's support is too wide, especially in
10
comparison with the rest of western Europe. Possibilities such as job-sharing and tele-working need to be
considered. The government and its social partners must explore all ways to meet parents' needs, says Dr.
Margret Fine-Davis of the Centre for Gender and Women's Studies at Trinity College in Dublin.

*(Based on information in Catherine Shanahan, "Pay Stay-at-Home and Working Parents." The Irish Examiner, September 11, 2005.)*

## WORDS IN DISCUSSION

*Apply the key words to your own life. Read and discuss each question in small groups. Try to use the key words.*

1. Have you ever had a serious **injury**?

   **EXAMPLE**

   *Two years ago, I **injured** my leg when I fell down the stairs. The pain was so bad, I fainted. I was rushed to the hospital. They were very **efficient**, and my leg is fine now.*

2. Is there a large **gap** or a small **gap between** your parents' ages?

3. Do you often **resign yourself to** doing work around the house? Is there any kind of housework you actually like?

4. A bad snowstorm is coming and you'll probably have to stay indoors for several days. What will you make sure you have a large **stock** of?

5. Do people pay **income tax** in your native country?

6. Do you work **efficiently** or do you often waste time and energy?

7. Name a reason why a family might **desert** their home.

8. You've been invited to **survey** a large group of famous people. What will the subject of your **survey** be?

9. Are your views usually **in accord with** those of your parents? Your siblings?

10. Is there something in your life you find to be **scarce**? Explain.

## ❚ WORDS IN WRITING

*Choose two topics and write a short paragraph on each. Try to use the key words.*

1. You're going to live in a **desert** for one week. Who and what will you take with you?

   **EXAMPLE**

   *If I'm going to spend a week in a **desert**, then I'll take lots of water, sunblock lotion, a tent, a big hat, sunglasses, dry food, and a few books. I'd like to invite my best friend so I won't be lonely.*

2. Describe a time you needed to **take stock of** your life. What decision(s) did you face at that time?

3. You have a great job, and now you have just won the lottery. Will you **resign** from your job? Why or why not?

4. Name a common way many people **injure** themselves in their own homes. How can home **injuries** be prevented?

5. What do you consider to be an acceptable **income** for a person living in your hometown?

| assign | decay | lean | pump | shield |
|--------|-------|------|------|--------|
| awkward | gender | peculiar | seed | swear |

## WORDS IN CONTEXT

*Use the sentences to guess what each key word means. Choose the meaning that is closest to that of the key word in **bold**.*

1. **assign**
   /əˈsaɪn/
   –verb

   • For homework, Miss Anderson **assigned** chapters two and three.
   • Our team was **assigned** the research for the new project.

   *Assign* means . . .   a. to give a choice   (b.) to give a job to do   c. to give papers

2. **awkward**
   /ˈɔkwəd/
   –adjective

   • Al is an **awkward** dancer; he looked scared when the girl asked him to dance.
   • Eleanor is very shy, so she feels **awkward** when she meets new people.

   *Awkward* means . . .   a. uncomfortable   b. graceful   c. relaxed and skillful

3. **decay**
   /dɪˈkeɪ/
   –verb

   • Because Mike's tooth had **decayed**, the dentist had to pull it out.
   • After leaves fall from trees in the forest, they **decay**.

   *Decay* means . . .   a. to be in fine condition   b. to be slowly destroyed   c. to disappear

4. **gender**
   /ˈdʒɛndə/
   –noun

   • Before their baby was born, Eliska and Luke did not know what the **gender** would be; they had no idea if they were going to have a boy or a girl.
   • The committee will not choose the new teacher on the basis of **gender** because we feel that either a man or a woman can do the job well.

   *Gender* means . . .   a. language   b. male or female   c. identity

5. **lean**
   /lin/
   –verb

   • When Angie whispered the secret, Josie **leaned** forward to hear it.
   • Mrs. Williams felt tired as she waited in line, so she **leaned** against the wall.

   *Lean* means . . .   a. to remain still   b. to jump   c. to bend or rest against

6. **peculiar**
   /pɪˈkyulyə/
   –adjective

   • Andrew has the **peculiar** habit of eating breakfast at night.
   • This soup has a **peculiar** taste; I can't decide if I like it.

   *Peculiar* means . . .   a. strange   b. normal   c. perfect

7. **pump**
   /pʌmp/
   –noun

   • Nakori used a **pump** to put more air into her bike tire.
   • This station is self-service; drive up to the **pump** and put gas into the car.

   *Pump* means . . .   a. air   b. a gas station   c. a machine that forces air or liquid into something

8. **seed**
/sid/
–noun

- My grandfather planted the apple **seed** in the ground behind our house, and now it has grown into a beautiful apple tree.
- **Seeds** that you plant in the spring will grow into flowers in the summer.

*Seed* means . . .

a. a flower

b. the stem

c. part of plant from which a new plant will grow

9. **shield**
/ʃild/
–noun

- A long time ago, a knight who went to war carried a **shield** to protect himself; if someone shot arrows at him, he could hold up his **shield** to block the arrows.
- During violent demonstrations, the police sometimes carry **shields** to protect themselves from stones or other objects people throw at them.

*Shield* means . . .

a. something that is a weapon

b. a kind of clothing

c. something that protects

10. **swear**
/swɛr/
–verb

- If a person **swears** in a television interview, the station covers the rude words with a beep because it is not legal to **swear** on television.
- Our grandmother was so upset when she heard Gabe **swear** that she threatened to wash his mouth out with soap.

*Swear* means . . .

a. to use polite language

b. to use unusual language

c. to use offensive language

## WORDS AND DEFINITIONS

*Match each key word with its definition.*

1. _____decay_____ to be slowly destroyed by a natural chemical process

2. _____ the fact of being male or female

3. _____ to give someone a job to do

4. _____ to use offensive language

5. _____ a small, hard object produced by plants, from which a new plant will grow

6. _____ to bend your body or rest it against something for support

7. _____ something that protects someone or something from being hurt or damaged

8. _____ strange and a little surprising

9. _____ moving or behaving in a way that is not relaxed or comfortable because you feel nervous or embarrassed

10. _____ a machine that forces air or liquid into something

# COMPREHENSION CHECK

*Choose the best answer.*

1. What does a **shield** do?
   a. It shoots.
   b. It protects. *(circled)*
   c. It hurts.
   d. It entertains.

2. Who is **awkward**?
   a. Helene, who speaks with perfect confidence.
   b. Nadine, who is a graceful dancer.
   c. Troy, who tries to dance and trips over his partner's feet.
   d. Marcos, who feels comfortable meeting his girlfriend's parents.

3. Who is **peculiar**?
   a. Vince, who wears a business suit to go to the office.
   b. Nina, who wears jeans around the house.
   c. Ella, who wears a heavy coat in winter.
   d. Zack, who wears a heavy coat in summer.

4. What should you never **lean** on?
   a. a desk
   b. a fence
   c. a sofa
   d. a hot stove

5. Which item has a **gender**?
   a. a child
   b. a mountain
   c. a table
   d. sunshine

6. What can a **pump** NOT put into a car?
   a. air
   b. gas
   c. sand
   d. fuel

7. Which situation involves **swearing**?
   a. "Kurt! Don't use bad words."
   b. "Maybe I'll study vocabulary tonight."
   c. "I am looking for some new sunglasses."
   d. "I am so disappointed that you broke my computer."

8. What is NOT **decaying**?
   a. Because Shelly eats candy constantly, her teeth are turning black.
   b. The dead fish is rotting on the beach.
   c. The new leaves are growing on the tree.
   d. The dead plant is turning brown.

9. Who is **assigning** something?
   a. "Yes, I accept the job."
   b. "Harry, your job is to wash the dishes."
   c. "Why should I work?"
   d. "You can help if you have some spare time."

10. Which description does not involve a **seed**?
    a. A watermelon has many of them.
    b. You peel the skin from a vegetable before you eat it.
    c. To grow tomatoes, we need to put them in the dirt.
    d. You don't want to eat this part of an orange.

# WORD FAMILIES

Now that you have studied the ten key words and their basic definitions, you are ready to learn words that belong to the same family as some of the key words. A word family includes words that look alike but have different functions (noun, verb, adjective, or adverb). Their meanings are related but different.

**A.** *Look at each model phrase and decide whether the word in **bold** is used as a noun, verb, adjective, or adverb.*

|  | NOUN | VERB | ADJECTIVE | ADVERB |
|---|---|---|---|---|
| **1. assign** | | | | |
| • **assign** responsibilities | | ✓ | | |
| • a new **assignment** | ✓ | | | |
| **2. awkward** | | | | |
| • an **awkward** teenager | | | | |
| • throw **awkwardly** | | | | |
| **3. decay** | | | | |
| • start to **decay** | | | | |
| • tooth **decay** | | | | |
| **4. peculiar** | | | | |
| • a **peculiar** habit | | | | |
| • little **peculiarities** | | | | |
| **5. pump** | | | | |
| • a gas **pump** | | | | |
| • **pump** gas into the car | | | | |
| **6. shield** | | | | |
| • a metal **shield** | | | | |
| • **shield** someone | | | | |

**B.** *Match the following sentences with the definition of the word in **bold**.*

___b___ 1. My sister wants to **shield** her children from bad movies.

_____ 2. In many gas stations, you can have someone **pump** gas into your car, or you can do it yourself.

_____ 3. Singing to himself is one of Jim's **peculiarities**.

_____ 4. I **awkwardly** tried to explain why I was forty-five minutes late to class.

_____ 5. The journalist traveled to Vietnam on a special **assignment**.

_____ 6. The dentist advised his patient to brush her teeth regularly to avoid tooth **decay**.

a. an unusual or slightly strange habit or quality, especially one that only a particular person, place, or thing has

b. to protect someone or something from being hurt, damaged, or upset

c. a job or piece of work that is given to someone.

d. to use a pump to make air or liquid move in a particular direction

e. in a strange way because you feel nervous or embarrassed

f. the process, state, or result of decaying

## SAME WORD, DIFFERENT MEANING

Most words have more than one meaning. Study the additional meanings of **assign**, **lean**, and **swear**. Then read each sentence and decide which meaning is used.

| | | |
|---|---|---|
| a. **assign** v. | to give someone a job to do |
| b. **assign** v. | to give something to someone |
| c. **lean** v. | to bend your body or rest it against something for support |
| d. **lean** adj. | having little fat |
| e. **swear** v. | to use offensive language |
| f. **swear** v. | to promise that you will do something |

_d_ 1. Swimmers have **lean** bodies.

_____ 2. When the judge asked Ron if he would be honest, Ron said, "I **swear** to tell the truth."

_____ 3. When we were sailing, the captain asked us to **lean** to the left to balance the boat.

_____ 4. Hank **swore** at his enemy.

_____ 5. The university **assigned** a small dorm room to Carol.

_____ 6. Lola **assigned** a chapter to each person in her study group.

## WORDS IN SENTENCES

Complete each sentence with one of the words from the box.

| | | | | |
|---|---|---|---|---|
| ~~assign~~ | decaying | lean | pumps | shield |
| awkwardly | gender | peculiar | seeds | swore |

1. My managers _____ assign _____ projects to me.

2. Carly doesn't let her five-year-old child watch the news; she wants to _____ him from violent stories.

3. When I had to give a speech in French, which I do not know well, I spoke _____.

4. During the wedding ceremony, Heinz _____ to love his wife for the rest of his life.

5. That's a(n) _____ idea; why did you suggest it?

6. Stef is on a diet, so she will eat only _____ meat.

7. At the beginning of the summer, the Stuntz family _____ water into their swimming pool.

8. When choosing a puppy, it's important to consider which _____ you want.

9. The old wooden dock was _____ in the water.

10. If you want to grow sunflowers, you should plant _____ in April.

# WORDS IN COLLOCATIONS AND EXPRESSIONS

*Following are common collocations (word partners) and expressions with some of the key words. Read the definitions and then complete the conversations with the correct forms of the collocations and expressions.*

1. **assign**
   - **assign (sb) the task of (doing sth)** — give somebody a job to do

2. **awkward**
   - **an awkward position** — an embarrassing position

3. **peculiar**
   - **be peculiar to** — to be a quality of only one particular person, place, or thing

4. **seed**
   - **plant the seeds of (sth)** — to start something that will grow and develop

5. **shield**
   - **shield (sb/sth) from** — to protect someone or something from being hurt, damaged, or upset

6. **swear**
   - **I could have sworn that** — said to mean that you were sure about something, but now you are not sure

1.   MOTHER:   I don't want you to go to that movie. I've heard that the actors swear a lot.

     SON:   But I'm seventeen, Mom! You can't _shield_ me _from_ bad language forever. And I already invited Julie on a date to see it. Please, don't put me in _____ by telling me I can't go. I don't know how I could explain it to Julie.

2.   BIRD WATCHER 1:   Look at the brilliant blue color of the bird's feathers. Extraordinary, isn't it?

     BIRD WATCHER 2:   Yes. That color _____ blue starlings. I've been waiting my whole life to see it.

3.   COLUMBUS:   This isn't India?! But _____ I was in India!

     INDIAN CHIEF:   Sorry, but you're wrong.

4.   ASSISTANT:   What's my assignment this week, Professor?

     PROFESSOR:   I'm going to _____ you _____ correcting the final exams.

5.   ADVISOR:   Why don't you want to be a philosophy major anymore?

     STUDENT:   The philosophy class I took last semester began to _____ doubt in my mind. It was so boring, I started to wonder if I really wanted to philosophize forever. So I decided I wanted to study engineering.

*Read this article about health. Complete it with words and expressions from the boxes.*

| awkward | be peculiar to | planting the seeds of | ~~pump~~ | shield |
|---|---|---|---|---|

## NATIVE AMERICANS CHOOSE NEW HABITS TO FIGHT DIABETES

Diabetes is a disease in which there is too much sugar in the blood. Diabetics control their blood sugar levels with insulin, a natural substance produced by the body that allows sugar to be used for energy. Some people with diabetes wear an insulin _____*pump*_____ , which is a portable machine that puts insulin into the body at programmed times. Now researchers are interested in ways not only to control the disease, but also to prevent it.

Diabetes affects people around the world. However, in the United States, high rates of diabetes seem to _____2_____ Native Americans. In some tribes the rate of diabetes among adults is more than 50 percent.

Although Native Americans know that they're more at risk for diabetes, some may feel _____3_____ about trying to prevent it. In fact, many fear that they can do nothing to stop it. Now health educators at the Native American Community Health Center in Phoenix are _____4_____ change by teaching how this disease can be overcome. They want to _____5_____ as many young people as possible from developing the disease.

| assign ... the task of | genders | lean | swear |
|---|---|---|---|

Much of the community health center's focus is on educating young people. For several years now, the center has run a summer camp that educates kids of both _____6_____ aged ten to sixteen on how to avoid diabetes through good eating habits and exercise. The kids are weighed and have their blood sugar levels taken at the start of the camp. In the general population, about a quarter of kids are overweight. Among the camp kids, about three-quarters weigh too much.

Not only does the camp give the message of healthy living, it also helps the kids feel proud of being Native American. The health educators explain that health involves the physical, emotional, and spiritual self. They also _____7_____ the young people _____ taking the messages home. Families can change their eating habits by choosing to eat more _____8_____ meat and more fresh fruit and by avoiding sweetened drinks.

The Native American Community Health Center holds reunions for the campers every few months to recheck their weight and blood sugar levels and reinforce what they've learned. Health educators _____9_____ that the camp experience can make a change in these kids' lives. Giving the children the skills to make good health decisions prepares them to fight diabetes.

*(Based on Mary Beth Faller, "Native Americans Are Rethinking Diabetes." The Arizona Republic online, November 1, 2005.)*

## WORDS IN DISCUSSION

Apply the key words to your own life. Read and discuss each question in small groups. Try to use the key words.

**EXAMPLE**

One thing that I **swore** I would do: _____*never lie to my family*_____

*A: I think it's too hard to **swear** never to lie. Don't you have to lie sometimes?*

*B: No. Honesty is really important to me, so it was easy for me to make that promise.*

1. How often I **pump** gas into my car: _____

2. Someone I can **lean** on for emotional support: _____

3. If I have children, the **gender** that I would like them be: _____

4. How often I **swear**, using rude words: _____

5. The kind of **seed** I like to eat: _____

6. A job I would like to be **assigned** to: _____

7. How often my family tries to **shield** me from problems: _____

8. A situation in which I feel **awkward**: _____

9. Something that I hope will never **decay**: _____

10. Something I do that is **peculiar**: _____

## WORDS IN WRITING

Choose two topics and write a short paragraph on each. Try to use the key words.

1. Tell a story about a time when you planted a **seed**.

**EXAMPLE**

*A few years ago I wanted to grow some wildflowers, so I bought a packet of **seeds**. The directions looked remarkably easy. I simply had to dig a small hole, throw in the seeds, and cover the seeds with dirt. I waited and waited for the flowers to appear, but they didn't. What step had I forgotten? Much too late, I remembered that **seeds** need water to grow.*

2. At what age do you think people feel the most **awkward**? What advice would you give people at this **awkward** age?

3. What do you find **peculiar** about the English language?

4. What parts of life, if any, do you believe parents should **shield** their children from?

5. Do you prefer to have male or female friends or friends of both **genders**? Explain.

# QUIZ 9

## PART A

*Choose the word that best completes each item and write it in the space provided.*

1. The economy has been bad, so jobs are _____scarce_____.
   - a. scarce
   - b. awkward
   - c. vain
   - d. punctual

2. Anita is always _____, so I'm a bit worried that she's late for the meeting.
   - a. scarce
   - b. awkward
   - c. peculiar
   - d. punctual

3. In many cultures a first name tells you a person's _____. For example, "ko" is a common ending in Japanese female names. So Yuko, Reiko, and Keiko are girls.
   - a. temper
   - b. income
   - c. gender
   - d. district

4. Many know Broadway to be New York City's theater _____.
   - a. merchant
   - b. district
   - c. branch
   - d. stock

5. Teachers _____ homework for further practice. It's important to study at home, too.
   - a. guarantee
   - b. injure
   - c. resign
   - d. assign

6. We bought _____ to grow tomato plants and herbs in our garden.
   - a. branches
   - b. seeds
   - c. shields
   - d. stocks

7. My mother can usually control her _____, but the salesman was speaking so rudely that she began yelling at him right there in the store.
   - a. temper
   - b. gender
   - c. income
   - d. stock

8. Isn't it _____ that Paul says he's broke but wears expensive clothes?
   - a. vain
   - b. awkward
   - c. peculiar
   - d. punctual

9. They _____ this product works or they'll give your money back.
   - a. guarantee
   - b. injure
   - c. resign
   - d. assign

10. Many American families today have two _____. The mother and father both need to work to pay all the expenses.
    - a. merchants
    - b. incomes
    - c. gaps
    - d. stocks

## PART B

*Read each statement and write **T** for true or **F** for false in the space provided.*

____F____ 1. A **coward** faces difficult problems and dangerous situations with courage.

_____ 2. A person who seriously **injures** himself or herself should get medical attention.

_____ 3. Two businessmen reach an **accord** when they continue to argue and compete with each other.

_____ 4. A **shield's** main purpose is to cause harm.

_____ 5. A **stock** of food and water may be useful during a major snowstorm.

_____ 6. You might feel **awkward** if you forgot the name of the person you're talking to.

_____ 7. A **vain** person complains about the way he or she looks and envies others.

_____ 8. People expect **justice** in a court of law.

_____ 9. A **pump** can help you put gas in your car.

_____ 10. Employers want and need **efficient** workers.

## PART C

*Complete each item with a word from the box. Use each word once.*

| branch | desert | knelt | ~~merchants~~ | survey |
|--------|--------|-------|---------------|--------|
| decay | gap | leaned | resign | swears |

1. Although the number of indoor malls is growing, many _____merchants_____ around the world still do business in open air markets.

2. Death Valley is in a _____, and the temperature there can reach nearly 120°F (50°C). It's the lowest and hottest place in North America.

3. Brianna _____ closer to read the information printed next to the painting.

4. The messenger _____ before the king and queen before delivering the news.

5. There may be jobs that pay better, but Ms. Lockett will never_____ from this school. She loves teaching here too much.

6. Will you please complete my _____? I'm writing a paper, and I'd like to find out if people today are spending more time using the Internet than watching TV.

7. I appreciate hunters who use all parts of the animal they kill and leave nothing to _____.

8. The ball rolled through a _____ in the fence.

9. The child grabbed the lowest _____ and began to climb the tree.

10. Jake never _____, except when he's in extreme pain.

## WORDS IN CONTEXT

*Use the sentences to guess what each key word means. Choose the meaning that is closest to that of the key word in **bold**.*

1. **decade**
/ˈdɛkeɪd/
-noun

   • The 1960s were an important **decade** in space history. In 1961 Yuri Gagarin became the first human in space. In 1969 Neil Armstrong walked on the moon.

   • My sister is one **decade** older than I am, so while her favorite songs are mostly from the 1980s, mine are from the 1990s.

   *Decade* means . . .   a. ten years (circled)   b. date   c. wartime

2. **fault**
/fɔlt/
-noun

   • I overslept, so it's my **fault** that the group missed the plane. I'm sorry.

   • The teacher asked me who had broken the desk, and though I knew, I didn't want to say whose **fault** it was.

   *Fault* means . . .   a. a complaint   b. responsibility for a mistake   c. a request for help

3. **feature**
/ˈfitʃɚ/
-noun

   • The parents wanted to know more about the car's safety **features**; the children cared only about the entertainment **features**.

   • I bought the more expensive coffee machine with timed turn-on and automatic turn-off **features**.

   *Feature* means . . .   a. talent or ability   b. a secret   c. an important or interesting part

4. **judge**
/dʒʌdʒ/
-noun

   • The United States Supreme Court is made up of nine **judges** who serve for life.

   • The **judge** said that the woman was guilty and sent her to prison for twenty-five years.

   a. the person in control of a court   b. a police officer   c. a lawyer

5. **labor**
/ˈleɪbɚ/
-noun

   • Uncle Jim tried to pay us for our **labor**, but we told him that we didn't mind helping him move the furniture. It was hard work but good exercise.

   • My grandmother grew up on a farm, and everyone in the family shared the **labor**. One of her jobs was to milk the cows.

   *Labor* means . . .   a. suffering   b. work   c. help

**6. pack**
/pæk/
-verb

- You have too much in your closet. Why don't you **pack** your winter clothes and put them in the attic? You don't need them now.
- Why haven't you **packed** yet for your trip tomorrow? Go get your suitcase.

*Pack* means . . .   a. to put things in the garbage   b. to sell   c. to put things into boxes or suitcases

**7. rank**
/ræŋk/
-noun

- General is the highest **rank** in the U.S. Army.
- It takes nine to twelve years to move up the twelve **ranks** in the Boy Scouts of America. Little boys start as Cub Scouts and can become Eagle Scouts as young men.

*Rank* means . . .   a. a skill   b. a position or level   c. a job

**8. respond**
/rɪ'spɑnd/
-verb

- The fire department quickly **responded** to the call for help.
- If the subway employees refuse to work for those wages, how will the city **respond**? Does the mayor have a plan of action?

*Respond* means . . .   a. to react   b. to offer money   c. to show concern

**9. swell**
/swɛl/
-verb

- Both of the boxer's eyes were beginning to **swell**. Could he still see?
- My finger got caught in the door. Now it's **swelling** and it really hurts.

*Swell* means . . .   a. to become painful   b. to slowly get bigger   c. to bleed

**10. tender**
/'tɛndɚ/
-adjective

- The steak wasn't very **tender**, so my knife wasn't much help.
- The vegetables were **tender** enough for me to chew even with my sore tooth.

*Tender* means . . .   a. easy to eat   b. tasty   c. cooked

## WORDS AND DEFINITIONS

*Match each key word with its definition.*

1. _____labor_____ work, especially work using a lot of physical effort

2. _____ an important or interesting part of something

3. _____ a period of ten years

4. _____ responsibility for a mistake

5. _____ a position or level within an organization

6. _____ easy to cut and eat

7. _____ to slowly increase in size, especially because of an injury

8. _____ the official in control of a court of law who decides punishments for criminals

9. _____ to react to something that has been said or done

10. _____ to put things into boxes, bags, etc. in order to take or store them somewhere

*Choose the best answer.*

1. Iomar is moving to a new apartment. What will he use to **pack**?

   a. mops and brooms

   b. boxes, bags, and suitcases

   c. his friend's car or truck

   d. a newspaper that lists available apartments in the city

2. Which is the most common way to **respond** to a compliment?

   a. crying

   b. asking for an explanation

   c. getting angry and walking away

   d. saying "thank you"

3. Uncle Martin is a sergeant. Aunt Trudy says that he's a very good police officer, so one day he'll have the **rank** of captain. Which is correct?

   a. The position of a sergeant is lower than a captain's.

   b. The position of a sergeant is higher than a captain's.

   c. Uncle Martin will soon retire.

   d. The position of a sergeant is at the same level as a captain's.

4. Which is the best description of a **judge**'s job?

   a. to keep the streets safe from criminal activity

   b. to help people prepare for court cases

   c. to help decide if a person is guilty of a crime and decide punishments

   d. to inform the public of criminal activity through news reports

5. All the following items are special **features** of cell phones EXCEPT

   a. the ability to take, send, and store pictures.

   b. a choice of games to play.

   c. the cost of the phone.

   d. the ability to give voice commands.

6. Which person is performing **labor**?

   a. a tourist walking around the city

   b. a construction worker repairing a roof

   c. a businessman reading a newspaper in a coffee shop

   d. a woman writing a letter to her favorite cousin

7. The last time Leif saw Francisco was a **decade** ago. That means that

   a. Leif and Francisco see each other often.

   b. only a few months have passed since their last meeting.

   c. Leif and Francisco have never met.

   d. ten years have passed since their last meeting.

8. The meat was **tender**; it was

   a. a pleasure to eat such a fine steak.

   b. hard to chew.

   c. raw, so I had the waiter take it back to the kitchen.

   d. so spicy that I drank two whole glasses of water to cool my mouth.

9. Michelle's mouth is beginning to **swell** a little;

   a. she doesn't usually wear lipstick.

   b. she has a nice smile.

   c. she has been talking a lot and is tired.

   d. the dentist pulled a tooth earlier today.

10. It's not my **fault** that the shower is broken.

    a. I'm sorry. I'll pay for the damage.

    b. I use it every day without any problems.

    c. You're the one who tried to fix it and made it worse.

    d. We were trying to fix it, but we caused some damage.

# WORD FAMILIES

Now that you have studied the ten key words and their basic definitions, you are ready to learn words that belong to the same family as some of the key words. A word family includes words that look alike but have different functions (noun, verb, adjective, or adverb). Their meanings are related but different.

**A.** *Look at each model phrase and decide whether the word in **bold** is used as a noun, verb, adjective, or adverb.*

| | NOUN | VERB | ADJECTIVE | ADVERB |
|---|---|---|---|---|
| 1. **feature** | | | | |
| • a safety **feature** | ✓ | | | |
| • to **feature** a new actor | | ✓ | | |
| 2. **judge** | | | | |
| • the **judge's** decision | | | | |
| • **judge** her work | | | | |
| • a fair **judgment** | | | | |
| 3. **labor** | | | | |
| • appreciate your **labor** | | | | |
| • **labor** for hours | | | | |
| 4. **pack** | | | | |
| • **pack** your suitcase | | | | |
| • a **pack** of cigarettes | | | | |
| 5. **rank** | | | | |
| • the **rank** of Colonel | | | | |
| • **rank** restaurants by quality of service | | | | |
| 6. **respond** | | | | |
| • **respond** positively | | | | |
| • give a **response** | | | | |

**B.** *Read the first half of each sentence and match it with the appropriate ending.*

___f___ 1. Do you want to play a game with me?

_____ 2. To finish their work by evening

_____ 3. The 1956 film *Love Me Tender* was the first movie to

_____ 4. The Wharton School at the University of Pennsylvania is a good business school; most people

_____ 5. Knowledge and skills are important when deciding a person's value. Don't

_____ 6. My mother was so shocked by the news of my brother's marriage, she showed

_____ 7. Derek has been playing the guitar for only one year. Saying he's not very skilled is

a. a harsh **judgment**.

b. **feature** Elvis Presley.

c. **rank** it among the best.

d. use appearance to **judge** others.

e. the men must **labor** hard.

f. I just bought a **pack** of cards.

g. no **response**.

## SAME WORD, DIFFERENT MEANING

Most words have more than one meaning. Study the additional meanings of **pack**, **respond**, and **tender**. Then read each sentence and decide which meaning is used.

| | | |
|---|---|---|
| a. **pack** *n.* | | a small container that holds a set of things |
| b. **pack** *n.* | | a group of people |
| c. **respond** *v.* | | to react to something that has been said or done |
| d. **respond** *v.* | | to say or write something as a reply |
| e. **tender** *adj.* | | easy to cut and eat |
| f. **tender** *adj.* | | gentle in a way that shows love |

__e__ 1. My chicken never turns out as **tender** as yours. How do you prepare it?

_____ 2. My mother doesn't like to tell people her age, so when she's asked about it, she usually **responds**, "How old do you think I am?"

_____ 3. The father had a **tender** look on his face as he held his new baby daughter.

_____ 4. The salesperson happily greeted the **pack** of tourists as they entered the store.

_____ 5. Ellen threw a pillow at Carl in anger. Carl surprised her when he **responded** by laughing.

_____ 6. How much does a **pack** of cigarettes cost?

## WORDS IN SENTENCES

Complete each sentence with one of the words from the box.

| | | | | |
|---|---|---|---|---|
| ~~decade~~ | featured | labored | ranks | swell |
| fault | judgment | pack | responded | tender |

1. A _____decade_____ passed before Clint asked Dora to marry him. They met in 1993 and got married in 2003.

2. It was obvious that Jill had _____ feelings for the homeless puppy. Sure enough, she asked our parents if she could keep it.

3. The clever politician _____ to the question in such a way that no one really understood if his final answer was yes or no.

4. A _____ of photographers stood outside the restaurant, waiting for the movie star and his girlfriend to finish their meal.

5. At first, I thought the painting was too simple, but over time I realized that my initial _____ failed to see the quality of the artist's work.

6. Actress Natalie Portman was _____ in *Leon the Professional* when she was barely thirteen.

7. This airline is very good. It _____ number one on most passengers' lists when it comes to efficient service and comfort.

8. Tina and Chris _____ all week to clean out the attic, which had held various family belongings for over forty years.

9. Don't say it's my _____ that we have nothing to eat. Your talking took my attention away from the kitchen, and that's why everything burned.

10. Melissa's arm began to _____ where the bee had stung her.

## ▌WORDS IN COLLOCATIONS AND EXPRESSIONS

*Following are common collocations (word partners) and expressions with some of the key words. Read the definitions and then complete the conversations with the correct form of the collocations and expressions.*

| | |
|---|---|
| 1. **fault** | |
| • **find fault with (sb/sth)** | to find something wrong about someone or something and complain about it |
| 2. **judge** | |
| • **pass judgment (on sb/sth)** | to give an opinion or criticize somebody or something |
| 3. **labor** | |
| • **a labor of love** | work that is done for pleasure, not for money |
| • **manual labor** | physical work |
| 4. **respond** | |
| • **respond (to sth) by (doing sth)** | to react to something that has been said or done |
| 5. **swell** | |
| • **swell with (emotion)** | to experience an emotion very strongly |

1. MORRIS: Sometimes I get tired of working in an office. Wouldn't it be great to work outdoors? I'd like to build a house or something like that.

   JOHN: Well, building a house requires a lot of _____manual labor_____. You might want to return to your comfortable office after one day of that kind of work.

2. MEMBER 1: A group of us asked the management if the gym could have earlier hours, so we can exercise before we go to work.

   MEMBER 2: I heard that the gym will likely _____ opening its doors an hour earlier in the morning.

3. MRS. WALLACE: Why don't we ever go to the theater?

   MR. WALLACE: Because you're so hard to please. You _____ everything: the actors, the music, the writing, and of course the price of the tickets.

4. CONRAD: Our neighbor is a sweet lady, but she really loves to talk about her grandchildren and how wonderful they are.

   PAULA: That's for sure. A single compliment about them will make Mrs. Fletcher _____ pride.

5.     VANCE:     I heard Dana talking about the new student. She doesn't seem to like her.

         OLIVER:     Dana doesn't always take the time to get to know a person. I've warned her more than once not to _____ too quickly.

6.     CLAIRE:     Simon told me that you wrote a book about your family.

         LEO:     I did. The book is about my family's history. It was a real _____. I'm not sure if it will ever get published, but that's not why I wrote it anyway.

## ▌WORDS IN A READING

*Read the film review. Complete it with words and expressions from the boxes.*

| | | |
|---|---|---|
| a labor of love | ~~found fault with~~ | ranks |
| decade | passed judgment | responded . . . to |

### FILM REVIEW: COPPOLA'S *THE OUTSIDERS*

The 1980s film *The Outsiders* is being re-released in theaters and on DVD, with additional scenes and a new soundtrack. When the original film came out, critics __*found fault with*__ it, not recognizing
$_1$
the strengths of the work. Perhaps they _____ too quickly. Today, *The Outsiders*
$_2$
_____ as one of the best teen melodramas of that _____.
$_3$                                                        $_4$

*The Outsiders* was _____ for the director, Francis Ford Coppola. In 1982, one of his
$_5$
films, *One from the Heart,* was not well received. In fact, he lost all his money because of that film. Hurting from the failure of this film, Coppola readily agreed to work on a new project: a school librarian and 110 children begged him in a letter to make a movie based on S. E. Hinton's novel *The Outsiders.* Coppola was reportedly healed by the process of making this film, and in contrast to the critics of that time, young viewers _____ very positively _____ his work. To this
$_6$
day, fans remain loyal to the film.

| | | | |
|---|---|---|---|
| features | pack | swells with | tender |

The movie _____ big stars including Patrick Swayze, Rob Lowe, Matt Dillon, Tom
$_7$
Cruise, and Emilio Estevez. At the time, however, this was a _____ of young actors with little
$_8$
film experience. Nevertheless, this group of boys managed to tell a powerful story about two small-town gangs in Oklahoma in the 1960s, the poor against the rich, otherwise known as the Greasers and the Socs.

The film _____ emotion, and one of the newly added segments only increases the
$_9$
depth of the actors' performance. A very touching scene shows two brothers, played by Howell and

Lowe, holding each other in bed. The closeness is innocently sweet and, according to *The New York Times*, this scene along with the rest of the movie honors something that is often absent from the big screen: "_____ male beauty."

<sub>10</sub>

*(Based on information in "An Expanded Version of Coppola's The Outsiders." The Week, September 23, 2005.)*

## ▌WORDS IN DISCUSSION

*Apply the key words to your own life. Read and discuss each question in small groups. Try to use the key words.*

1. Name a **decade** of great music.

   ### EXAMPLE

   *I listen to popular songs on the radio, but I like a lot of singers and groups from the 1960s. That was a great **decade** for music. That's when Elvis and the Beatles were really popular.*

2. Name a helpful **feature** on most cell phones.

3. If you hurt your ankle and it begins to **swell**, what should you do?

4. When someone asks a very personal question that you don't want to answer, how do you **respond**?

5. When you meet someone for the first time, do you ever **pass judgment** too quickly?

6. Canada, Australia, and the United States celebrate **Labor** Day. Does your country have this holiday? When?

7. Think of three popular vacation spots. How would you **rank** them? Which is the best of the three?

8. Can you easily admit a mistake when it's your **fault**?

9. How much does a **pack** of gum cost? How often do you buy one?

10. Do you know how to cook? How can you make sure that meat turns out **tender**?

## ▌WORDS IN WRITING

*Choose two topics and write a short paragraph on each. Try to use the key words.*

1. Name three things you **pack** on any trip you take.

   ### EXAMPLE

   *I always **pack** my camera, my diary, and a good book when I go on a trip. Some things make great pictures, so you need a camera. Other things are more interesting to describe in words, so you need a diary. Finally, a book can always help pass the time no matter where you are.*

2. Is there a memory that makes you **swell with** pride?

3. Do you easily **find fault with** movies? What kinds of movies do you particularly dislike and why?

4. What's the hardest you've ever had to **labor**? Describe the work you did.

5. In what area do you have enough knowledge and experience to **judge** somebody or something? Do you often give advice in this area?

## ▌WORDS IN CONTEXT

*Use the sentences to guess what each key word means. Choose the meaning that is closest to that of the key word in* **bold**.

**1. debate**
/dɪˈbeɪt/
*-noun*

- There is a lot of **debate** in the United States about gun control; some people argue that guns should be illegal, and others feel that they should be legal.
- People cannot agree about the future of our town; at the last town meeting, there was a very heated **debate** about building a new stadium.

*Debate* means . . .  ⓐ discussion          b. physical fighting     c. friendly conversation

**2. draft**
/dræft/
*-noun*

- Julian wrote a **draft** of the letter, made corrections, and then copied it.
- This is only the first **draft** of our business plan; it's not the final version.

*Draft* means . . .  a. something not in          b. something complete   c. the beginning of
                       finished form                                      something

**3. glory**
/ˈglɔri/
*-noun*

- An Olympic athlete achieves **glory** when he wins a gold medal.
- Some people who are praying say, "**Glory** to God."

*Glory* means . . .  a. mild respect          b. criticism          c. honor and praise

**4. hollow**
/ˈhɑloʊ/
*-adjective*

- This old tree is **hollow**; you can put your hand inside it.
- The column is **hollow**; nothing but air is inside it.

*Hollow* means . . .  a. empty inside          b. round          c. solid

**5. ink**
/ɪŋk/
*-noun*

- When I saw the blue **ink** on Linda's fingers, I knew that she had been writing.
- You cannot write with a pen that has no **ink**.

*Ink* means . . .  a. the plastic part          b. the colored liquid   c. a stain
                    of a pen                     in a pen

**6. mental**
/ˈmɛntəl/
*-adjective*

- Although the elderly woman is too weak to leave her hospital bed, her **mental** abilities are still strong.
- Jason is fine physically, but his **mental** health isn't good. He "sees" all sorts of strange things.

*Mental* means . . .  a. relating to the body     b. relating to the spirit   c. relating to the mind

**7. refer**
/rɪˈfɚ/
-verb

- Moon Sung **refers** to Seoul as "my hometown."
- I was surprised when Mohammed **referred** to his brother; I had assumed that he was an only child.

*Refer* means . . .
    a. to ask a question about
    b. to tell an answer about
    c. to mention or speak about

**8. scold**
/skoʊld/
-verb

- Our teacher often **scolds** us for forgetting our homework.
- Mom **scolded** Alex for wearing his dirty boots inside the house.

*Scold* means . . .
    a. to discuss in a calm voice
    b. to angrily criticize someone
    c. to ask about

**9. soul**
/soʊl/
-noun

- Many people believe that our **souls** continue to exist after our bodies die.
- Fred is ugly, but Tessa loves him because he has a beautiful **soul**.

*Soul* means . . .
    a. a person's body
    b. a person's speech
    c. the part of a person that is not physical

**10. virtue**
/ˈvɚtʃu/
-noun

- Mother Theresa was a woman of high **virtue**; she was always honest and good.
- The Dalai Lama has lived a life of **virtue**.

*Virtue* means . . .
    a. wealth
    b. ideas
    c. moral goodness

## ▌ WORDS AND DEFINITIONS

*Match each key word with its definition.*

1. _____mental_____ relating to the mind or happening in the mind

2. _____ the importance, praise, and honor that people give someone they admire

3. _____ colored liquid used for writing or printing

4. _____ the part of a person that is not physical and contains his or her thoughts, feelings, character, etc.

5. _____ to mention or speak about someone or something

6. _____ having an empty space inside

7. _____ a piece of writing, a drawing, or a plan that is not yet in its finished form

8. _____ to angrily criticize someone about something they have done

9. _____ moral goodness of character or behavior

10. _____ a discussion or argument on a subject in which people express different opinions

# ▌COMPREHENSION CHECK

*Choose the best answer.*

1. Which person is **scolding** someone?
   a. "Let's play."
   (b.) "Don't chew with your mouth open!"
   c. "The answer is five."
   d. "You look lovely."

2. Where is there NOT **ink**?
   a. on a paper
   b. in a pencil
   c. in a pen
   d. in a computer printer

3. Which activity requires the most **mental** effort?
   a. running a race
   b. lying on the beach
   c. taking a math test
   d. dancing the tango

4. Which item is **hollow**?
   a. an empty jar
   b. a rock
   c. an orange
   d. a new bottle of shampoo

5. Which person did NOT make a **draft**?
   a. Shin Wook, who wrote his essay a second time.
   b. Neslihan, who e-mailed the first version of her report to her professor.
   c. Kuo jui, who made his first plan for traveling around the U.S.
   d. Raquel, who volunteered to help in the hospital.

6. What is the best job for a person of very high **virtue**?
   a. rock star
   b. thief
   c. religious leader
   d. lawyer

7. What do people use in **debate**?
   a. their hands
   b. words
   c. guns
   d. nothing

8. Who achieves **glory**?
   a. the reporter who writes about the race
   b. the people watching the race
   c. the loser of the race
   d. the winner of the race

9. Which is part of the **soul**?
   a. skin
   b. teeth
   c. feelings
   d. blood

10. If Fai **refers** to graduate school during our conversation, she
   a. asks about it.
   b. avoids the topic of graduate school.
   c. thinks about it but says nothing.
   d. mentions graduate school.

# WORD FAMILIES

Now that you have studied the ten key words and their basic definitions, you are ready to learn words that belong to the same family as some of the key words. A word family includes words that look alike but have different functions (noun, verb, adjective, or adverb). Their meanings are related but different.

**A.** *Look at each model phrase and decide whether the word in* **bold** *is used as a noun, verb, adjective, or adverb.*

| | NOUN | VERB | ADJECTIVE | ADVERB |
|---|---|---|---|---|
| 1. **debate** | | | | |
| • a serious **debate** | ✓ | | | |
| • to **debate** a topic | | ✓ | | |
| 2. **glory** | | | | |
| • a day of **glory** | | | | |
| • **glorious** victory | | | | |
| 3. **mental** | | | | |
| • have **mental** problems | | | | |
| • be **mentally** ill | | | | |
| 4. **refer** | | | | |
| • to **refer** to something | | | | |
| • an interesting **reference** | | | | |
| 5. **virtue** | | | | |
| • a life of **virtue** | | | | |
| • a **virtuous** life | | | | |
| 6. **soul** | | | | |
| • good for the **soul** | | | | |
| • a **soulful** poem | | | | |

**B.** *Read the first half of each sentence and match it with the appropriate ending.*

___c___ 1. In the lecture on African languages, the professor made a

_____ 2. I respect Hugh for spending his vacation with his grandmother; it was

_____ 3. Before Luke went bungee jumping he wanted to

_____ 4. The beautiful woman in the painting looked at us sadly with her

_____ 5. On TV tonight, the politicians will

_____ 6. Kang loved the movie's

a. **soulful** eyes.

b. prepare himself **mentally** so that he would be confident when he jumped.

c. **reference** to a dying tribal language.

d. **glorious** ending.

e. **debate** about health care reform.

f. **virtuous** of him to do that.

## SAME WORD, DIFFERENT MEANING

*Most words have more than one meaning. Study the additional meanings of **draft**, **glory**, and **virtue**. Then read each sentence and decide which meaning is used.*

| | | |
|---|---|---|
| a. **draft** *n.* | a piece of writing, a drawing, or a plan that is not yet in its finished form |
| b. **draft** *v.* | to order someone to fight for his or her country during a war |
| c. **glory** *n.* | the importance, praise, and honor that people give someone they admire |
| d. **glory** *n.* | a beautiful and impressive appearance |
| e. **virtue** *n.* | moral goodness of character or behavior |
| f. **virtue** *n.* | an advantage that makes something better or more useful than something else |

__e__ 1. Jane wants to teach her children the importance of **virtue**.

_____ 2. I'd like to see the **glory** of Rome sometime in my life.

_____ 3. My Uncle Joe was **drafted** into the army during World War II.

_____ 4. What are the **virtues** of Sam's plan?

_____ 5. The **glory** of winning the marathon made Halima cry happy tears.

_____ 6. Please turn in the second **draft** of your essay by December 15.

## WORDS IN SENTENCES

*Complete each sentence with one of the words from the box.*

| | | | | |
|---|---|---|---|---|
| debated | ~~glorious~~ | ink | refers | soulful |
| drafted | hollow | mentally | scolded | virtues |

1. Janetta's graduation day was _____glorious_____ .

2. Keng _____ Vit after he ate all the cookies.

3. Allen is _____ ill, so he should talk to a psychiatrist.

4. When Laura heard Max's _____ singing, she fell in love with him.

5. Although this plan is not perfect, it has its _____ .

6. Oh, no! My pen burst and I have _____ all over my hands.

7. Sulafa often _____ to Saudi Arabia in our conversations.

8. Wilson hates war, so he hopes he will never be _____ .

9. Roberto knocked on the wall to find out if it was _____ .

10. Jong Sun and Jin Hyuk _____ about cars for twenty minutes; Jong Sun argued that the BMW was better than the Porsche, but Jin Hyuk disagreed.

# WORDS IN COLLOCATIONS AND EXPRESSIONS

*Following are common collocations (word partners) and expressions with some of the key words. Read the definitions and then complete the conversations with the correct form of the collocations and expressions.*

1. **debate**
   - **debate whether (or not)** — to think about something carefully (before making a decision)

2. **draft**
   - **the final draft** — the final form of a piece of writing, a drawing, or a plan

3. **hollow**
   - **a hollow promise** — an insincere promise

4. **mental**
   - **make a mental note** — to make an effort to remember

5. **refer**
   - **refer (sb/sth) to (sb/sth)** — to send someone to another place or person for information or advice

6. **soul**
   - **the soul of (sth)** — a special quality that gives something its true character

1. CHARLOTTE: I'm going to Paris next week! Where do you suggest that I go on my free afternoon there?

   ANNETTE: You should explore the city on foot. By walking through the neighborhoods, visiting the little shops and cafes, you can get a feel for ____*the soul of*____ the city.

2. WIFE: We're out of milk, honey. Do you want me to write it on the shopping list?

   HUSBAND: No, that's all right. I'll _____ to pick some up tonight. I'm sure I'll remember.

3. PROFESSOR: Larry, _____ of your paper is due on Monday.

   LARRY: It is? Okay, I'll bring it in on Monday, I promise.

   PROFESSOR: I hope that's not _____. Your last three papers have been late. It can't happen again.

4. MARIA: I want to learn as much as possible about dinosaurs.

   PROFESSOR: I'm afraid that's not my specialty. However, I can _____ you _____ my friend Sal Kline, who is an expert at the natural history museum.

5. SELAH: Are you going to marry William, Goi?

   GOI: I often ask myself if William and I could really make each other happy. I _____ or not we are really right for each other. I'm just not sure yet.

## WORDS IN A READING

*Read this article about literature. Complete it with words and expressions from the boxes.*

| debated whether | final draft | ~~glorious~~ | referred | scold | virtue |
|---|---|---|---|---|---|

### HOW DO YOU PICTURE THE LIFE OF PI?

Yann Martel was completely surprised when *Life of Pi*, his novel about a sixteen-year-old boy named Pi stranded at sea in a lifeboat with a Bengal tiger, won the 2002 Man Booker Prize. Following this _____glorious_____ success, *The Times* and his publishers are holding a competition to illustrate* a
_1_
new edition of *Life of Pi*. Martel is excited about the competition: it's another way of sharing his story.

In the three years he has spent traveling around the world talking about his book, he has often been surprised by readers' reactions to his story. After a reading in Berne, Switzerland, a woman raised her hand and _____ to the story of a boy and a tiger in a lifeboat crossing the Pacific as a
_2_
metaphor** on marriage. "Husbands are like the tiger in the story: difficult. There's plenty to
_____ them for." Even stranger, a man once gave Martel a stamp-collecting magazine in
_3_
which the man had written an article that _____ Pi's relationship with the tiger is like
_4_
the relationship of a stamp collector with his favorite stamp.

Martel realizes that once he writes the _____ of a story and it is published, the
_5_
reader will interpret it in his or her own way. He feels that the _____ of illustrations is
_6_
that they can help the imaginations of those who read *Life of Pi*.

| hollow | ink | mental | the soul of |
|---|---|---|---|

The only negative side Martel can think of is that pictures might limit readers. He knows that when a book is turned into a movie, people often visualize the story in terms of the movie; they lose the
_____ image they had formed in their imagination. In the worst case, pictures could give
_7_
readers a(n) _____ idea of the story, emptied of their own imaginations. However, Martel
_8_
is optimistic that pictures, like words, are only the beginning of "the meeting between reader and book, that makes a book come to life."

In this way, whoever wins this competition and draws the pictures for the new edition of Martel's book will react to the book with his or her own imagination. Because of this, Martel is very open-minded about the illustrations: whether they are lifelike or abstract; whether they are made with paint
or _____.
_9_

---

\* **illustrate**   to make illustrations (pictures) for something
\*\* **metaphor**   a way of describing something by comparing it to something else that has similar qualities without using "like" or "as"

Martel is excited by this competition because it will show him how different people see his book. How will artists portray _____ the book? Will the tiger be scary or friendly; will the

10

ocean be threatening; will the island be something out of Frankenstein, or will it be a paradise?

*(Based on information in "How Do You Picture the Life of Pi?" The Times, October 8, 2005.)*

## ▌ WORDS IN DISCUSSION

*Apply the key words to your own life. Read and discuss each question in small groups. Try to use the key words.*

### EXAMPLE

How many **drafts** I usually write of an essay: ___4___

*A: My first **draft** is just freewriting. My ideas develop in my second and third **drafts**. Finally, my grammar and spelling are perfect in the final **draft**.*

*B: Wow! I only write an essay once. I don't have the patience to do several **drafts**.*

1. A topic which people in my native country often **debate** about: _____

2. How certain I am that my **soul** will still exist after I die: _____%

3. How much I enjoy challenging **mental** work: _____

4. If I write a love letter, the color **ink** that I will use: _____

5. What I would do if I were **drafted** to fight in a war: _____

6. What our teacher says when he or she **scolds** us: _____

7. A person I often **refer** to when I am talking with my friends: _____

8. How interested I am in learning about the **virtues** of being vegetarian: _____

9. My mother owns a small statue which she believes is solid gold. I discover that the statue is **hollow**. What I do: _____

10. Someone is going to achieve **glory** tomorrow. The person whom I want it to be: _____

## ▌ WORDS IN WRITING

*Choose two topics and write a short paragraph on each. Try to use the key words.*

1. Do you prefer to write with pen and **ink** or a computer? Explain.

### EXAMPLE

*Like many people, I use a computer more than I use a pen and paper. This is because I can write faster on the computer. However, I enjoy writing with a pen. If I am writing a personal letter, I prefer to use pen and **ink**. This seems more personal.*

2. What topic is often **debated** in your city or country? Explain why.

3. Imagine a moment of future **glory** in your life. Describe it well.

4. Describe something that you have worked on which was **mentally** challenging.

5. Describe someone whom you believe is **virtuous**.

Chapter 29    263

## WORDS IN CONTEXT

*Use the sentences to guess what each key word means. Choose the meaning that is closest to that of the key word in **bold**.*

**1. ambition**
/æmˈbɪʃən/
-noun

- Diogo's **ambition** has pushed him to work hard and earn the respect of his teammates. He hopes to be named captain next season.
- Mrs. Wallace is worried that her son has no **ambition**. He doesn't study much in school, and he recently stopped his guitar lessons.

*Ambition* means . . . a. desire to succeed    b. courage    c. intelligence

**2. character**
/ˈkærɪktɚ/
-adjective

- I was surprised to learn that the general has a calm, friendly **character**.
- The older buildings give the town a Spanish **character**.

*Character* means . . . a. personality    b. location    c. reputation

**3. conquer**
/ˈkɑŋkɚ/
-verb

- The state of New Jersey was originally Dutch land, but the British **conquered** the Dutch in the second half of the seventeenth century.
- Attila the Hun had much power in Central Europe, but he couldn't **conquer** Gaul, today's France. The Romans played a part in stopping him.

*Conquer* means . . . a. to win control of    b. to settle in peace    c. to influence

**4. despair**
/dɪˈspɛr/
-noun

- Losing his job filled Jerry with **despair**. "I'm too old to find another job. What will happen to me?" he thought sadly.
- Veronica couldn't pay her bills. She began to cry in **despair**.

*Despair* means . . . a. a need to fight    b. a bad dream    c. a loss of hope

**5. image**
/ˈɪmɪdʒ/
-noun

- Rob always wears a suit when he travels to keep a professional **image**.
- The new advertisements were an effort to recreate the company's **image** as a modern department store for the young family.

*Image* means . . . a. fame or popularity    b. way of presenting yourself    c. success in business

**6. minimum**
/ˈmɪnəməm/
-adjective

- Joan's parents and teachers are disappointed that she continually does the **minimum** amount of work and never tries to test the limits of her mind.
- The electrician promised he could do the work at a **minimum** cost.

*Minimum* means . . . a. the smallest    b. necessary    c. the highest

7. **pinch**
/pɪntʃ/
-verb

- When the woman came over to **pinch** the baby's cheeks, the baby smiled at her.
- My classmate **pinched** my arm to wake me up before the teacher saw that I had fallen asleep.

*Pinch* means . . .    a. to hit or kick    b. to massage lightly    c. to tightly press

8. **pride**
/praɪd/
-noun

- The architect looked at the finished building and smiled with **pride**.
- Most fans wore the team colors and waved team flags to show their **pride**.

*Pride* means . . .    a. satisfaction and pleasure    b. excitement    c. worry and doubt

9. **scorn**
/skɔrn/
-noun

- After telling the teacher who had cheated on the test, Lee had to face the **scorn** of her classmates.
- The criminal felt the **scorn** of the people as she walked from the courthouse to the police car. Many angry words were shouted at her.

*Scorn* means . . .    a. selfishness    b. strong criticism    c. emotional weakness

10. **series**
/ˈsɪriz/
-noun

- After a **series** of terrible arguments, the partners decided to sell the business, and each went his own way.
- A **series** of robberies in the same area led the police to believe that one person was responsible for all of them.

*Series* means . . .    a. a plan or schedule    b. a discovery    c. a group of events or actions

## WORDS AND DEFINITIONS

*Match each key word with its definition.*

1. _____*pinch*_____ to squeeze or press someone's skin very tightly between your finger and thumb

2. _____ a feeling that you have no hope at all

3. _____ the smallest possible (number, amount, or degree)

4. _____ strong criticism of someone or something that you think is not worth any respect

5. _____ all the qualities that make someone or something different from any other

6. _____ a group of events or actions of the same kind that happen one after the other

7. _____ the way a person, organization, or product presents itself to the public

8. _____ a strong desire to succeed

9. _____ to win control of a land or country by force

10. _____ a feeling of satisfaction and pleasure in something done by you or someone connected to you

# COMPREHENSION CHECK

*Choose the best answer.*

1. Which situation is NOT a cause for **despair**?

   a. "I can't find a well-paying job, and I have bills to pay."

   b. "I hurt my friend's feelings, and she won't talk to me."

   c. "There was a fire in my apartment, and I have no insurance."

   d. "I need to decide when to take my vacation and where I'm going."

2. In 1588, Philip II of Spain sent his ships to **conquer** England;

   a. he and his people were welcomed by the Queen herself.

   b. the attack failed.

   c. England had asked for Spain's help.

   d. he spent his time there studying the land and the people.

3. Vacations are all about having **minimum**

   a. worry and responsibility.

   b. free time.

   c. fun and relaxation.

   d. expenses.

4. Neil says that he's looking for someone with a strong **character**. His ideal woman

   a. is not only beautiful, but has firm opinions, humor, and lots of energy.

   b. can lift 200 pounds.

   c. comes from a rich family.

   d. has a successful career.

5. Matt has a lot of **ambition**;

   a. he likes his position at work and plans to keep it for many years.

   b. he's determined to become a vice president and partner.

   c. his salary pays the bills and allows some extra money for entertainment.

   d. he complains about taking work home in the evenings and on weekends.

6. Anna Marie **pinched** her cheeks

   a. because they itched.

   b. to help the cuts heal.

   c. with a little bit of lotion.

   d. to bring a little color to her face.

7. If Francine has nothing but **scorn** for laziness, she

   a. doesn't like to work.

   b. doesn't respect those who do little work.

   c. takes a lot of breaks at work.

   d. offers to help others complete their work.

8. This athlete has a positive **image** because he

   a. answers yes to most questions.

   b. hides from journalists and photographers.

   c. is very friendly during TV interviews.

   d. wants to make $10 million a year.

9. Jonas feels a lot of **pride**

   a. because his daughter was accepted at Harvard University.

   b. because his daughter failed chemistry.

   c. when his son takes his car without asking.

   d. when his children go to sleep early.

10. A visiting professor is giving a **series** of lectures this week. That means that

    a. the same lecture will be repeated several times.

    b. there will be only one evening to hear him speak.

    c. there will be several times we can hear him speak.

    d. he'll give a test after every lecture.

# WORD FAMILIES

Now that you have studied the ten key words and their basic definitions, you are ready to learn words that belong to the same family as some of the key words. A word family includes words that look alike but have different functions (noun, verb, adjective, or adverb). Their meanings are related but different.

**A.** *Look at each model phrase and decide whether the word in* **bold** *is used as a noun, verb, adjective, or adverb.*

|  | NOUN | VERB | ADJECTIVE | ADVERB |
|---|---|---|---|---|
| 1. **ambition** | | | | |
| • great **ambition** | ✓ | | | |
| • an **ambitious** man | | | ✓ | |
| 2. **despair** | | | | |
| • fall into **despair** | | | | |
| • begin to **despair** | | | | |
| • become **desperate** | | | | |
| 3. **minimum** | | | | |
| • the **minimum** price | | | | |
| • reach the **minimum** | | | | |
| 4. **pinch** | | | | |
| • **pinch** her cheeks | | | | |
| • a **pinch** of salt | | | | |
| 5. **pride** | | | | |
| • filled with **pride** | | | | |
| • be **proud** | | | | |
| 6. **scorn** | | | | |
| • suffer the **scorn** of others | | | | |
| • to **scorn** other people | | | | |

**B.** *Read each sentence and match the word in* **bold** *with the correct definition from page 268.*

___c___ 1. My brother is a very modern father. He **scorns** the old ways of our parents and raises his own children very differently from how he and I were raised.

_____ 2. Fabiana made a **desperate** request for financial help, but the university told her that her grades were too low to receive a scholarship.

_____ 3. I put a **pinch** of pepper into the soup to add flavor.

_____ 4. The manager said that mistakes naturally happen but that the company expects human error to be at a **minimum**.

_____ 5. My teammates and I began to **despair** when the score became 6 to 1. We knew then that we'd never win.

_____ 6. Dillon is an **ambitious** young man. He plans to finish college in three years instead of four and then go to law school.

_____ 7. At Felix's high school graduation, his parents told him how **proud** they were of him.

a. a small amount that you can hold between your finger and thumb

b. the smallest number, amount, or degree possible

c. to show in an unkind way that you think that a person, idea, or suggestion is stupid or not worth considering

d. having a strong desire to be successful or powerful

e. to feel that there is no hope at all

f. feeling pleased with your achievements, family, country, etc. because you think they are very good

g. willing to do anything to change a very bad situation

## | SAME WORD, DIFFERENT MEANING

*Most words have more than one meaning. Study the additional meanings of **character, conquer,** and **series**. Then read each sentence and decide which meaning is used.*

| | | |
|---|---|---|
| a. | **character** *n.* | personality; the qualities that make someone or something different from any other |
| b. | **character** *n.* | a person in a book, play, movie, etc. |
| c. | **conquer** *v.* | to win control of a land or country by force |
| d. | **conquer** *v.* | to gain control over a feeling, problem, or other difficulty |
| e. | **series** *n.* | a group of events, actions, or things of the same kind that happen one after the other |
| f. | **series** *n.* | a set of television or radio programs with the same characters or on the same subject |

___e___ 1. A **series** of bad decisions by the board of directors led to the company's ruin.

_____ 2. I started skiing only last month, but I've already **conquered** my fear of steep hills.

_____ 3. My grandfather often spoke in a loud and commanding voice, but there was a really soft side to his **character** that not everyone knew.

_____ 4. I like to stay home on Thursday nights and watch my favorite TV **series**.

_____ 5. I've read *The Catcher in the Rye* many times; I like and understand the **character** Holden Caulfield very well.

_____ 6. Russia has always been a difficult land to **conquer** because of its size and climate.

## | WORDS IN SENTENCES

*Complete each sentence on page 269 with one of the words from the box.*

| | | | | |
|---|---|---|---|---|
| ambitious | conquered | image | ~~pinch~~ | scorned |
| character | desperate | minimum | proud | series |

1. If you want the sauce to be spicy, you can add a(n) _____pinch_____ of red pepper.

2. When the public learned about the actor's criminal history, it ruined his good-boy _____.

3. My great-grandmother likes to remember how as a child she and her whole family would listen to a radio _____ for entertainment.

4. Lucas says that one day he'll be sitting in the White House and he'll control the whole country. Don't you think that's rather _____?

5. You could tell by the big smile on the little girl's face that she was _____ she could ride a bike all by herself.

6. At first, I questioned whether I could manage a shop of my own, but I'm glad I _____ those doubts because today I'm very happy running my own hair salon.

7. We keep noise at a(n) _____, so I'm not sure why our neighbor complained.

8. The race car driver made a(n) _____ attempt to win, but ended up crashing into the wall instead.

9. In literature class, we have to choose one _____ from Shakespeare's *Hamlet* and write a two-page description.

10. What I remember most about my grandmother was that she _____ anyone who wasted things. She liked people who appreciated what they had.

## ▌WORDS IN COLLOCATIONS AND EXPRESSIONS

*Following are common collocations (word partners) and expressions with some of the key words. Read the definitions and then complete the conversations on page 270 with the correct form of the collocations and expressions.*

| | | |
|---|---|---|
| 1. | **conquer** | |
| | • **conquer your fear (of sth)** | to take action despite being afraid (of something) |
| 2. | **despair** | |
| | • **in despair** | the state of having no hope at all |
| 3. | **minimum** | |
| | • **keep (sth) to a minimum** | to maintain the smallest amount or degree possible |
| 4. | **pride** | |
| | • **proud of (sb/sth)** | feeling pleased with your achievements, family, country, etc. because you think they are very good |
| | • **take (great) pride in (sth)** | to receive great pleasure from (an action, a possession, or a relative) |
| 5. | **series** | |
| | • **a series of (sth)** | a number of events or a group of actions of the same kind that happen one after the other |

1. ROOMMATE 1: What's this? I found it on the coffee table.

   ROOMMATE 2: It's a two-page essay I wrote for my French teacher. I never thought I could write so much in another language. I'm really _____*proud of*_____ it.

2. RADIO HOST: So you're saying you can't pay your rent, right?

   CALLER: That's right. I lost my job last year. I've been trying to find another job, but now I'm sick, and I've given up all hope.

   RADIO HOST: Okay, listeners. Our caller is _____. Can you help? The line is open for your calls.

3. THERESA: As usual, I'm sure my mother will _____ her cooking this year at Thanksgiving. She loves to set a beautiful table.

   PHILLIP: I'm looking forward to it. Thank you for the invitation.

4. FAN 1: So the young player from Germany is the favorite to win today's match, right?

   FAN 2: Yes. He's already won _____ games, and some think no one can beat him.

5. LIONEL: I hate high places. When I stay at hotels, I always ask for a room on the first or second floor.

   TERRY: And you live in an apartment on the ground floor! Maybe you should do something like bungee jumping to _____ of heights.

6. MR. NELSON: We should go away somewhere to relax. Maybe a cruise?

   MRS. NELSON: With the kids in college, we don't have much money to take a vacation, so we'd have to _____ all costs _____.

## WORDS IN A READING

*Read this article about a young chef and TV host. Complete it with words and expressions from the boxes.*

| ambition | ~~character~~ | minimum | series | takes pride in |
|---|---|---|---|---|

### COOKING WITH RACHAEL RAY

Rachael Ray is fast becoming a major name in the cooking world. Her fun, energetic

_____*character*_____ separates her from the calmer and more serious personalities one usually finds on
    1

cooking shows. But that's not the only thing. Rachael _____ making wonderful meals
                                                              2

with _____ effort and cost. The titles of her TV shows, *30-Minute Meals* and *$40 a Day*,
         3

say it all. Rachael's success is based on keeping mealtime simple.

In contrast to her cooking style, Rachael's life is quite complex at the present. The young woman has ten cookbooks, four TV shows, and a magazine to her credit. Rachael enjoys the challenge of handling all these projects, claiming, "I've got so much energy I don't know what to do with it."

Though Rachael has a lot of _____, success didn't come quickly. She started with the most basic jobs in the food industry. Working behind food counters and on kitchen production lines, she waited for an opportunity. One came when she created a cooking course to help the sales at a gourmet market in Albany, New York. A local TV station helped her turn the popular course into weekly segments for the evening news, which in turn led to her first TV _____.

| conquer their fear of | despair | image | pinch | scorns |

From the beginning of her TV career, Rachael was liked by viewers. She makes cooking simple and enjoyable. Rachael _____ complicated processes and does not even take the time for exact measurements. A _____ of this and a handful of that—and the result is always a great meal that looks as good as any made by a gourmet chef.

Her style of cooking looks thrown together on the spot, as does her TV _____—she tapes her shows in everyday clothes and with her hair down—but just as her simple dishes deliver a rich taste, her relaxed on-screen manner is truly a work of art. Her casual approach to working in the kitchen makes it easy for the nonexperts to _____ cooking. As Rachael prepares her easy yet creative meals, she usually makes a mess, which is refreshing and entertaining to viewers. The mess is not a cause for _____; Rachael laughs and says, "That's why I have a big dog!"

*(Based on information in Bob Spitz, "Turning Up the Heat." Reader's Digest, November 2005.)*

## ❚ WORDS IN DISCUSSION

*Apply the key words to your own life. Read and discuss each question in small groups. Try to use the key words.*

1. Name a fear you have yet to **conquer**.

   **EXAMPLE**

   *I've never **conquered** my fear of spiders. I've hated them since childhood.*

2. Give one word to describe your **character**.

3. Name a reason to **pinch** your nose shut.

4. Do you have a favorite TV **series**? If so, which one and why do you enjoy watching it?

5. What do you do to **keep** stress **to a minimum** in your life?

6. Name someone you know who is very **ambitious** and give an example of his or her **ambition**.

7. What is a common cause for **despair**?

8. What **image** do you want people to have of you?

9. Name a habit you **scorn** in others.

10. Name something or someone you are **proud of**.

# ▎WORDS IN WRITING

*Choose two topics and write a short paragraph on each. Try to use the key words.*

1. In which professions do people worry most about their **image**?

   **EXAMPLE**

   *I think everyone worries about their **image**, but maybe some worry more than others. People like actors make money because of their **image**. People like politicians can lose their position if something hurts their **image**. In my opinion, if you're good at your job, you shouldn't have to worry about what people think about you.*

2. Describe a **character** from a well-known book or movie.

3. What's something you **take pride in**?

4. Describe a **series of** actions that are a part of your morning routine.

5. Was there ever a time you felt **desperate**? What caused your **despair**?

## PART A

*Choose the word that best completes each item and write it in the space provided.*

1. Ned has a lot of _____ambition_____. He wants to go to Harvard Business School and start his own company after graduating.
   - a. pride
   - b. scorn
   - c. despair
   - d. ambition

2. Lorna has an odd habit when she talks about her father. Sometimes she _____ to him as Daddy, and other times she says Papa.
   - a. pinches
   - b. responds
   - c. refers
   - d. scolds

3. It's Devin's _____ that the dishes broke. He dropped them.
   - a. soul
   - b. decade
   - c. fault
   - d. draft

4. Our store workers are taught to _____ politely and calmly to customer complaints.
   - a. pack
   - b. respond
   - c. refer
   - d. scold

5. Winning an Academy Award brings _____ to actors, directors, and producers.
   - a. virtue
   - b. glory
   - c. despair
   - d. labor

6. The people in church that day prayed for the _____ of all who died in the war.
   - a. virtues
   - b. drafts
   - c. faults
   - d. souls

7. The "Roaring Twenties" was a special _____ for American women. They worked outside the home, cut their hair short, and danced in skirts just below the knee.
   - a. image
   - b. decade
   - c. despair
   - d. series

8. The loss of a loved one can lead to a feeling of _____.
   - a. glory
   - b. scorn
   - c. despair
   - d. pride

9. Our father _____ us for not calling home to say we'd be late.
   - a. packed
   - b. pinched
   - c. conquered
   - d. scolded

10. Prisoners often perform _____, from cleaning up parks to making furniture.
    - a. labor
    - b. glory
    - c. fault
    - d. virtue

## PART B

*Read each statement and write **T** for true or **F** for false in the space provided.*

**T** 1. An insect bite can sting and make your skin **swell**.

_____ 2. A **judge** works in a prison.

_____ 3. When going on a trip, people usually use suitcases to **pack** their belongings.

_____ 4. Someone who is generous, kind, and interested in helping the community is a person of **virtue**.

_____ 5. Army officers hold **ranks**.

_____ 6. Boxers **pinch** each other. The heavier the boxer, the stronger he **pinches**.

_____ 7. Politicians must be concerned about their **image** when public support is needed.

_____ 8. Heroes earn people's **scorn**.

_____ 9. A banana is long and **hollow**.

_____ 10. Some pencils use **ink**.

## PART C

*Complete each item with a word from the box. Use each word once.*

| character | debate | feature | minimum | series |
|---|---|---|---|---|
| conquered | drafts | mental | pride | ~~tender~~ |

1. The grilled chicken was very _____tender_____ and flavorful. Everyone complimented the chef.

2. Some frozen foods aren't bad. They provide a healthy meal with _____ effort.

3. Ben made a _____ of mistakes that made our supervisor question his ability to handle his new position. In the past Ben always made good decisions.

4. Our TV has a _____ that allows us to watch two channels at the same time.

5. My coach taught me that physical strength isn't enough to be a good wrestler because the sport also involves a _____ game.

6. Some argue that the American West was _____ at a high price; taking control of the land greatly hurt the Native American way of life.

7. We all think that my baby nephew's _____ will be just like his grandfather's. That's not a bad thing since I think my father is wonderful, though a bit stubborn.

8. Radio shows often encourage _____. You can call in and argue your point of view.

9. It took three _____ before Johanna felt satisfied with her English paper.

10. Winning the World Cup can fill a soccer team as well as a whole country with _____.

# APPENDIX: Understanding Word Parts

Many academic words came to the English language from Greek or Latin. These words are made up of different parts that have special meanings.

**EXAMPLE**

*un*believ*able*
prefix      suffix

It is easy to discover the meaning of a word and its part of speech if you know common prefixes (word beginnings) and suffixes (word endings).

## WORD BUILDER 1: Prefixes and Meaning

*How many prefixes (word beginnings) do you already know? Test your knowledge and then check your answers below. Write the letter of the correct meaning next to each word.*

|   | | PREFIX | EXAMPLE | MEANING |
|---|---|---|---|---|
| _C_ | 1. | **ab-** | **ab**sent | a. together |
| | 2. | **ap-** | **ap**proach | b. not |
| | 3. | **bene-** | **bene**fit | c. away from |
| | 4. | **co-** | **co**mmunity | d. to, nearness to |
| | 5. | **dis-** | **dis**trust | e. good |
| | 6. | **ex-** | **ex**port | f. one |
| | 7. | **pre-** | **pre**vious | g. in favor of |
| | 8. | **pro-** | **pro**pose | h. out |
| | 9. | **uni-** | **uni**te | i. see |
| | 10. | **vis-** | **vis**ible | j. before |

**ANSWER KEY:**   1c, 2d, 3e, 4a, 5b, 6h, 7i, 8g, 9f, 10i

## WORD BUILDER 2: Suffixes and Word Families

*How many suffixes (word endings) do you already know? Test your knowledge without looking at the chart that follows.*

| SUFFIX | EXAMPLE FROM THIS BOOK | PART OF SPEECH | SUFFIX | EXAMPLE FROM THIS BOOK | PART OF SPEECH |
|---|---|---|---|---|---|
| 1. -able | _available_ | _adj._ | 7. –ful | _____ | _____ |
| 2. –age | _____ | _____ | 8. –ity | _____ | _____ |
| 3. –al | _____ | _____ | 9. –ize | _____ | _____ |
| 4. –ance | _____ | _____ | 10. –ly | _____ | _____ |
| 5. –ate | _____ | _____ | 11. –ment | _____ | _____ |
| 6. –ation | _____ | _____ | 12. –or | _____ | _____ |

## SUFFIX REFERENCE CHART: 12 Important Suffixes to Know

| SUFFIX | PART OF SPEECH | MEANING | EXAMPLES FROM THIS BOOK | SPECIAL USE* |
|---|---|---|---|---|
| 1. -able | *adjective* | able to | **avail**able, manag**eable** | √ |
| 2. -age | *noun* | action | encour**age**, pass**age** | |
| 3. -al | *adjective* | like or relating to | critic**al**, tradition**al** | √ |
| 4. -ance | *noun* | act or state of being | insur**ance**, nuis**ance** | |
| 5. -ate | *verb* | cause or make | calcul**ate**, mig**rate** | |
| 6. -ation | *noun* | act or state of being | gener**ation**, reput**ation** | √ |
| 7. -ful | *adjective* | full of | boast**ful**, grace**ful** | √ |
| 8. -ity | *noun* | state of being | punctual**ity**, van**ity** | √ |
| 9. -ize | *verb* | make | colon**ize**, critic**ize** | |
| 10. -ly | *adverb* | like | bitter**ly**, effective**ly** | |
| 11. -ment | *noun* | act or result | judg**ment**, require**ment** | √ |
| 12. -or | *noun* | one who | edit**or**, govern**or** | |

*** Special Uses of Some Suffixes:**

**-able** turns a verb into adjective: drink+ **able**= drinkable
　　　　　　　　　　*verb*　　　　　　*adj.*

**-al** turns a noun into an adjective: music + **al**= musical
　　　　　　　　　　*noun*　　　*adj.*

**-ation** turns a verb into a noun: create + **ation**= creation
　　　　　　　　　　*verb*　　　　　　　*noun.*

**-ful** turns a noun into an adjective: beauty + **ful**= beautiful
　　　　　　　　　　*noun*　　　*adj.*

**-ity** turns an adjective into a noun: punctual + **ity**= punctuality
　　　　　　　　　　*adj.*　　　　*noun*

**-ment** turns a verb into a noun: judge + **ment**= judgment
　　　　　　　　　　*verb*　　　　*noun*

# WORD INDEX

Here you can find the words that are taught in this book and the chapters in which they are introduced. You can see that every key word comes from the General Service List (GSL) of the 2,000 most common words in English, or the Academic Word List (AWL).

**A**

| | | |
|---|---|---|
| absence 16 | GSL |
| accord 26 | GSL |
| accurate 3 | AWL |
| accuse 9 | GSL |
| achieve 23 | AWL |
| acquire 11 | AWL |
| administration 19 | AWL |
| agriculture 21 | GSL |
| aid 20 | AWL |
| affect 10 | AWL |
| aim 7 | GSL |
| alternative 12 | AWL |
| ambition 30 | GSL |
| analyze 1 | AWL |
| appoint 6 | GSL |
| approach 7 | AWL |
| assign 27 | AWL |
| assist 1 | AWL |
| associate 16 | GSL |
| assume 13 | AWL |
| astonish 6 | GSL |
| attitude 5 | AWL |
| authority 9 | AWL |
| available 2 | AWL |
| awkward 27 | GSL |

**B**

| | | |
|---|---|---|
| bar 13 | GSL |
| basis 20 | GSL |
| bear 24 | GSL |
| behave 17 | GSL |
| bend 16 | GSL |
| benefit 4 | AWL |
| bitter 11 | GSL |
| boast 12 | GSL |

| | | |
|---|---|---|
| boundary 12 | GSL |
| branch 25 | GSL |
| bribe 9 | GSL |
| brief 9 | AWL |
| broad 8 | GSL |
| burst 22 | GSL |

**C**

| | | |
|---|---|---|
| calculate 6 | GSL |
| caution 20 | GSL |
| challenge 6 | AWL |
| character 30 | GSL |
| claim 19 | GSL |
| classic 3 | AWL |
| coarse 15 | GSL |
| colony 15 | GSL |
| comment 8 | AWL |
| commerce 22 | GSL |
| community 12 | AWL |
| concentrate 2 | AWL |
| concept 6 | AWL |
| conquer 30 | GSL |
| conscience 13 | GSL |
| conscious 20 | GSL |
| consist 18 | AWL |
| constant 23 | AWL |
| construct 1 | AWL |
| consultant 2 | AWL |
| consume 11 | AWL |
| contrast 4 | AWL |
| contribute 5 | AWL |
| convenience 4 | GSL |
| corporation 23 | AWL |
| coward 25 | GSL |
| credit 19 | AWL |
| creep 22 | GSL |
| critic 3 | GSL |

| | | |
|---|---|---|
| crush 10 | GSL |
| culture 20 | AWL |
| current 7 | GSL |
| custom 7 | GSL |

**D**

| | | |
|---|---|---|
| data 2 | AWL |
| debate 29 | AWL |
| debt 1 | GSL |
| decade 28 | AWL |
| decay 27 | GSL |
| deceive 13 | GSL |
| declare 10 | GSL |
| despair 30 | GSL |
| discipline 11 | GSL |
| display 13 | AWL |
| distinguish 20 | GSL |
| distribute 1 | AWL |
| draft 29 | AWL |
| drag 6 | GSL |
| drama 16 | AWL |
| dust 15 | GSL |

**E**

| | | |
|---|---|---|
| earnest 19 | GSL |
| edit 2 | AWL |
| effective 8 | GSL |
| efficient 26 | GSL |
| elect 14 | GSL |
| empire 15 | GSL |
| encourage 3 | GSL |
| ensure 14 | AWL |
| essential 14 | GSL |
| establish 5 | AWL |
| excessive 17 | GSL |
| exclude 18 | AWL |
| exhibit 3 | AWL |
| expert 17 | AWL |